ARISTOTLE

ARISTOTLE
THE POWER OF PERCEPTION

DEBORAH K. W. MODRAK

THE UNIVERSITY OF CHICAGO PRESS
CHICAGO AND LONDON

The University of Chicago Press, Chicago 60637
The University of Chicago Press, Ltd., London
© 1987 by The University of Chicago
All rights reserved. Published 1987
Paperback edition 1989
Printed in the United States of America

98 97 96 95 94 93 92 91 90 89   6 5 4 3 2

Library of Congress Cataloging in Publication Data
Modrak, Deborah K. W.
  Aristotle : the power of perception.
  Bibliography: p.
  Includes index.
  1. Aristotle—Contributions in theory of perception.
2. Perception (Philosophy)—History.   I. Title.
B491.P38M62   1987   121'.3'0924   86-19208
ISBN 0-226-53338-7 (cloth)
ISBN 0-226-53339-5 (pbk.)

TO MY CHILDREN
Joseph and Judith Modrak

Contents

Preface ix

1 What the Issues Are 1
    1. Recent Scholarship on Aristotle's Philosophy of Mind 4
    2. The Case for a Single Theory 9
    3. Aristotle and Modern Philosophy of Mind 15
    4. Objectives and Strategy 19

Part I. The Perceptual Faculty

2 The Theoretical Framework 23
    1. The Theoretical Foundations 25
    2. Perception in General 38
    3. The Psychophysical Model of Perception 39
    4. Reductive Materialism: Ancient and Modern Versions 43
    5. Hylomorphism and Psychophysicalism 49

3 The Five Senses and the Common Sense: Perception and Apperception 55
    1. The *Logos* Doctrine 56
    2. *Koinē Aisthēsis* 62
    3. The Physiological Basis of the Common Sense 71
    4. Theory and the Common Sense 76
    5. Epistemological Issues 77

4 *Phantasia* 81
    1. What *Phantasia* Is 82
    2. *Mnēmē, Anamnēsis* and Dreaming 87
    3. *Phantasia* and Voluntary Movement 95
    4. Sensory Representation 99
    5. *Phantasia* and the Foundational Principles 107

Part II. Thought and Consciousness

5 Thinking and Perceiving — 113
1. The Nature of the *Noētikon*   113
2. The *Noētikon* and the *Aisthētikon*   117
3. The Autonomy of Thought   124
4. Mental Representation   127
5. The Noetic Faculty and the Foundational Principles   130

6 Consciousness — 133
1. The Common Sense and the Unity of Experience   134
2. Reflexive Consciousness   145
3. Is Aristotle's Conception of Consciousness Different from Ours?   149
4. Consciousness and the Foundational Principles   152

Part III. Perception, Thought and Knowledge

7 The Epistemological Consequences — 157
1. Perception as the Source of Knowledge   158
2. The Genetic Account of the *Posterior Analytics* II, 19   161
3. Psychologism and Realism   171
4. The Epistemological Consequences of the Foundational Principles   176
5. Psychological Solutions to Epistemological Problems   178

Conclusion — 180

Abbreviations — 182

Notes — 183

References — 227

Index — 239

Preface

To see a vermilion sunset, to hear a chorus, to picture a goat-stag, to dream about thunder and lightning, to remember the hot, dry wind—these experiences and many more are exercises of the perceptual faculty, if Aristotle is right. While no immediate harm would be done were we to approach Aristotle's account of the perceptual faculty from the perspective of a narrowly defined and modern notion of perception, the breadth of Aristotle's vision and the comprehensiveness of his theory of perception would elude us. If instead we recognize that the "perceptual" for Aristotle is a very broad category and if we investigate the full range of activities he ascribes to the perceptual faculty, we can hope to do justice to his views. As a psychologist, Aristotle is primarily occupied with the analysis of sense perception, perceptual judgment, reflexive awareness, imagination, memory and dreams. The only other feature of human psychology that seriously interests Aristotle is thought. Even here the explanation he gives is deeply influenced by his conception of the perceptual system. Aristotle models his account of the rational faculty on his account of the perceptual faculty, and he makes thinking dependent upon the presentation of images through the imagination. Aristotle develops a model of cognitive activity to explain perception, which he then extends to include all other forms of cognition. Aristotle's theory of perception is thus at the heart of his psychology.

One reason to study Aristotle's theory of perception is the intrinsic appeal of the topic; another is the relevance of this theory to other parts of Aristotle's program. If we wish to examine his account of cognition, to evaluate his conception of psychology, or to compare his philosophy of mind to ours, we must come to terms with Aristotle's comprehensive treatment of "perception."

I am deeply grateful to the Center for Hellenic Studies. While in residence there, I completed the research for this book. I was also supported by a grant from the American Council of Learned Societies, and I would like to thank the Council as well as the National Endowment for the Humanities, which provided the funds for that fellowship. Finally, I wish to thank the University of Rochester for the Mellon Faculty Fellowship and research leave that enabled me to finish the work.

The manuscript has benefited enormously from the critical scrutiny of other scholars. When I presented parts of it in his seminar, Myles Burnyeat provoked me by brilliant criticism to rethink my positions and reformulate my arguments. David Glidden and Ralf Meerbote made numerous, incisive comments on the second chapter. Marjorie Grene read the first complete draft. Her insightful comments and cogent criticisms were invaluable. The present text owes much to the very knowledgeable and thorough critique of Charles Kahn, who as first reader for the University of Chicago Press, called my attention to weak arguments, poorly documented interpretations, and repetitious passages. I am, of course, entirely responsible for the interpretation presented here and all the mistakes that remain.

I also wish to thank Anna Harrison and Lynne McCoy for typing the manuscript.

There are many whose names do not appear here to whom I am also indebted. The teacher who challenged a jejune interpretation, the philosopher who pressed a telling objection, the student who found a text baffling—all of these and many more contributed to my development as a scholar. Equally important was the encouragement of friends and family.

1

What the Issues Are

The perennial problem in the philosophy of mind is to determine the ontological status of the mind. The first question Aristotle addresses in the *De Anima* is that of the ontological status of the *psuchē* (soul). In *De Anima* I, he considers this question obliquely, while finding fault with other philosophers' views. Despite differences in detail, a common theme runs throughout Aristotle's criticisms of his predecessors: they failed to recognize the unique character of the *psuchē*. Their accounts run aground on the Scylla of materialism or the Charybdis of dualism or both.[1] The materialists cannot account for motivation (406b15–25), and the dualists cannot explain soul-body relations (407b12–24).[2] The *psuchē* is not made of air or fire, as some of the pre-Socratics thought, nor is it a separate immaterial substance as the Platonists held. In *De Anima* II, Aristotle offers an account that promises a way out of the dilemma posed in the first book.[3] The *psuchē* is the form of the body; as such, it is neither a material nor an immaterial substance of the same ontological type as the body (412a15–22).[4]

In the philosophy of mind, the distinction between dualism and materialism is usually taken for granted, as is the usefulness of classifying an account of the mental as a dualist or a materialist theory. Approaching Aristotle's psychological writings within this tradition, modern scholars have attempted to categorize Aristotle as either a dualist or a materialist.[5] Matson (1966, 93) includes Aristotle in the sweeping judgment that "in the whole classical corpus there exists no denial of the view that sensing is a bodily process throughout" (cf. Slakey 1961). Solmsen, on the other hand, concludes that in Aristotle's psychology neither the functioning of the individual senses nor the functioning of the common sense depends upon physiological processes (1961, 170).[6] Kahn refuses to follow either of these lines of interpretation, but nonetheless he finds it worthwhile "to relate the Aristotelian terms body and *psuchē* to the modern distinction between body and mind" (1966, 45). At a recent conference on the *De Anima*, one speaker argued that material causes are more important than formal causes in Aristotle's psychology while another denied that psychological changes involve physical changes.⁷ The motivation of these commentators is clear: to place Aristotle's philosophy of mind squarely in one philosophical tradition or the other. This project is ill conceived because, as I shall argue, Aristotle is neither a materialist nor a dualist.⁸ To treat the dichotomy between materialist and dualist approaches as irreconcilable and to read Aristotle's psychology in light of this dichotomy distorts his position almost beyond recognition and obscures the sophistication of his analyses of mental phenomena.

Fortunately for Aristotelian exegesis, recent developments in the philosophy of mind have caused some philosophers to question the wisdom of approaching the analysis of mental phenomena from either a reductive materialist stance or a dualist one. The typical modern critic of the traditional dichotomy is a proponent of psychological functionalism. The central thesis of functionalism is that mental states are functional states of organisms. Some recent commentators, notably Sorabji (1974) and Nussbaum (1978), have found a precedent in Aristotle's philosophy of mind for functionalism. Aristotle, like the modern functionalist, refuses to endorse either reductive materialism or dualism, and for this reason the functionalist interpretation of Aristotle's position is closer to the mark than its competitors. But (as we shall discover in chap. 2) Aristotle's approach also resists assimilation to modern psychological functionalism.⁹

My objective is to investigate Aristotle's philosophy of mind as expressed in the theory of perception. Aristotle expends far more effort on the analysis of the perceptual faculty than on any other psychological phenomenon. This faculty is not simply the capacity for sense perception; its functions are many and various. Because we possess a perceptual faculty, we are able to sense, to perceive, to imagine, to dream, to remember and to engage in goal-directed behavior. The reflexive awareness of these activities is also a function of the perceptual faculty. The range and diversity of the activities Aristotle assigns to the perceptual faculty account for the central position of the theory of perception in Aristotle's psychology. To understand the latter theory without understanding the former would be impossible.

We will have to work to uncover Aristotle's theory of perception. Aristotle approaches the activities of the perceptual faculty in his usual analytic manner. Thus, he examines various functions of the perceptual faculty individually. Sense objects, the five senses, the common sense, the imagination and memory are taken up in turn. Some of these discussions occur in the *De Anima*; others occur in the psychological treatises of the *Parva Naturalia*, namely, the *De Sensu*, the *De Memoria*, the *De Somno*, the *De Insomniis* and the *De Divinatione per*

Somnum. Moreover, in some cases the same topic is discussed in several different treatises.[10] These factors make Aristotle's general theory of the perceptual faculty relatively obscure and inaccessible. Recent commentators, for the most part, have concentrated on particular functions of the perceptual faculty, for instance, sense perception or reflexive awareness, or on specific texts, for example, *De Anima* III, 3. As a result of Aristotle's style of presentation and the methodology of modern scholarship, Aristotle's detailed explanations of particular, perceptual activities now stand out in sharp relief from the shadowy, background theory of perception.

On the other hand, it seems reasonable to assume that Aristotle invokes one and the same psychic faculty to explain different cognitive activities in order to subsume all these explanations under a general explanatory model. Insofar as we concern ourselves solely with the specific activities of the perceptual faculty, we will fail to grasp the significance of Aristotle's strategy in assigning many different functions to this faculty. If we fail to come to terms with the background theory of perception, we impoverish our understanding of the particular cognitive activities falling under the perceptual faculty. My objective is to elicit the general theory of perception underlying Aristotle's explanations of particular, cognitive phenomena. Then using this theory as a point of reference, we may hope to approach Aristotle's detailed explanations of perceiving, imagining, and remembering from a perspective comparable to his.

This project will prove worthwhile even if the assumption that there is a clearly defined notion of the perceptual faculty at work should prove unfounded. If Aristotle has recourse to a unified theory of the perceptual faculty, then placing a cognitive activity such as sense perception within the larger context of the functions of that faculty enables him to give a more adequate (because more comprehensive) explanation of the activity than he would give were he to propound an explanation that applied only to the cognition in question. If Aristotle appeals to the perceptual faculty in particular cases without having any general theory of its operations, the appeal amounts to mere hand waving. Should the latter be the case we cannot know that it is so without investigating Aristotle's descriptions of the perceptual faculty and the cognitions assigned to the perceptual faculty.

I know of no better way to test the hypothesis that Aristotle has a unified theory of the perceptual faculty than to attempt to articulate the theory, and this is what I propose to do. I shall examine all the texts pertaining to the perceptual faculty and analyze all the functions of the perceptual faculty. This is an ambitious undertaking but well worth the effort for it will significantly deepen our understanding of Aristotle's psychology and philosophy of mind. I shall argue that there is a core theory of perception that supports Aristotle's analyses of individual perceptual capacities and that lends coherence and comprehensiveness to these analyses. The core theory consists in five basic principles that provide the theoretical foundation for Aristotle's explanations of specific perceptual phenomena. As we shall discover in subsequent chapters, Aristotle frequently invokes these principles in his psychological writings; even in contexts where he does not explicitly assert the core theory of perception, he structures his explanations in accordance with them.

Another benefit to be derived from examining the texts that describe the functions of the perceptual faculty is a heightened appreciation for recent scholarship on the *De Anima* and the *Parva Naturalia*. We will be in an excellent position to review and evaluate this work. Aristotle's psychological writings were the subject of the Seventh Symposium Aristotelicum in 1975 and of numerous papers published over the last twenty years.[11] For the most part, other scholars have concentrated on narrowly defined topics and have left unanswered broadly based questions of the sort to be discussed here. The evaluation of the progress made by these scholars will be facilitated by considering their contributions from the perspective of the general theory of the perceptual faculty. Several issues have been of particular concern to modern scholars: the relation between mind and body in Aristotle's philosophy of mind, the nature of perception, reflexive awareness and consciousness, imagination and the connections between perceiving, thinking and knowing. I will address all of these issues in subsequent chapters. For the moment, a quick review of recent developments and open problems should suffice to set the stage for our investigations.

1. Recent Scholarship on Aristotle's Philosophy of Mind

A topic of perennial interest to philosophers is the mind-body problem. Aristotle's answer seems to be straightforward: the *psuchē* (mind/soul) is the form of the body ("psychological hylomorphism"). Yet recent commentators have disagreed about the proper interpretation of this doctrine, about its significance for Aristotle, and about its coherence. Some commentators question the extent of Aristotle's commitment to psychological hylomorphism. In the *De Anima* and elsewhere, Aristotle asserts the primacy of form over matter.[12] In other explanatory contexts, he emphasizes the importance of the formal cause and largely ignores the material cause, but in the psychological treatises, explanations in terms of material causes seem to predominate.[13] For instance, hearing is explained by appeal to the movement of the air enclosed in the inner ear, and voluntary action is explained by appeal to muscular changes due to internal changes in bodily temperature (*De An.* 420a3–20; *De Motu An.* 701b2–702a10). Moreover, whether Aristotle could have consistently adhered to the program of giving hylomorphic analyses of psychological states, should he have so desired, is a matter for debate.[14]

The history of recent scholarship on Aristotle's conception of the mind-body relation finds scholars in the 1960s criticizing Aristotle for being a reductive materialist and scholars in the 1970s rejecting Aristotle's alleged materialism in favor of hylomorphism. Slakey (1961, 470) claimed that, for Aristotle, perception simply is "an event in the sense organs." Not only is Aristotle's theory of perception a materialist theory on this reading but Slakey also found it to be a rather simple-minded and unsatisfactory materialist theory. According to Slakey, "an object which is perceived to be x makes the sense organ involved in its perception to be itself x" (p. 475). Red objects make the eyes red, and hot objects make the body hot. With certain reservations, Hamlyn (1968a, 113) concurred with Slakey's analysis, and he too was critical of Aristotle: "It is not easy to see how the eye can receive colour when we see, or the ear sound when we hear." Barnes (1971–72, 104–6) rejected the prevailing view that Aristotle opted for reductive materialism in the case of the perceptual faculty. The eye does not literally become purple nor does the ear resound with music. Barnes construed Aristotle's hylomorphism as a version of the attribute theory of mind, albeit a somewhat eccentric version, for (on Barnes's reading) the possession of certain psychological states, for example, thought, need not imply the possession of a body.[15] Sorabji (1974) agreed with Slakey and Hamlyn against Barnes that the sense organs literally take on the sensible qualities which are perceived; however, he agreed with Barnes that Aristotle is not a reductive materialist. The psychological event is something over and above the physiological change. This "something else" is, or should be, captured by the formal description of the psychological state. Sorabji then looked for formal descriptions of psychological activities that did not make implicit or explicit reference to physiology; finding none in the text, he urged functional descriptions on Aristotle.

Ackrill (1972–73) accepted Aristotle's hylomorphism and made no attempt to assimilate it to any other, more modern approach to mind-body relations. Then he went on to argue that Aristotle's descriptions of the *psuchē* and of the body are inconsistent with one of the presuppositions of hylomorphism, namely, that it is possible to give conceptually distinct descriptions of the form and the matter of the composite. According to Ackrill, in the case of psychological hylomorphism, this presupposition is false because it is incompatible with Aristotle's conception of organic substances. Physiological descriptions, according to Aristotle, make tacit reference to psychological structures. A severed hand is a hand in name only.[16] Hence, Ackrill argues, no attempt by Aristotle to describe the matter of a psychological state can be successful.

Despite holdouts, there seems to be a growing consensus among Aristotelian scholars that we should take Aristotle's psychological hylomorphism seriously. There is, as yet, however, little agreement about the precise contours of his philosophy of mind. Part of the difficulty (as I shall argue in chap. 2) is the poor fit between Aristotle's hylomorphism and our theories of mind (cf. Sorabji 1974, 64; Barnes 1971–72, 101–4). Aristotle is not a psychophysical reductionist in the modern sense. Granted, Aristotle sometimes finds it convenient to talk about the bricks and stones making up a house as if they were the house, and for similar reasons he sometimes finds it useful to talk about the jelly making up the eye as if it were the eye.[17] Nevertheless, the relation between form and matter is not the relation of identity, nor is the matter of a composite identical with the composite.

Nor again is Aristotle's philosophy of mind easily depicted as an ancient version of one of the nonreductionist theories of mind championed by modern philosophers. It is not rightly described as an attribute theory of mind. For Aristotle, psychological states are states of living creatures, but like any other substantial form the *psuchē* is not an attribute. The form determines the character of the composite, and thus the form is not on the same ontological level as the properties of the composite (Modrak 1979, 1984). On the other hand, if Aristotle is a functionalist at all, he is not a psychological functionalist in the modern sense.[18] Aristotle is not concerned to give functional descriptions of psychological states that make no reference to physiology.[19] Unlike a modern psychological functionalist, he identifies psychological states with psychophysical states. Although the formal description of the state does not explicitly mention the material substratum, the full description of the state does. Not only would the full description of seeing, for example, mention the color seen, it would also mention the change in the eye jelly. The recognition that all attempts to subsume Aristotle's philosophy of mind under modern theories of one sort or another have failed should encourage us to take a fresh look at his position.[20]

Not only are there these general issues to consider in relation to Aristotle's philosophy of mind, there are a number of open problems that directly concern the functions of the perceptual faculty. Sorabji

(1971) pointed out that Aristotle defines the special senses with reference to their proper objects, and he contended that this was problematic in the case of the sense of touch. Finding Aristotle's practice in this regard unexceptional, Kosman (1975) argued that the sense object also determines the character of the sensing. He used this insight to explicate Aristotle's account of reflexive awareness in *De Anima* III, 2. If Kosman is right, Aristotle would be ill advised to adopt the nonlocalization criterion for touch that Sorabji prefers to Aristotle's object-centered criterion.

Aristotle's notion of *phantasia* (imagination) has come under scrutiny of late (Rees 1971; Schofield 1978; Nussbaum 1978; Watson 1982). Hamlyn (1968a) could not find a coherent conception of *phantasia* in the chapter (*De An.* III, 3) devoted to the definition of *phantasia*. Schofield (1978) refuted Hamlyn and argued that if we take the notion of *phantasia* to be the notion of nonparadigmatic sensory experience, then this chapter presents a consistent doctrine. For Schofield, nonparadigmatic sensory experience is sensory experience about which the percipient is or should be skeptical. Nussbaum (1978) took a different tack; she based her position on the importance of *phantasia* in action contexts, and she held that *phantasia* is the interpretative aspect of perception. I have argued elsewhere for an interpretation closer to Schofield's than Nussbaum's, although I rejected the identification of nonparadigmatic sensory experience with unreliable sensory information (Modrak, forthcoming). On my reading, representations through *phantasia* need not be misleading, and so I, unlike Schofield and like Nussbaum, was able to explain the central place Aristotle assigns *phantasia* in goal-directed behavior. Insofar as the consistency of Aristotle's notion of *phantasia* is at issue, the case for coherence appears to have carried the day, but the role of *phantasia* in lending coherence to the theory of the perceptual faculty remains to be recognized and evaluated.

Aristotle uses the notion of *phantasia* as a device to include a number of cognitive activities under the functions of the perceptual faculty. Typically, when Aristotle assigns a particular cognitive activity (other than sense perception) to the perceptual faculty, he points out that the object of the activity is a *phantasma*. *Phantasmata*, like the objects of direct perception, are complexes of sensible characters. The *phantasma* as the internal counterpart of the perceptible qualities of an external object is the link between the apprehension of sensible qualities in ordinary perception and the employment of sensible qualities in the internal representations of fantasies, dreams and memories. If there is a unified conception of the perceptual faculty at the center of Aristotle's account of perceiving, imagining, remembering and dreaming, its existence is in part due to his notion of *phantasia* as sensory representation. I will undertake a thorough investigation of these issues in chapter 4.

Aristotle's conception of consciousness has also been the subject of heated debate of late. Some commentators deny that Aristotle has any conception of consciousness at all; others attribute a concept of consciousness to him but not a Cartesian concept; still others would attribute a Cartesian conception to him.[21] Kahn (1966) located Aristotle's notion of consciousness in the activities of the common sense, and Hardie (1976) found both a general and a reflexive (Cartesian) concept of consciousness in Aristotle's writings (see also Modrak 1981a). Yet Rorty (1979) found nothing at all like a Cartesian notion of consciousness in Aristotle and insisted that the Cartesian conception of consciousness originated in the seventeenth century. In the face of such disagreements, the topic of consciousness deserves our attention. Aristotle's conception of consciousness must be gleaned from his analyses of particular types of cognition since his analytic approach to psychology leads to the investigation of specific cognitive activities and not to the systematic study of consciousness, which requires a synthesis of the various aspects of "mental" life. In chapters 2, 3, and 4 we will look at all the functions Aristotle assigns the perceptual faculty and in chapter 5 at the functions he assigns the noetic faculty; this will leave us in an excellent position to determine, in chapter 6, whether Aristotle has a notion of consciousness and to what extent his notion of consciousness resembles ours.

Aristotle's theory of perception also has important consequences for his epistemology. In the *De Anima* and elsewhere, Aristotle asserts that knowledge depends upon perception: "Were one to perceive nothing, one would neither learn nor understand anything," (432a7–8; cf. *Pst. Anal.* I, 18). Aristotle elaborates this thesis further in the *Posterior Analytics*, making perception the ultimate source of the first principles of art and science. A critical text in this connection is *Posterior Analytics* II, 19 (cf. *Met.* I, 1); in the opening lines of this chapter, Aristotle announces that he intends to explain how we come to know the first principles of science. He then describes an inductive process that enables us to derive abstract universals from our perceptions of sensible particulars. Aristotle concludes with a description of the apodictic certainty of first principles. The chapter seems to divide into a discussion of induction (*epagōgē*) and intuition (*nous*).[22] The connection between the two sections is a matter of controversy. A few years ago there was general agreement among commentators that Aristotle had pushed his empiricist account of the acquisition of basic concepts and first principles as far as possible in the first part of the chapter; then, having recognized that induction could not provide apodictic certainty, he had fallen back upon a "Platonic" intuition (*nous*) of first principles in the concluding section. Among others, Lee (1935), Le Blond (1939), and Randall (1960) endorsed this reading of II, 19.

Discomforted by the Platonic character of *nous* on these earlier accounts of Aristotle's epistemology, scholars in the 1970s took another look at *Posterior Analytics* II, 19. Kosman (1973) argued that *nous* is realized in the mental activity of *epagōgē*. Lesher (1973) elaborated on this view and argued that *nous* is involved whenever we reason inductively from particular cases to universal principles (cf. Engberg-Pedersen 1979). Kahn (1981) concurred and held that the two parts of II, 19 describe the two stages of the inductive process. But the question is not yet settled. Like earlier commentators, Barnes (1975) found only an attenuated connection between the two parts of the chapter. The proper interpretation of II, 19 cannot be decided on the basis of that text alone or even on the basis of the *Posterior Analytics* alone. The interpretation of II, 19 ultimately rests on Aristotle's notions of perception, induction and intellection. By the end of this study, we will be in an excellent position to bring Aristotle's psychological theory to bear on the interpretation of his epistemology.[23]

In short, as a consequence of recent scholarship on Aristotle's philosophy of mind, theory of perception, and epistemology, the problems are more clearly defined than ever before. The solutions to these problems are not yet clear and in many cases demand a broad perspective on the Aristotelian corpus and the critical literature. After providing the latter, I hope to make some progress toward the resolution of the outstanding problems.

2. The Case for a Single Theory

In 1923 W. W. Jaeger (1948) made an eloquent case for Aristotle's development as a philosopher. The works of Aristotle as they have come down to us, he argued, do not present a single, unchanging philosophical perspective but instead illustrate a continuous philosophical progression.[24] Jaeger divided Aristotle's philosophical career into three periods. During the early period, Aristotle was a member of Plato's Academy and wrote dialogues modeled on Platonic dialogues and expressing similar philosophical positions. There was a middle, transitional period when Aristotle was away from Athens and began to develop his own philosophical positions. This period also found him taking an interest in the natural sciences. In the final period, Aristotle returned to Athens and came to his own as a philosopher. This period saw the elaboration of the doctrines we associate with Aristotelianism, including the distinction between form and matter and the application of this distinction to a number of philosophical problems, from the analysis of change to the relationship between mind and body.

Jaeger paid scant attention to the *De Anima* and largely ignored the psychological treatises of the *Parva Naturalia*.[25] Nuyens ([1948] 1973) brought Jaeger's developmental thesis to bear on the interpretation of Aristotle's psychology, and he found three comparable periods in it. The first is characterized by Platonic dualism, where the soul and the body are opposed to each other; the second is characterized by psychophysical instrumentalism, where the soul cooperates with the body and gives it life; the third is characterized by hylomorphism, where the soul and the body form a unity (pp. 57–58). Nuyens considered the relationship between the treatises of the *Parva Naturalia* and the *De Anima* and arrived at the following conclusions: (1) the *De Juventute*, the *De Respiratione* and the *De Longitudine Vitae* belong to the instrumentalist period;[26] and (2) the other five treatises of the *Parva Naturalia* belong to the same period as the *De Anima*, that is, to the final, hylomorphic stage of Aristotle's career. Nuyens supported these contentions with numerous textual citations. He established that the doctrines of the *De Juventute* and the *De Respiratione* are similar to doctrines found in the biological works such as the *De Partibus Animalium*, which he assigned to the instrumentalist period, and he demonstrated that the doctrines of the *De Sensu* and the *De Memoria* are similar to the doctrines of the *De Anima*, which he assigned to the last period. However, Lulofs (1943; 1947) and later Ross (1955, 11–14) pointed out that parts of the *De Somno* and the *De Insomniis* seem to belong to the instrumentalist period.[27] While agreeing with Nuyens that parts of the *De Sensu* and the *De Memoria* belong to the same period as parts of the *De Anima*, Ross (1955, 15–18) argued that *De Anima* II was a later work than any found in the *Parva Naturalia*.[28] He claimed that a "two-substance view" of the soul is found throughout the *Parva Naturalia* and that this view is inconsistent with the hylomorphism of *De Anima* II. Still later, Block (1961), who agreed with Ross that the psychological treatises of the *Parva Naturalia* belong to a different period than the *De Anima*, concluded that the psychological theory of the *Parva Naturalia* is more sophisticated and hence later than that of the *De Anima*.

If any of these accounts are right and Aristotle espoused different psychological theories in different treatises, then the project of reconstructing the psychological theory that shapes all of Aristotle's theorizing about psychological phenomena is ill conceived. My project rests on the assumption that the psychological theses found in the *Parva Naturalia* and the *De Anima* can be profitably viewed as a continuous exposition of one psychological theory.[29] Fortunately, recent scholarship favors the unitarian approach to be followed here. For instance, Kahn (1966) argued for unitarianism as did Sorabji (1972; see also Hardie 1964).

The seeds for dissension about the cogency of the developmental hypothesis were sown by its proponents. Their disagreements undermined the very distinctions they wished to maintain. Lulofs would divide two quite short works, the *De Somno* and the *De Insomniis*, into smaller parts in order to fit them into the Nuyens scheme.[30] Ross is skeptical about dividing these works, but he would assign a later date to *De Anima* II than to the other parts of the *De Anima*. If the method originally intended to produce a division of Aristotle's works into three periods produces numerous divisions, there is some reason to doubt the wisdom of the original scheme of classification.

Part of the appeal of the unitarian interpretation is that it allows us to use one psychological treatise to elucidate another. The psychological writings fit together nicely. The *De Anima* sets the stage for Aristotle's psychology and presents the general theory. The first book surveys the theories of Aristotle's predecessors and rejects both materialist and dualist approaches to the philosophy of mind; the initial chapters of the second book present Aristotle's hylomorphic doctrine as a genuine alternative to materialism and dualism. The Aristotelian *psuchē* is a complex of vital capacities, which Aristotle groups under four headings: the nutritive soul, the sensitive soul, the noetic soul and the locomotive soul (*De An.* II, 2–3). Aristotle discusses all of these faculties both in the *De Anima* and elsewhere.

Many of the topics mentioned in the *De Anima* reappear as the subjects for separate treatises. The *De Motu Animalium* completes the *De Anima*'s explanation of voluntary motion; the *De Memoria* gives a detailed account of memory and recollection.[31] The *De Anima* devotes a chapter to the nutritive faculty, the functions of which are the subject of detailed investigation in the biological treatises.[32] The analysis of cognitive capacities dominates Aristotle's attention in the *De Anima*, and the theories of sense perception and noetic activity are presented in some detail. Nonetheless, in the *Parva Naturalia* Aristotle sees fit to return to some of these topics: the *De Sensu* consists in a lengthy excursus on the nature of sense objects; apperception is taken up in the

De Somno as well as in the *De Sensu;* and the *De Insomniis* gives an account of dreaming that complements the discussion of *phantasia* in *De Anima* III, 3.

Aristotle's handling of the case of apperception is instructive in this regard; in three different treatises (the *De Anima*, the *De Sensu* and the *De Somno*) Aristotle puzzles about our ability to perceive two different sensibles simultaneously and to recognize their differences; he wonders how it is possible for a percipient to see a white color, to taste a sweet flavor, and simultaneously to recognize that the qualities white and sweet are different types of sensibles. In the *De Anima*, Aristotle offers a metaphor by way of explanation: the faculty making the judgment is like a boundary point. In the *De Somno*, he gives a more detailed and technical answer: there is a capacity common to all the senses that can be exercised in relation to sensible qualities presented through several different sense modalities and thus can be employed to make apperceptual judgments.[33] Clearly, it is to our advantage, if we wish to understand Aristotle's position on this particular question, to look at all three passages together. More generally, our understanding of the *De Anima* will be greatly enhanced by bringing the *Parva Naturalia*'s detailed descriptions of psychological phenomena to bear on the interpretation of the *De Anima*, and conversely, the general psychological theory of the *De Anima* provides a framework in which to interpret other treatises dealing with more narrowly defined topics.

The advantages that the unitarian approach affords to the interpreter of Aristotle's psychology provides a strong prima facie argument for the thesis that Aristotle espouses a single psychological theory which finds expression in the *Parva Naturalia* as well as the *De Anima*. The prima facie argument for unitarianism would of course be defeated were the Nuyens-Ross view, that some of the doctrines asserted in the *Parva Naturalia* are inconsistent with those asserted in the *De Anima*, to prove correct. These scholars base their arguments primarily on the alleged contrast between the conception of the *psuchē* found in the biological writings and the hylomorphic conception of the *De Anima*. Allegedly, the former involves a dualistic and instrumentalist conception of the soul where the soul is primarily located in the heart, while the hylomorphic view identifies the soul with the form of the body. Ross takes any instrumentalist language or any reference to the heart as the seat of the *psuchē* to be incompatible with the hylomorphic view. This leads him to assign a singularly late date to *De Anima* II, which is the only work where he finds a thoroughgoing commitment to hylomorphism (1955, 17).

However, the case for the distinction between the biological and hylomorphic conceptions of the *psuchē*, which is at the heart of the Nuyens-Ross interpretation, is not as strong as its proponents would have us believe. We should consider the following counterarguments. In the first place, Aristotle often lapses into nontechnical language and as a result sometimes creates the impression that he is endorsing a position that he is not endorsing. Instrumentalist descriptions are more commonsensical than hylomorphic descriptions, hence the mere use of instrumentalist language need not imply instrumentalism in the technical sense in which it excludes hylomorphism. In the second place, it is agreed that the soul as the form of the body is the principle of life (cf. *De An.* 415b8); but just as some parts of the body are more crucial to the survival of the organism than others, the form as realized in these parts might be more important. In *Metaphysics* VII, a late work by all accounts and in a context where the hylomorphic view is in evidence, Aristotle describes the soul as being immediately present in the heart or perhaps in the brain but not in both (1035b26–28).[34] When Aristotle speaks of the soul's being in the heart, he seems to mean nothing more than that the proper functioning of the heart is essential to the survival of the organism.

In the third place, it is arguable that the instrumentalism of the biological treatises is compatible with hylomorphism and that Aristotle's espousal of instrumentalism need not be equated with the acceptance of dualism.[35] The failure on Aristotle's part to mention psychological hylomorphism in a psychological or biological context is not tantamount to the rejection of this doctrine. Even in *De Anima* II, Aristotle does not explicitly invoke psychological hylomorphism in the analysis of particular psychological phenomena.[36] Moreover, his discussion of nutrition in the fourth chapter is instrumentalist; the soul is the cause of digestion and of the heat required for digestion (416a9–15). What the proponent of the developmental hypothesis must establish is that the treatises of the *Parva Naturalia* in contrast to the *De Anima* express views that are inconsistent with psychological hylomorphism.

Ross argues that a two-substance view of the *psuchē* and the body is found in the *Parva Naturalia*, which is incompatible with the *De Anima*'s hylomorphism. Throughout the *Parva Naturalia*, we find passages that seem to treat the *psuchē* as a distinct substance and passages where Aristotle uses *psuchē* as if it refers to a substance. For instance, psychological states are said to be common to body and *psuchē* in the *Parva Naturalia*. However, we find analogous passages in the *De Anima* (cf., e.g., *De An.* 408b15–18 to *De Som.* 454a9–10). Here are two passages, the first from the *De Anima* and the second from the *De*

Sensu, that seem to make precisely the same point in nearly the same language:

> And it seems that all the affections of the soul are with the body, anger, gentleness, fear, hope, enthusiasm, and further joy and both loving and hating for at the same time as these the body is somehow affected. (403a16–19)

> It seems that the most significant properties . . . of animals are common to soul and body, for instance perception and memory and anger and desire and appetite in general, and in addition to these, both pleasure and pain. (436a8–11)[37]

De Anima I also finds Aristotle saying that memory originates in a bodily movement that reaches the soul, whereas recollection originates in the soul and extends to the body (408b15–18). This description is as suggestive of dualism as any found in the *De Memoria*'s detailed and similar account of memory and recollection.[38] In *De Anima* II we encounter the notorious pilot passage: "And further it is unclear whether the soul is the actuality [*entelecheia*] of the body just as the sailor is of the ship" (413a8–9).[39]

From this cursory survey of similar texts, it should be evident that Aristotle's dualist descriptions are not limited to the "earlier, biological" works but are also found in such "later, hylomorphic" works as *De Anima* II and *Metaphysics* VII. If such descriptions show that Aristotle subscribes to a two-substance view of the *psuchē* and the body, then he subscribes to a two-substance view throughout his career. Since Aristotle accepts psychological hylomorphism and gives dualist descriptions of psychological phenomena in the same works, we may conclude that Aristotle is hopelessly confused about mind-body relations. Or we may conclude that psychological hylomorphism is compatible with dualist language and instrumentalism.[40] In neither case do we have any reason to adopt the developmental hypothesis.

Presumably, Aristotle believed that the two types of description were compatible. On his behalf, let us try to sketch an account on which the simultaneous endorsement of psychological hylomorphism and instrumentalism makes sense. First, for the sake of exposition, Aristotle often eschews technical terms and adopts a more conversational tone. In ordinary discourse, the soul is frequently described as though it were a separate substance.[41] In certain contexts, Aristotle would gain little by bringing his technical (i.e., hylomorphic) notion of *psuchē* into the discussion. If his findings are compatible with psychological hylomorphism, no harm is done by the use of popular terminology.[42] Second, Aristotle emphasizes the propaedeutic character of the general definition of the soul, namely, the soul is the form or actuality of the body (*De An.* 414b20–33). The analysis of specific psychological phenomena in terms of the capacities of specific bodily organs presupposes psychological hylomorphism. Such analyses are found in the *De Anima*, the *Parva Naturalia* and the biological treatises. A case in point is the description of the development of the human embryo in the *De Generatione Animalium*, where the nutritive soul comes into existence with the heart and the digestive system, the sensitive soul develops with the growth of the perceptual organs, and Aristotle worries about the status of *nous*, which has no organ to enform (736b5–29).[43] The entire description is framed within the conceptual framework of psychological hylomorphism.[44] Nor is this an isolated instance. In general, Aristotle treats psychological hylomorphism and psychophysical instrumentalism as complementary hypotheses not as mutually exclusive ones.

Clearly, the developmental view cannot be sustained in application to the psychological doctrines of the *De Anima* and the *Parva Naturalia*. Moreover, we were able to explain Aristotle's practice of invoking both types of descriptions in the same treatise. It is to our advantage to use passages from the *Parva Naturalia* to explicate doctrines found in the *De Anima* and conversely. Thus, with all due respect to the advocates of the various versions of the developmental hypothesis, I here adopt a unitarian approach to Aristotle's philosophy of mind.

3. Aristotle and Modern Philosophy of Mind

To formulate a position that is consistent with the objectives and methodology of modern physical science has been a major concern of modern philosophers of mind.[45] With its emphasis on reduction, its success at explaining macroscopic events by appealing to submicroscopic ones, and its hope of carrying this project still further to achieve a single, unified theory, modern physical science is inhospitable to dualism. During the last fifty years, defenses of dualism were scarcely to be found in the (secular) philosophical literature. Instead philosophers argued among themselves and with psychologists about how best to give a characterization of the mind that is either straightforwardly materialist or at least compatible with materialism.

In the 1960s, reductive materialism in the form of the Psychophysical Identity Theory seemed to be the best strategy.[46] The central thesis of the Psychophysical Identity Theory is that mental states are simply states of the central nervous system. However, critics of this approach soon pointed out that psychophysical identity statements of the form "pain is a firing of the C-fibers" gave rise to certain conceptual puzzles, for pains seem to have properties that brain events do not have and vice versa.[47] Even more troubling was the growing suspicion shared by neurophysiologists as well as by philosophers that the project of trying to isolate a type of cerebral activity to be identified with each particular psychological state was doomed to failure. The complexity of neurological function, the versatility of the brain, and the differences between species made it seem quite unlikely that such correlations would be forthcoming even in a highly developed neurophysiology.[48] It seemed more likely that psychophysical correlations would be established for single occurrences and that neurophysiology would be a source of token-token identity statements instead of the type-type identity statements required by the Psychophysical Identity Theory. For instance, in the future it may be possible to identify with a specific event in my brain my current belief that it is raining today, but it will not be possible to generalize from my case and attribute the same brain state to another person who holds the same belief. Meanwhile, other philosophers raised questions about the "empirical" nature of the identification process. They argued that we could never distinguish on empirical grounds between the case where a particular psychological state is constantly correlated with a particular brain state and the case where the psychological state and the brain state are one and the same state. Should we choose to describe this situation in terms of identity, we do so for conceptual reasons and not because the Psychophysical Identity Theory has more empirical support than alternative theories of mind.[49]

Recently, psychological functionalism has replaced the Psychophysical Identity Theory as the dominant theory of mind. At least in part, its appeal is due to the belief that functionalism is compatible with the empirical investigation of minds and that functionalism does not require a materialist reduction of minds to brains.[50] At this juncture, Aristotle's philosophy of mind becomes of particular interest since he too was trying to avoid both the problems inherent in dualism and the problems inherent in reductive materialism. Moreover, Aristotle's approach to the analysis of psychological states seems to resemble the modern functionalist's approach. According to psychological functionalism, mental states are functional states of organisms, namely, states that are defined in terms of their causal role; as functional states, mental states are not defined in terms of intrinsic characteristics.[51] Aristotle defines the *psuchē* in terms of certain capacities that are characteristic of living things of a particular type (cf. Grene 1963, 243). To have a *psuchē* is to be alive; in the case of animals, to have a *psuchē* is to be capable of perception, self-movement, reproduction, growth and digestion.⁵² Vital capacities of this sort are also defined by their causal role.⁵³

Like the modern functionalist, Aristotle steers clear of both dualism and physicalism. As a conglomerate of vital capacities, the *psuchē* is definitely not a distinct substance. By describing the *psuchē* in terms of capacities for vital functions, Aristotle avoids the identification of the soul with the body; the capacity to digest food is conceptually distinct from the realization of this capacity in any particular physical structure.

Not surprisingly, a number of modern philosophers have construed Aristotle's views as an ancient version of psychological functionalism (Nussbaum 1978; Sorabji 1974). There have been a few dissenters, but on balance the similarities between Aristotle's psychology and modern functionalism have received more comment than the differences.⁵⁴ To decide whether Aristotle is a psychological functionalist is not a task to be undertaken in an introductory chapter. In chapter 2 I will examine Aristotle's treatment of sense perception in relation to modern functionalism. It will be easier to decide whether Aristotle is a functionalist or not when we are clearer about his views.

There is another respect in which modern philosophy is directly relevant to our concerns as interpreters of Aristotle's philosophy of mind. It teaches us two lessons. The first, namely, the desirability of finding a tertium quid between dualism and reductive materialism, has already been discussed. The second is the desirability of preserving the descriptive power of sentences employing the mental predicates of ordinary language. This lesson is clear from a thumbnail sketch of the recent history of the philosophy of mind. The modern era began with logical behaviorism.⁵⁵ The logical behaviorists, most notably Ryle (1949) and Wittgenstein (1953), construed psychological descriptions as descriptions of behavioral dispositions. According to the behaviorists, terms that appear to refer to the mental states of a person in fact ascribe behavioral tendencies to the person. The logical behaviorists reasoned that if we can explain the use of mental terms without positing the existence of mental states, we can eliminate such states from our ontology. The behaviorist reduction was abandoned after the best efforts of its enthusiastic supporters failed to produce persuasive behaviorist paraphrases of descriptions employing mental predicates.

The Psychophysical Identity Theory eliminated mental states by making them states of the central nervous system. Since there are conceptual obstacles to identifying mental events under phenomenal descriptions with brain events, the proponents of the Identity Theory proposed to translate phenomenal descriptions of mental events into "topic-neutral" language (Smart 1959; Armstrong 1968).[56] These descriptions of psychological states would not presuppose the mental character of the state. Should it turn out that the referents of the terms denoting mental states in a topic-neutral sentence were states of the central nervous system, it would be conceptually unproblematic. Once more the philosophical community rejected the translation program because the proposed translations did not seem to express the same propositions as the original sentences.

Psychological functionalism seems to offer a way around this recurrent problem. Functionalists recognize different levels of descriptions: the mental predicates of ordinary language, the functional descriptions of cognitive psychology, and the physiological descriptions of neural science. Some proponents of functionalism believe that mental descriptions are in principle eliminable in favor of functional ones (Shoemaker 1975). Other proponents believe that functionalist descriptions of mental states can be used to secure the identity of a mental state with a neural state (Lewis 1972).[57] Nonetheless, it is generally agreed that the reduction of one level of description to another is not entailed by the functionalist thesis. Critics of functionalism have argued, moreover, that the reduction of one level to another will not prove possible (Block and Fodor 1972; cf. Davidson 1970). Aristotle also appeals to different levels of description. In Aristotelian terms, the formal definition of a psychological state and its material definition are conceptually distinct. For instance, the formal definition of anger is "the desire for retaliation," whereas the material definition is "the boiling of blood around the heart." For Aristotle, these descriptions are the two components of the full psychological definition of anger. His definitions of psychological states have all the descriptive force of ordinary phenomenal descriptions because the latter are incorporated in the former. In itself, this is an advantageous feature; however, it opens Aristotle's analysis up for objections about the cogency of appealing to different levels of description similar to the ones raised in connection with modern functionalism.

In these and other respects, I shall make use of the tools of modern philosophy of mind to clarify Aristotle's positions. This practice need not, and hopefully will not, lead to anachronism. Even if, at the end of the day, we decide that Aristotle's philosophy of mind is quite unlike any twentieth-century theory, we will have furthered our understanding of Aristotle's positions by bringing state-of-the-art analytic tools to bear on the Aristotelian corpus. In addition, since Aristotle and the modern philosopher of mind share certain objectives, the examination of Aristotle's analyses of specific psychological states should help define the conceptual issues confronting the modern philosopher.

4. Objectives and Strategy

This book is primarily about Aristotle's theory of perception as presented in the *De Anima* and the *Parva Naturalia*. The psychological activities Aristotle assigns to the perceptual faculty are many and diverse. This prompts the question, When Aristotle assigns all of these activities to the same psychic faculty, does he intend to invoke a single explanatory model? This question is at the heart of my project. The only way to answer it is to attempt to discover the common conceptual foundations underlying Aristotle's analyses of the specific functions of the perceptual faculty. If the attempt fails, then the answer to our question will be no; if the attempt succeeds, the answer will be yes.

I argue in chapter 2 that the theoretical foundation consists in five explanatory principles—the Psychophysical Principle, the Actuality Principle, the Sensory Representation Principle, the Analytic Principle and the Normative Psychophysical Principle. In the subsequent chapters we shall see this explanatory model at work in Aristotle's account of the five senses; his description of the common sense, including apperception; his account of *phantasia*, including dreaming and remembering; his discussion of thought; and his treatment of consciousness.[58] The final chapter explores the epistemological consequences of Aristotle's conception of the perceptual faculty.

I
THE PERCEPTUAL FACULTY

2

The Theoretical Framework

The preceding chapter set out the general issues to be investigated in connection with Aristotle's philosophy of mind and theory of perception. The first item on our agenda is to uncover the theoretical foundations of Aristotle's treatment of perception. If the amount of space Aristotle devotes to the discussion of the perceptual faculty is symptomatic of his concern, then he finds the functions of the perceptual faculty of the soul more interesting than any other psychological capacities. The functions of the perceptual faculty of the soul include sense perception, reflexive awareness, imagination and memory. Aristotle describes each one in some detail. *De Anima* II, 5–III, 2, the entire *De Sensu* and large portions of the *De Memoria*, the *De Somno* and the *De Insomniis* are devoted to the discussion of these capacities. Moreover, the perceptual faculty is the only psychic faculty analyzed in sufficient detail to enable us to treat Aristotle's discussion of it as a theory of a particular type of psychological function and to evaluate this theory on the grounds of comprehensiveness, coherence, explanatory power and simplicity.

At first glance, it might seem that Aristotle's theory of perception will fail on all or at least most of these counts and on some others as well. Despite the relatively extensive treatment, Aristotle's discussion of perception and related faculties often appears sketchy, fragmentary and otherwise unsatisfactory. A careful examination of the texts in question, however, reveals a successful effort to lay the foundations for a comprehensive and self-consistent theory of sensing, perceiving, imagining and remembering.

As a first step toward coming to terms with Aristotle's conception of the perceptual faculty, I have abstracted the most important of the assumptions that shape his theorizing about perception. These include fundamental tenets that he repeatedly invokes to justify further claims about the nature of perceiving as well as prescriptive principles that he invokes in his criticisms of other philosophical treatments of the soul and follows in his own analysis. Just as Aristotle does not draw a sharp distinction between rules of inference and axioms in the *Posterior An-*

alytics, he accords descriptive and prescriptive principles the same status in the psychological treatises.

The skeleton of the theory consists in three foundational principles and two prescriptive ones. These principles inform Aristotle's treatment of the perceptual faculty and account for its unity and coherence.[1] They provide the cohesion and comprehensiveness that warrant the ascription of a "theory" of perception and perceptual consciousness to Aristotle. In brief, the principles are as follows.[2]

Foundational Principles

A. Descriptive Principles

1. *Psychophysical Principle.*[3] Many states, if not all, that are ordinarily assigned to the soul are psychophysical states, namely, psychical states with physical realizations.[4]
2. *Actuality Principle.* A cognitive faculty is potentially what its object is actually.[5]
3. *Sensory Representation Principle.*[6] If a cognitive activity has a sense object as its focal object, the psychic faculty involved is a perceptual faculty.[7]

B. Prescriptive Principles

4. *Analytic Principle.* A psychological explanation should begin with an account of the constituent parts of the phenomenon under consideration and then make this account the basis for extending the explanation to cover more complex phenomena of the same sort.[8]
5. *Normative Psychophysical Principle.* Psychological explanation at its most complete will take the psychophysical character of psychological states into account.[9]

These are the principles that determine the character of Aristotle's analysis of the functions of the perceptual faculty of the soul. Establishing their role in the psychological theory of the *De Anima* and the *Parva Naturalia* is one objective of the book as a whole and the primary objective of this chapter. The second objective is to evaluate the cogency of Aristotle's approach to psychological phenomena. Aristotle's brand of psychophysicalism will come under particular scrutiny. To bring out the unique features of his position I shall contrast Aristotelian psychophysicalism with pre-Socratic materialism and Platonic dualism and compare it with twentieth-century materialism. Psychophysical analysis, as Aristotle understands it, is a form of hylomorphic analysis, so the final section is devoted to the discussion of recent critiques of psychological hylomorphism.

1. The Theoretical Foundations

The foundational principles have substantial textual support as well as modern analogues. These features provide us with a good starting point, so let us now consider each principle from both perspectives. The descriptive and prescriptive versions of the Psychophysical Principle will be discussed at the same time since Aristotle tends to conflate the two; the other principles will be discussed in turn.

"It seems that all the affections [*pathē*] of the soul involve the body—passion, gentleness, fear, pity, confidence and further, joy and both loving and hating" (403a16–18). Aristotle makes this statement in the first chapter of the *De Anima*. A similar pronouncement is made in the first chapter of the *De Sensu*: "The most important characteristics of animals seem to be common to soul and body, for example, sense perception and memory and passion and desire and appetite generally as well as pleasure and pain" (436a7–10). The thesis that many, possibly all, psychological states have physiological bases is evident in much, if not all, of Aristotle's theorizing about psychology.[10] Yet Aristotle does not emphasize the role of the body to the exclusion of the mind. Hence he criticizes Democritus for giving a purely mechanical account of animal motion that makes no reference to choice or thought (*De An.* 406b24–25). In explanations of cognitive or affective states, physiological states are of interest to the psychologist just insofar as they are amenable to formal descriptions ascribing beliefs, intentions and feelings to the subject.

By the end of the first chapter of the *De Anima*, both the descriptive and the prescriptive forms of the Psychophysical Principle have found expression. At 403a19–25, Aristotle cites as evidence for the Psychophysical Principle our susceptibility to certain emotions when we are in certain physiological states. Subsequently, the principle in both its forms is shown to be a powerful tool in the critique of his predecessors' views, which without exception, according to Aristotle, involve the misguided reduction of psychological states to purely physical states or the equally misguided construal of psychological states as purely psychical states.[11]

Affirming the psychophysical character of psychological states enables Aristotle to extend an analytic tool that he has found useful in a number of other contexts—the distinction between matter and form—to the analysis of the relationship between mind and body and to the analysis of particular psychological faculties. Aristotle's psychological hylomorphism has a number of advantages—some of which will be mentioned in a moment, others of which should become clearer in subsequent chapters as we examine the details of Aristotle's theory. Psychological hylomorphism also provides a handle on Aristotle's construal of psychophysicalism, for the relation of form to matter is discussed at some length in other (nonpsychological) contexts; we can draw upon these discussions to gain greater clarity about the relation of mind to body.

In the *Physics*, the distinction between matter and form is the device for distinguishing between the substratum or subject that underlies a change and the characteristic that is acquired in the course of the change.[12] The man who learns music is the matter for an alteration brought about by the acquisition of the form of musicalness. In the *Metaphysics*, form is identified with the principle of organization that makes a thing what it is and matter with the stuff that is so organized.[13] The form of a house is its function, to be a shelter for people and animals; the matter of a house is whatever stuff it is made out of (1043a14–21). Despite differences in application and differences in import in different treatises, hylomorphic analysis always involves the differentiation of the material basis of an object or state from the structure or functional organization that determines its character.

In *De Anima* I, 1, having affirmed the psychophysical character of psychological states, Aristotle goes on to discuss different approaches to defining such states. The dialectician's definition in terms of the form (*eidos*) is contrasted to the natural scientist's definition in terms of the matter (*hulē*). The former defines anger as the desire for retaliation; the latter, a boiling of the blood or heat around the heart (403a30–31). Aristotle decides that the psychologist should employ both types of definition. The relation between the components of a psychological definition is the same as the relation between the formal and material descriptions of other composites. Although the formal and material descriptions of a composite are both true of that composite, the form is not identical to the matter. The desire for retaliation is not identical to the boiling of blood, nor is a shelter for people and animals identical to bricks and stones. Nor is the form identical to the composite. A shelter is realized in bricks and stones, but qua form it also exists as the object of the architect's art (*Met.* 1032a28–b14) and qua embodied form it may exist in many different types of material. Anger qua psychical (formal) state is the desire for retaliation; anger qua psychological (composite) state is the desire for retaliation realized in a boiling of blood around the heart.

In the second book of the *De Anima*, when Aristotle begins his own account of psychological faculties, he makes the soul the form of the body.¹⁴ This has several advantages. First, it ensures the unity of the animal as a whole (cf. 414a14–20). Body and soul are not sandwiched together to make an animal; rather the body is the material substratum that is organized in a particular way, and the principle of organization is its soul. Aristotle compares the animal to the eye, its soul to sight, and its body to the pupil (412b18–22).¹⁵ The formal description of an eye is a functional description in terms of the capacity to see.¹⁶ The material description picks out the physical structure that underlies the function.

As the functional organization of an animal, the animal soul is integrally bound up with the body (cf. 412b6–8). The soul is the capacity to carry out all the physiological and psychological functions that constitute living for a particular kind of creature. The more complex the organism, the more complex the soul. Plants have the simplest form of soul, and thus they are capable of nutrition, reproduction and growth. Animals have a more complicated form of soul, for they are able to perceive and move about as well as possessing the nutritive capacities. The souls of human beings are still more complex and include the capacity for reasoning.

The soul so conceived is not open to the criticism that Aristotle raises against dualist accounts:

> And yet some such explanation [of mind-body interaction] would seem to be required, as it is owing to their relationship that the one acts, the other is acted upon, that the one is moved and the other causes it to move; and between two things taken at random no such mutual relations exist. The supporters of such theories merely undertake to explain the nature of the soul. Of the body which is to receive it they have nothing more to say: just as if it were possible . . . for any soul taken at random to pass into any body. (*De An.* 407b17–23; cf. 414a20–25)

Having made the *psuchē* a unified complex of vital capacities that accounts for a biological individual's being alive and being the kind of organism it is, Aristotle is on solid ground applying the Normative Psychophysical Principle to the explanation of particular capacities. Just as it is possible to describe the animal in terms of its form or matter, or both, it is also possible to describe its psychological states in these terms. The formal and material descriptions pick out different aspects of the psychophysical state, which like the animal is a single thing. As a consequence, Aristotle's treatment of all psychological phenomena (with the possible exception of noetic activity) is shaped and unified by a single methodological assumption.¹⁷

Aristotle's analysis of specific psychic capacities proceeds in accordance with the Psychophysical Principle. The capacity is described formally and assigned to the bodily system that it enforms, and both are attended to in the explanation of that aspect of psychic function. The formal description of the capacity to see is in terms of the actualization of color, which is described by a ratio of black/dark to white/light.[18] Because the matter of the eye is organized in a particular way, such that it is receptive to various ratios of black/dark to white/light, the eye is capable of seeing (*De An.* 422b23–24).[19] Although it is possible to describe the form or function of an eye without referring to the physical structure of the eye, the instantiation of the form depends upon the existence of a bodily organ that is so enformed. Even in the case of thinking—the one psychical state that Aristotle refuses to assign to a particular bodily organ–a general dependence on the body is affirmed (403a8–10). Aristotle often speaks as if thought were an emergent property that depends in a quite direct way upon perceptual capacities that are realized through physiological processes (cf. 429b10–17). In contexts where he affirms the distinctive character of noetic activity, Aristotle still insists that human thought always employs *phantasmata* (sensory representations).[20]

The Psychophysical Principle has a modern analogue in psychological functionalism. The central tenet of functionalism is the thesis that mental states are functional states to be defined in terms of their causal roles.[21] A strict functionalist definition of a psychological state makes no reference to physiological states or to phenomenal features. On the other hand, many functionalists are materialists who believe that the psychological states given functional analyses can ultimately be identified with neurophysiological states.[22] At first glance, Aristotle's position seems to be remarkably similar. He gives formal descriptions of psychological states that do not mention physiological features, and he also believes that most psychological states have physical realizations. However, the differences between Aristotelian hylomorphism and modern functionalism tell against the assimilation of the one to the other. In the first place, an adequate psychological definition according to Aristotle mentions the form of the psychological state, and the formal description mentions phenomenal and intentional features.[23] Aristotle has no interest in defining mental states in terms of behavioral outputs.[24] He defines perceptual states in terms of the apprehension of sensible qualities, thus to hear is to be aware of differences in pitch.[25] Aristotle makes no attempt to define the internal state in terms of its causal role with respect to behavior or other internal states; to do so would be to reduce the formal/psychical description to a purely functional one. This project would be flatly rejected by Aristotle as utterly misguided. In the second place, just as Aristotle allows the formal definition to refer to phenomenal features of the experience, he includes a physiological description in the full definition of a psychological state. Psychological states are construed as functional states of certain bodily organs. In this respect, Aristotle's position is closer to the construal of functional states found traditionally in the biological sciences than to that of many modern philosophers of mind.[26]

Another theoretical assumption that shapes Aristotle's psychology is the Actuality Principle, the thesis that a cognitive faculty is potentially what its object is actually. Like the Psychophysical Principle, the Actuality Principle makes its first appearance in the first chapter of the *De Anima*. There it motivates a series of questions.

> It is also difficult to determine which of these are naturally different from each other, and whether we ought to investigate the parts first or the functions of these, for instance, thinking or the intellect, perceiving or the perceptual faculty and similarly concerning the others. And if the functions are first, again someone might ask whether we ought first to investigate the corresponding objects, for instance, the object of perception before the faculty of perception and the object of thought before the intellect. (402b10–14)

In the second book, Aristotle makes the order suggested above his own (415a18–22). When in the fifth chapter Aristotle turns to the analysis of the senses, he begins with a discussion of their objects.

Although well attested to in his analyses of cognitive faculties, the Actuality Principle is not defended by Aristotle. The explanation lies in part in the conception of psychic faculties he inherits from his philosophical predecessors. Aristotle finds the pre-Socratic philosophers asserting a garbled form of the Actuality Principle.

> But the earlier physical philosophers did not speak well in this case, thinking nothing white nor black exists without sight, not flavor without taste. In one way they spoke correctly but in another they did not. For the sense and its object are said in two ways, as potentialities and as actualities; in the latter case what they said happens but in the former case it does not. (426a20–25)

The pre-Socratic version of the Actuality Principle collapses the distinction between reality and appearance (cf. *Met.* 1009b1–1010a5). Aristotle avoids this untoward consequence by appealing to the distinction between actual and potential sense objects.

Although this fact is not mentioned by Aristotle, Plato also appeals to cognitive objects to individuate cognitive faculties. This consequence of the Actuality Principle plays an important part in the argument in *Republic* V to show that knowledge and belief have different objects.

> In the case of a faculty I look to that alone which it is related to and what it accomplishes and in this way I call each of them a faculty and that which is related to the same thing and accomplishes the same thing I call the same faculty and a faculty which is related to and accomplishes another thing, I call other. (477cd)

Similar epistemological considerations probably motivate Aristotle's advocacy of the Actuality Principle. If, in fact, a faculty is known and defined in relation to its object, then acceptance of the Actuality Principle ends speculation about what features the faculty might have in itself that *ex hypothesi* are not taken into account in the definition.

In the *Theaetetus*, Plato espouses a theory of perception that contrasts the dispositions for seeing and for being seen to actual seeing and being seen.

> then it is that, as the vision from the eyes and the whiteness from the thing that joins in giving birth to color pass in the space between, the eye becomes filled with vision and now sees and becomes not vision, but a seeing eye, while the other parent of the color is saturated with whiteness and becomes, on its side not whiteness, but a white thing, be it stick or stone or whatever else may chance to be so colored. (*Theaet.* 156de)

The seeing eye comes into existence simultaneously with the colored object, whereas the existence of the eye that can see is independent of the existence of the object that can be seen, and conversely (156a–157a).[27] Plato speaks of the seeing and the being white as twin products of the interaction of the sense organ and the external object. Aristotle in *De Anima* III, 2 exploits the notion of simultaneous realizations of the potential for perceiving possessed by the percipient and the potential for being perceived possessed by the object to argue that there is a single realization of both, that seeing, the second actuality of sight, and the nameless second actuality of color (viz., color-as-perceived) are one and the same (425b26–426a19).[28] To describe the process as a seeing is to describe it in relation to the percipient; to describe it as a being white is to describe it in relation to the object. The Actuality Principle provides Aristotle with a justification for treating the "twins" of the *Theaetetus* as two different descriptions of the same process. If the faculty is potentially what its object is actually, the eye's seeing would be an actualization of color.[29] There is a single event that from one point of view is a seeing and from another, a coloring.

Terms meaning actuality, namely, *entelecheia* and *energeia*, are first encountered in *De Anima* II, 1 as part of the general account of the soul; slightly later they are encountered again in the discussion of perception in general in II, 5.[30] Having originally described the soul as the form of the body in *De Anima* II, 1, Aristotle revises this definition twice; in both of the later versions "first actuality" (*entelecheia hē protē*) is substituted for "form." The final definition asserts that the soul is the first actuality of a natural body having organs (412b5–6). A first actuality is likened to the possession of knowledge as distinguished from its use, which is analogous to a second actuality. As the form of the body, the soul is the complex of vital capacities that are characteristic of the type of living thing in question. The exercise of the capacities making up the soul is the second actuality of the body. Second actualities are teleologically prior to first actualities, that is, the first actuality exists for the sake of the second. "Animals do not see in order that they may have sight, but they have sight that they may see" (*Met.* 1050a10–11). Since a first actuality is defined in terms of the corresponding second actuality (cf. *Met.* 1049b12–16), the processes through which vital capacities are realized are epistemologically prior to the capacities.[31]

> And if we ought to say what each of these is, for instance, what the intellectual faculty is or the perceptual or the nutritive, we ought to say before this what thinking and perceiving are, for, with respect to definition, operations and actions are prior to their faculties. And if so, still prior to these we ought to consider the corresponding objects, for we ought to give an account of these first for the same reason. (*De An.* 415a16–21)

The epistemological priority of the object is due to its ontological priority.[32] When a person tastes something salty, for instance, the characteristics of the salt determine the characteristics of the event of tasting in which the sense is exercised.

In *De Anima* II, 5, Aristotle argues that changes from first to second actualities are unique in that the move to second actuality preserves and completes the nature of the capacity, while in other types of change the original state is destroyed in the process. Since the faculty is potentially what its object is actually, there are no object-independent characteristics to be lost in the transition from dispositional to occurrent cognitive state and object-dependent characteristics are actualized, not lost, in the change. Audition, the first actuality of the ear, is the receptiveness to ratios of sharp to flat pitch, and a sound is a ratio of sharp to flat pitch.

Aristotle extends the Actuality Principle to the physical processses that are the material causes of perception (cf. *De Part. An.* 647a6–10). The external object that acts on a sense does so by virtue of having certain characteristics (potentially perceptible features) that affect the medium between the percipient and the object. The medium in turn affects the sense organ. A characteristic shared by the object, the medium and the organ is required by the Actuality Principle. In the case of sight, this characteristic is transparency. Transparency is possessed by the external object to a limited extent (*De Sens.* 439a22–30); by the medium, either water or air, to a great extent (*De An.* 418b4–20); and by the organ of sight, which is made up of water (*De An.* 425a4).

The conception of cognitive objects that is expressed in the Actuality Principle also has an analogue in contemporary theories of mind. In the late nineteenth century, Franz Brentano, an Aristotelian scholar and psychologist, argued that intentionality (being directed upon an object) is the distinctive characteristic of the mental.[33] Although the universality of this feature of mental life has been challenged, it is now widely accepted for cognitive states.[34] Two theses are combined in the modern conception of the intentionality of mental acts: (1) the mental act is directed upon an object and (2) the object need not exist in the extramental world but is projected into the world by the cognitive act.[35] The person who fears death does not fear the thought of dying but actually dying. Aristotle accepts a stronger variant of (1). The Actuality Principle makes the awareness of an object a necessary feature of a cognitive act; it also makes the character of a mental act dependent upon its object. Undoubtedly, Aristotle accepts an analogue of (2). He assumes that the cognitive object is apprehended as existing in the world or as being related to actually existing things in one way or another. Neither (2) nor its Aristotelian analogue follow from the Actuality Principle; however, in the case of perception, where the Actuality Principle is interpreted in light of a causal theory of perception, Aristotle has a theoretical justification for (2).[36] There is a further point of disagreement between Aristotle and Brentano. Aristotle invokes the Actuality Principle in discussions of the physical basis of perception (*De An.* 422a7, 422a34–422b10; *De Sens.* 438b26–439a4).[37] This use of the Actuality Principle has no analogue in modern treatments of intentionality; it does, however, illustrate Aristotle's thoroughgoing commitment to psychophysicalism.

The third foundational principle to be discussed is the Sensory Representation Principle. According to this principle, if the focal object of a mental act is a sensory object, then the cognition is an exercise of one of the constituent faculties of the perceptual faculty of the soul. Unlike the Psychophysical and Actuality Principles, the Sensory Representation Principle is not asserted as a general principle; yet it is equally important. The wide range of activities assigned to the perceptual faculty is a direct consequence of this principle. The influence of the Sensory Representation Principle, however, is less obvious in *De Anima* II than elsewhere. The assignment of sense perception to the perceptual faculty of the soul does not occasion why-questions of the sort that are provoked by Aristotle's assertion in *De Anima* III, 2 that perceptual self-consciousness is a form of perception or by the claim that it must be a sense that recognizes the difference between white and sweet (426b12–15). The modern reader is often puzzled by such claims—why assign apperceptual judgments to a perceptual faculty? The answer is given at 426b15: the faculty that is exercised in an apperceptual judgment must be a sense because its objects are sensibles.[38] This is the Sensory Representation Principle in a nutshell.

The Sensory Representation Principle is evident in Aristotle's treatment of *phantasia* (imagination) in the *De Anima* and the *Parva Naturalia*. *Phantasia* differs in several important respects from imagination as we conceive it (see *De An.* III, 3); among other things, *phantasia* includes the illusory or distorted impressions of external objects (428a12–15).[39] Its other major function is the presentation of *phantasmata*, namely, complexes of sensible characters (see chap. 4). Because its object is a complex of sensible characters, *phantasia* is assigned to the perceptual faculty of the soul—as is made clear in the *De Insomniis* where the *phantastikon* (faculty of imagination) is explicitly subsumed under the perceptual faculty (459a15–23). Memory and dreaming are assigned to the perceptual faculty in the *Parva Naturalia* on similar grounds. (*De Mem.* 450a9–15; *De Ins.* 458b10–459a22). Both involve the apprehension of *phantasmata*, so Aristotle makes both of them functions of the *phantastikon*.

The Sensory Representation Principle engenders a broad conception of the perceptual faculty because Aristotle subscribes to a notion of sensory representation.[40] All the cognitive activities falling under the perceptual faculty employ sensory representations. Representation is the depiction or description of objects and states of affairs involved in perception, memory, dreams and thoughts. Sensory representation is the depiction of objects or states of affairs through the use of sensible characters (colors, sounds, flavors, etc.). Sensible characters are properties that physical objects possess in relation to percipient beings; sensible characters are actualized as the objects of perception and are preserved as the objects of *phantasia*. That the apprehension of complexes of sensible characters can function as a mode of internal representation is evident from Aristotle's account of animal movement. In the sublunar realm only human beings are rational; all other creatures must manage without the noetic faculty of the soul. Nonetheless, other animals move about, find food, water and shelter, mate and care for their young. Aristotle invokes *phantasia* to explain these complex behaviors.[41] *Phantasia* plays the role in animal behavior that thinking plays in human behavior. Aristotle even occasionally suggests that *phantasia* is a rudimentary kind of thinking (*tis noēsis*) (*De An.* 433a10).[42] To put Aristotle's point in modern terminology: the animal has a capacity for internal representation such that it is able to represent objects in the world, not present to the senses, and to envisage possible courses of action through *phantasia*. This capacity must depend upon sensory representation alone because (nonhuman) animals cannot employ the abstract mode of representation, which is constitutive of rationality.

The distinction between the perceptual faculty and the rational faculty rests ultimately on the difference between these two modes of representation—one of which is solely dependent upon sensible characters as the vehicles of representation; the other of which, while still dependent upon *phantasmata*, primarily employs a language-like vehicle.[43] According to Aristotle, a distinctive mark of rationality is the ability to reason discursively (*De An.* 434a5–11, *De Mem.* 453a10–14). This leads him to argue that *phantasia* is not a form of belief (*doxa*) because belief carries conviction (*pistis*) but *phantasia* does not (*De An.* 428a20–22). Conviction involves the recognition of the grounds on which the judgment rests, and this requires a representation sufficiently complex to allow the thinker to make a judgment based on consciously held reasons. Such logical and conceptual complexity exceeds the representational capacities of an organism limited to sensory representation. Nonetheless, the complexity of the behaviors Aristotle explains by appeal to the perceptual faculty implies a broad notion of sensory representation.[44]

The comparison of the Sensory Representation Principle to modern conceptions and practices will be more easily made if we distinguish between the function of the Sensory Representation Principle, namely, the assimilation of a number of different mental processes to perceptual functions, and the notion of sensory representation itself. The Sensory Representation Principle as such does not have a counterpart in modern philosophy or psychology. Giving a unified account of the subset of mental states constituted by perceiving, remembering, dreaming and imagining is no longer seen as desirable. The notion of sensory representation, on the other hand, has a modern analogue in the recognition of a pictorial mode of internal representation. Whether and to what extent human thinking involves pictorial representation is currently a source of controversy among philosophers and psychologists. There has been a widespread tendency on the part of philosophers to assimilate states having sensory contents, such as perceivings and imaginings, to states employing symbolic representation.[45] However, recent findings by psychologists are causing some members of the philosophical community to reconsider the earlier opposition to a sensory mode of representation.[46] In general, psychologists have exhibited a greater willingness to allow thought to employ images. Some have even made iconic representation the mode of thought in young children.[47] A number of psychologists now believe that some internal representation is pictorial, and in support of their position they cite an ever-growing body of experimental data.[48] The reservations about mental imagery found in modern philosophical literature are alien to Aristotle, who finds the notion of sensory representation unproblematic and appeals to it in explanations of a wide variety of psychological phenomena.

The Sensory Representation Principle has a further advantage. By assimilating cases of apperception and other cognitions involving sensory contents to cases of perception, the Sensory Representation Principle enables Aristotle to use the theory of sense perception as the foundation for his account of a number of complex cognitive activities. Thus the Sensory Representation Principle dovetails nicely with the Analytic Principle, the only methodological principle that remains to be discussed.

The Analytic Principle recommends the division of the phenomenon to be explained into its most fundamental parts and then the construction of an explanation of the whole from the explanations of the parts.[49] Tailored to fit the occasion, the Analytic Principle is asserted by Aristotle early in *De Anima* II. No sooner does Aristotle give a general definition of soul than he questions the utility of this approach and stresses the importance of analyzing individual psychic faculties:

> It is clear that there will be one definition of the soul in the same way that there will be one definition of figure. . . . But as in the case of figures, a common definition might be produced which would fit all of them but would not be peculiar to any figure. And similarly in the case of the types of soul mentioned. For it would be absurd, both in this case and in the others, to investigate the common definition, which will not be peculiar to any existing thing and will not be according to the proper and indivisible species, neglecting such a definition. (*De An.* 414b20–28)

The investigation of psychological phenomena requires a general conception of the nature of the soul so that the investigator can pick out the items to be studied. The soul is a complex of vital capacities, according to Aristotle; as such, it includes all the capacities that distinguish living things from nonliving things. Aristotle groups these capacities together under four generic faculties—the nutritive, the perceptive, the noetic and the locomotive faculties. Then, following the practice he recommends, Aristotle examines each in turn. Within these groupings, he looks at the constituent functions, starting again from the most pervasive. The general description of perception in II, 5 quickly gives way to the detailed treatment of the individual senses in the following chapters.

The Analytic Principle not only shapes Aristotle's psychology, it embodies an explanatory ideal found in a number of Aristotelian treatises. The groundwork for the Analytic Principle is laid in the *Posterior Analytics*, where Aristotle takes up the general requirements a discipline must meet to count as a science (*epistēmē*).[50] As envisaged there, a completed science is an axiomatic system of propositions, expressing necessary truths and explicating the nature of a particular kind of entity, for instance, change or number.[51]

Commentators often point to the discrepancies between Aristotle's practice of science and the epistemology of the *Posterior Analytics*.[52] Nonetheless, there is ample evidence that Aristotle always believed that a science should be centered on a single genus, with the notions that constitute the genus isolated and defined. It is illustrated time and time again in the Aristotelian corpus.[53] A typical treatise begins by establishing the genus to be discussed—the *psuchē* in the *De Anima*, the good for persons in the *Nicomachean Ethics*, change in the *Physics*.[54] Then, having clarified what is properly included under the genus in question, Aristotle turns to the determination of the proper parts of the genus and subsequently defines these. Both the model of explanation described in the *Posterior Analytics* and Aristotle's procedure in other treatises attest to his commitment to the ideal expressed in the Analytic Principle.

Aristotle's adherence to the Analytic Principle is evident in his treatment of sense perception. Aristotle takes the basic perceptual capacities to be the five senses and offers an analysis of each in turn; he then makes the senses the basic building blocks in the account to follow in *De Anima* III and elsewhere of the more complex perceptual phenomena.[55] He fills out the account of sense perception by hypothesizing cooperative activity on the part of several senses. Although such activity is attributed to the common sense, Aristotle is careful to point out that the common sense is not another sense over and above the joint activity of the five senses (*De An.* 425a14–18; see Modrak 1981c).

The influence of the ideal expressed in the Analytic Principle on the subsequent history of philosophy and the history of science is too obvious to need further discussion. In the twentieth century, the Analytic Principle has given way in many quarters to reductionism—the call for the subsumption, whenever possible, of one type of explanation under another type that deals with more fundamental entities, for instance, the subsumption of the biological sciences under the physical ones. In the most austere form of reductionism, the ideal is the reduction of all types of explanations to explanations in terms of the configurations of elementary particles (see Oppenheim and Putnam 1958). The form reductionism has taken in the modern philosophy of mind is the doctrine that theories employing terms referring to mental states are in principle eliminable in favor of theories employing only neurophysiological concepts (Smart 1959; Rorty 1965; Armstrong 1968). The reduction of psychological explanations to neurophysiological ones is viewed as a first step toward the ultimate reduction of psychological explanations to physical explanations in terms of subatomic particles. The reductionist program of modern philosophy is motivated by concerns similar to the ones that motivate Aristotle's espousal of the Analytic Principle, namely, the desire to explain complex phenomena by appeal to simpler ones. In spite of this similarity, Aristotle is not a reductionist in the modern sense. He would reject as misguided any attempt to reduce psychology to physiology.

These five principles—the Psychophysical Principle, the Actuality Principle, the Sensory Representation Principle, the Analytic Principle and the Normative Psychophysical Principle—provide the theoretical skeleton that underpins the discussion of the various functions of the perceptual faculty of the soul in the *De Anima* and the *Parva Naturalia*. They are the source of the unity and simplicity of Aristotle's theory of perception. The accounts of sense perception, apperception, imagination and memory are unified by a shared set of methodological assumptions. The Sensory Representation Principle insures that all these faculties have the same kind of object—a sensory content. The Analytic Principle results in a comprehensive theory of perceptual functions that is built upon the account of the five senses. Simplicity is achieved because the common theoretical foundation allows Aristotle to posit only a few basic capacities and types of objects to explain all the cognitive functions assigned to the perceptual faculty of the soul.

2. Perception in General

By the end of *De Anima* II, 3, Aristotle has set out the general methodology to be followed in subsequent chapters. With the theoretical framework in place he is ready, in *De Anima* II, 5, to begin to construct an explanatory account of perceptual experience.[56] The topic is "the whole of perception." Here one finds the first application of the Actuality Principle to the senses and an account of change and of actuality and potentiality that can best be explicated against the background conception of the psychophysical character of the mental. Much of this chapter is devoted to the explication of the remark that perception is a kind of alteration (*alloiōsis tis*).[57] Here, as in a similar passage in the *Physics*, Aristotle's choice of words suggests that perception qua alteration differs from the standard case of alteration.[58] This suggestion is realized a few lines later, when Aristotle calls attention to the several senses in which a thing may be said to have a potentiality for changing in a particular respect and the several senses in which a thing may be said to undergo an alteration. One form of alteration is "to the negative states and the other to the habits and nature" of the subject of change (*De An.* 417b13–16). The first is illustrated by the change from ignorance to knowledge through learning; the second, by the change from dispositional to occurrent knowledge.[59]

The example may be clearer than the criterion Aristotle gives for distinguishing between kinds of alteration. What he needs and is trying to formulate is a general description of a unique kind of alteration, a description that will fit perceiving as well as the exercise of knowledge. As far as the latter is concerned, Aristotle could get the desired result by distinguishing between changes that are under an agent's conscious control and those that are not. Aristotle is tempted by this solution (cf. 417a27–b8), but since in the case of perception he cannot adopt it, he abandons it. He opts instead for a difference between changes that involve the destruction of some characteristic of the subject and changes that simply involve the "preservation of that which is so potentially by that which is so actually." In the latter case, at least one structural feature of the original state must be preserved in the terminal state.

A common subject matter is the only feature that might plausibly be attributed to both the dispositional knowledge of a particular fact about the Greek language and the exercise of this knowledge. When the grammarian exercises his knowledge, the grammatical fact is the object of his cognitive activity. In the case of dispositional knowledge (the knowledge the grammarian has when he is not exercising his knowledge), there is no conscious awareness of the object of knowledge and ipso facto no object of awareness. But if the grammarian may be truly described as knowing a particular fact when not thinking about it, then some property of the grammarian must make this description true. The existence of a cognitive structure that would enable the mind to be actively aware of the fact in the future would meet this requirement. The nature of the cognitive faculty is preserved in its exercise because its nature qua cognitive faculty is having a certain structure that it shares with its object.[60]

To sum up: the account in *De Anima* II, 5 of perception in general turns on (1) the identification of perception with alteration and (2) the specification of a special sense of alteration to fit the exercise of a cognitive faculty. Both follow in a quite direct way from Aristotle's psychophysicalism, which is formulated partly in response to his predecessors. Plato had allowed the body a role in perception, and the pre-Socratics had typically identified perceiving with bodily change (cf. Beare 1906). Aristotle agrees that perceiving is the alteration of a sense organ, but he reformulates the position, making perception the alteration of a sense organ under a psychophysical description. This makes the percipient's experience, namely, the awareness of sense objects, an integral part of the analysis. Thus, Aristotle proposes to distinguish between ordinary physical changes and the sort of change involved in perceiving qua awareness. Spelling out the difference between the two requires the Actuality Principle, for it postulates a unique relation between the cognitive state and its object. This relation justifies the claim that the exercise of a cognitive faculty preserves the faculty and hence is an actualization as distinguished from an ordinary alteration.

3. The Psychophysical Model of Perception

If my account of Aristotle's psychophysicalism is correct, we would expect to find all three types of description—psychical, physiological and psychophysical—employed by Aristotle when he turns to the analysis of sense perception in *De Anima* II, 7–11. In light of Aristotle's general preference, expressed in the Analytic Principle, for components over wholes, we would expect the discussion to be centered on the physiological substratum and on the psychological function that determines the character of a perceptual state. A quick survey of these chapters will bear out both expectations. As a heuristic device, I propose to make a distinction between a formal and a material level of discourse and to see if it is possible to piece together a physical and a psychical story for each sense.

The first question then is: Can one find in *De Anima* II both physical and psychological descriptions for the trio of sense organ (*aisthētērion*), sense (*aisthēsis*) and sense object (*aisthēton*) whose treatment is central to the analysis of sense perception? The *aisthētērion* clearly has a physical description as a body of a certain sort; it also has a formal description as that which has the capacity for receiving the sensible form without the matter (*De An.* 424a17–25; 425b23–24).[61] The sense object has a formal description as a sensible quality, but it also has a physical description as a characteristic of an external object that produces certain changes in the medium and consequently in the organ.[62] The sense is amenable to both types of descriptions—as a power of a bodily organ and as a capacity to experience sensible qualities of a certain type. Or, if the exercise of a sense is under consideration, sensing is on the one hand an alteration of a bodily organ and on the other an actualization of a perceptual capacity (cf. sec. 2).

Despite some vagueness about the mechanisms involved, the physical story is told in some detail. Each of the five senses is a power of a specific bodily organ. The organs are the eyes or perhaps more precisely the eye jelly, the ears, the nose, the tongue and the nameless organ of touch within the body.[63] The five peripheral organs are connected to a central organ in the region around the heart (*De Som.* 455a19–26; *De Part. An.* 656a28). In *De Anima* II, Aristotle assumes a version of the causal theory of perception. The external object of perception causes the change in the sense organ, which is the material cause of the perception. Aristotle concentrates on the process by which the object acts on the peripheral sense organ—presumably as a consequence of extending the Actuality Principle to the material basis of perception—and so he looks for physical characteristics shared by the object, the medium and the organ. The eye jelly consists of liquid because the eyes must be capable of being affected by the change brought about in a transparent medium by colored objects.[64] The inner ear is made up of air because sound is propagated through confined air. The nose is dry and the tongue moist for similar reasons.

The sense object under a material description is simply the characteristic of the external object of perception that brings about the change in the medium, which is communicated to the organ.[65] Color is the property of causing a particular change in a transparent medium, air or water, in the presence of light. In the *De Sensu*, color is identified with the limit of the transparent at the surface of bodies (439a30–31).[66] Sound is the setting of a mass of air into motion (*De An.* 419b9ff.). Odor is the giving off of a smoky vapor (*De Sens.* 438b25). Flavor is a property of liquids due to the presence of dry particles in them (*De*

Sens. 441b19). The objects of touch are physical properties such as temperature and solidity (*De An.* 423b27–29). As is evident from this quick survey, the material causes of perception are not neglected. Aristotle appeals to bodily organs, to external objects of perception, and to changes in a material medium and organ to explain sense perception.

By comparison, the psychical or formal side receives short shrift. Its presence is most evident in the treatment of the proper object(s) of each sense. As a consequence of the Actuality Principle, the description of a sense is based on the description of its proper object. Proper objects are sensible qualities. The proper object of sight is color; of hearing, sound; of taste, flavor; of smelling, odor; and of touch, the tangible qualities. An instance of the proper object of a sense falls along a continuum between two opposite qualities that determine the limits of that proper sensible.[67] Black and white are the fundamental pair of sensible qualities determining color; any color whatsoever may be represented as a ratio of black to white.[68] Sounds are defined by the sharp and the flat.[69] The fundamental pair for flavor and odor are the sweet and the bitter.[70] Even though Aristotle fails to reduce the tactile objects to a single pair of opposites, the analysis of them is also in terms of pairs of opposites: the hot and the cold, the wet and the dry, the hard and the soft.[71] As usual, Aristotle is concerned to give a uniform and systematic account of similar phenomena.

It is significant that in the case of the senses and their proper objects this account turns on "raw feels"—how the world is subjectively experienced, how it smells, tastes and sounds. When we perceive, we recognize (*gnōrizein*) and distinguish (*krinein*) sensible qualities.[72] Aristotle might have endorsed a purely mechanical model of perception where the body simply registers certain physical characteristics of its immediate environment, but he did not. For him, to perceive is to be conscious (*De Som.* 454a1–7).

At this point, it should be clear that we can reconstruct Aristotle's discussion of the individual senses as a two-tiered theory of psychological form and physiological substratum. Each sense is systematically and simultaneously considered from two perspectives—as the capacity of a bodily organ to be affected in a particular way by objects in its environment and as the capacity to have certain kinds of subjective experiences. Nonetheless, a reductive materialist reading of *De Anima* II, 7–11 has not yet been ruled out, for the various forms of perception might still turn out to be nothing over and above physiological changes under material descriptions. Since the physical story is told in greater detail, one might wonder whether in practice Aristotle takes the Psychophysical Principle to entail an irreducibly psychophysical model or the reduction of the psychological to the physiological.[73] Here I will quickly survey some of the general considerations against a reductive materialist interpretation of Aristotle's psychology. Unfortunately, these arguments alone will not suffice to rule out an Aristotelian version of reductive materialism. In the next section I show why it would be a mistake to attribute any form of reductionism to Aristotle.

First, *De Anima* I, 1 gives "the desire for retaliation or something of the sort" as a sample definition of the formal cause of anger (403a30–31). The *Rhetoric* (1378a30–32) states the definition in greater detail: "anger is a desire accompanied by pain for revenge for a conspicuous slight directed without justification toward oneself or towards what concerns one's friends."[74] This definition quite clearly refers to intentional states—a conscious desire for a specific end and beliefs about one's situation in the world, what has befallen one, and what one hopes to bring about. It is precisely such items that Aristotle claims a reductive materialist theory cannot take into account (*De An.* 406b25). Shortly before stating the formal definition of anger, Aristotle groups perception together with anger and a number of other psychological activities, describing them as activities that involve both body and soul (*De An.* 403a7). Hence we would not expect the formal definition of a perceptual state to be eliminable in favor of a physiological definition.

Second, Aristotle's willingness to countenance psychological states that have no bodily counterparts and his willingness to sometimes use idioms that suggest the soul is the subject of experience also reveal his openness to explanations and descriptions couched in purely psychological terms. Thinking, Aristotle argues in *De Anima* III, 4, has no bodily organ. This fact alone makes a physicalist construal of Aristotle's conception of thought very difficult, if not impossible, to maintain (see chap. 5).

Equally troublesome are the passages that treat the soul as a subject, from the notorious pilot passage (*De An.* 413a8–9) to more innocuous passages such as *De Sensu* 438b10 where Aristotle says that "the soul or the perceptual faculty of the soul is not on the surface of the eye." Although I do not believe these passages commit Aristotle to substance dualism, he comes to talk in this way because he employs psychical descriptions and sometimes slips over into using descriptions that appear to refer to psychical subjects.[75] These descriptions are the psychical counterparts of the psychological descriptions that seem to refer to purely physiological processes. Both types of description can and should be treated as elliptical.

Third, Aristotle explicitly appeals to experience in presenting his theory of perception. For instance, he begins the discussion of the sense of smell by acknowledging the difficulties of treating a sense that is relatively poorly developed in humans:

> In the case of the sense of smell and its object it is less easy to define these than the things already mentioned, for it is not so clear what sort of thing smell is as it is in the case of sound or color. The cause is that our sense of smell is not accurate but is worse than that of many animals. (*De An.* 421a7–10; cf. *De Sens.* 441a1–3)

Aristotle starts from the subjective experience of human percipients and works back to a theory of perception that takes account both of the phenomenal characteristics of objects of perception and the physical/physiological substratum of perception. He uses words such as *color* and *sound* to identify the features of the world-as-experienced, which he wants to discuss. Then he concentrates upon giving an account of the physical causes of perception.

In order to reject once and for all the view that in spite of himself Aristotle subscribes to reductive materialism, we should determine the particulars of how his position differs on the one hand from pre-Socratic materialism and on the other from the reductive materialism of the twentieth century.

4. Reductive Materialism: Ancient and Modern Versions

From the endorsement of the Psychophysical Principle in *De Anima* I to the analysis of the five senses in *De Anima* II, Aristotle's commitment to psychophysicalism does not waver. Aristotle's brand of psychophysicalism has rightly been described as sui generis. Its unique character will be more easily seen in contrast to other accounts of the mental. I propose first to look at psychophysicalism as Aristotle understood it in contrast to his predecessors' views and then to bring out the implications of his position by comparing it to modern accounts. Aristotle is keenly aware that he is not the first philosopher to raise and attempt to answer questions about the nature of the soul. His claim to eminence is that his account succeeds where others have failed. The second contrast is to twentieth-century materialist theories. The variety of possible materialist stances and the implications of each have become much clearer in the last forty years. Armed with these distinctions, we will be in a good position to determine the precise contours of Aristotle's materialism and hence of his psychophysicalism.

Aristotle developed his psychological theory in response to pre-Socratic materialism and Platonic dualism.[76] Aristotle's strategy (in *De Anima* I) is to use two attributes of ensouled creatures, namely, the capacity for self-movement and the capacity for perception, as touchstones for testing the theories of earlier thinkers who took these attributes to be the distinguishing marks of the *psuchē* (403b25–28).[77] Using this method, Aristotle highlights the inadequacies of the ancient versions of reductive materialism.

If Aristotle is to be trusted, most of his predecessors believed that the soul moves the body by being itself in motion (403b29–405a29). Among others, he mentions Anaxagoras, the Pythagoreans, Heracleitus, Democritus and Plato's *Timaeus* in this connection. Democritus constructed the soul out of rapidly moving, spherical atoms whereas the *Timaeus* employed circles of the same and the different.[78] Nevertheless, the earlier philosophers agreed that the soul is in motion; this feature is fatal to their accounts, Aristotle argues, because the concept itself is incoherent (405b31–407b26).

Aristotle finds a further difficulty with reductive materialist accounts of self-movement. Of necessity they ignore cognitive and affective states, such as beliefs and desires, that seem to play a central role in motivating actions (cf. Plato, *Phdo.* 99ab). "[A]nd more generally the soul does not seem to move the animal in this way but through choice [*prohairesis*] and thought [*noēsis*]" (*De An.* 406b24–25).

Earlier treatments of cognition do not fare any better under Aristotle's scrutiny. The typical pre-Socratic account of perception makes perception the result of the reception by bodily organs of effluences from external objects. Some pre-Socratics hold that the receptive organ and the stimulus share a common structure, whereas others hold that opposites perceive opposites. In either case, the hypothesized components of the *psuchē* are few while the objects perceived are many, and this is problematic—for reasons Aristotle points out in criticism of Empedocles: "But then it is of no help that the elements exist in the soul, unless the proportions [*logoi*] and the combination were also present; for each will recognize its like, but nothing will recognize bone or man, unless these are also present in the soul" (410a7–10). Furthermore, we have a number of different senses, but physicalist theories reduce all forms of perception to the sense of touch (*De Sens.* 442a29–b3).[79]

The underlying objective of Aristotle's multifaceted criticisms of his materialist predecessors is to demonstrate that any theory that identifies the soul with a material substance or identifies psychic states with states of matter will fail to give an adequate account of movement and perception.

Aristotle's psychology embodies his rejection of the materialism of the pre-Socratics and the dualism of the Platonists. Recognizing the bankruptcy of these approaches, Aristotle sets out to steer a middle course by propounding a psychophysical theory. Aristotle uses formal descriptions to capture the psychical features of psychological states and material descriptions to capture the physiological features; he combines the two into one description to capture all the characteristics of the irreducibly psychophysical state.

This conception of psychological explanation leads Aristotle to construct a psychophysical model of perception. We can easily establish the presence of this model in the *De Anima* and the *De Sensu*, but exactly what the model entails is much less clear. By contrasting Aristotle's position to that of the modern psychophysical identity theorist, I hope to bring out the salient features of Aristotle's position.

The psychophysical identity theory is typically asserted as part of a general reductionist strategy where the objective is the reduction of all explanatory theories to physics, to explanations in terms of elementary, submicroscopic particles. As part of this program, psychophysical identity statements would serve as bridge principles in the reduction of psychology to neurophysiology.[80] Optimally these statements would assert the identity of particular types of psychological phenomena with particular types of physiological phenomena (type-type identity statements). However, in some cases statements asserting the identity of a particular instance of a psychological state with a neurophysiological state (token-token identity statements) might be the best scientists could do.

The best way to compare Aristotle's position to the modern identity theorist's position is to decide whether Aristotle accepts either type-type or token-token identifications of the psychological with the physiological. There is some reason to doubt that Aristotle does, for to accept the identification of the psychical with the physical would seem incompatible with psychological hylomorphism. On the other hand, since physicalist interpretations of Aristotle's theory of perception abound, it seems reasonable to investigate the question further. Since what we mean by *psychological* is ambiguous with respect to the psychical (formal) and psychological (psychophysical) in Aristotle's sense, we should investigate whether Aristotle identifies psychical states under formal descriptions with physiological states under material descriptions; we should also investigate whether he identifies psychological states under composite descriptions (which combine the formal and material descriptions) with physiological states under material descriptions.

Aristotle appears to accept identity statements of the latter sort, that is, statements that assert the identity of the (composite) psychological state with a physiological state. For instance, Aristotle would no doubt accept as true a statement of the form "seeing red is such-and-such a change in the eye jelly of a living organism."[81] The first question is: If this statement expresses an identity, does it express a token-token or a type-type identity? Certain considerations suggest the latter. Presumably, were Aristotle interested in identifying mental with physical states, he would be primarily interested in type-type identity statements, for his intent is to offer a general theory about the character of psychological states. To make claims about particular instances that cannot be generalized to claims about the type in question would not further his objectives.[82] But other features of his account are inimical to establishing type-type identities. Aristotle recognizes differences between species. Smelling the pungent odor of fish bait may correspond to the same type of change in the noses of two human beings, but the fish's experience of the odor of the bait is another matter. Aristotle is quite explicit on this subject—different species may employ different physiological structures to the same end, the apprehension of a particular type of sense object.[83] Fish possess a sense of smell, but in their case this sense is not dependent upon inhaling air. If type-type identities are construed, as they often are, as holding across species, then "identity statements" of the sort that Aristotle would accept are more properly described as token-token identities.[84]

There is a further peculiarly Aristotelian restriction on the identification of the psychological with the physiological. While it is true to say that one and the same event is both a seeing and the occurrence of certain changes in a properly functioning eye, the physiological description depicts a physical system with psychological capacities, namely, a bodily structure that is capable of the awareness of color. The possession of this capacity cannot be reduced to characteristics of the materials making up the visual system.[85] The transparent in the eye is affected by color in the same way that the transparent medium is, that is, it transmits the ratio of white to black found in the object, but unlike the medium the eye is able to see. Although this capacity can be explained by the structure of the eye and the integration of the eye into the biological system that is the living animal, it is not thereby reduced to a purely mechanical response. The visual system possesses the structure it does because its constituent matter is enformed by the capacity to see (cf. Cooper, forthcoming).

Perceptual capacities are attributed to physiological systems on the basis of states of awareness. The latter are by definition the actualizations of sensible qualities, of colors, sounds, odors, flavors and tangible qualities. The object of the experience determines the character of the experience (the Actuality Principle), and the object is identified by its phenomenal characteristics. To smell is to be aware of odor, so Aristotle attributes a sense of smell to terrestrial animals and to fish, despite the fact that smelling is realized in different physiological processes in the two cases.

Just as the identification of the physiological process with a perceiving is dependent upon the applicability of a psychological description, so the identification of a physical characteristic such as the limit of the transparent with a (potential) sense object is dependent upon the applicability of a phenomenal description to the characteristic. The characteristics of physical objects that bring about experiences of such items as colors or sounds in percipients, insofar as they are dispositions to bring about these experiences, are potential objects of sense. The same physical characteristics may also bring about changes in nonpercipient substances. Aristotle wonders whether "something that is unable to smell can be affected by odor or something that is not able to see by color" (*De An.* 424b3–5). He decides it is impossible that odor should produce any effect other than smelling or color any effect other than seeing. Since colors and odors are perceived through a medium, Aristotle is certainly not denying that the physical characteristics that bring about these perceptions affect anything else, but he is arguing that qua odor or color, that is, qua dispositions to cause perceptual experiences of a certain sort, these physical characteristics can bring about no changes other than smelling and seeing respectively.[86]

To summarize the difference between Aristotle and the modern psychophysical identity theorists: Aristotle would allow us to conclude from a true statement to the effect that *B* sees red that certain changes are taking place in *B*'s eye jelly; he would even allow us to draw this conclusion from the psychical description of *B*'s state as the apprehension of a certain *logos* of black to white. In this respect, Aristotle's position is the same as the identity theorist's, but in other respects it is not.[87] Were Aristotle a modern identity theorist, he would hold that seeing red just is a particular motion of the eye jelly. Aristotle's actual view is that a *logos* of black to white enforms a certain motion of the eye jelly and that both should be mentioned in the psychologically adequate description of the seeing. What the modern identity theorist treats as two alternative descriptions of the same physiological state, one couched in mental terms and one couched in physiological terms, Aristotle would treat as alternative and incomplete descriptions of the same psychophysical state.[88]

On the other hand, we should not draw sweeping ontological conclusions from the fact that terms referring to phenomenal features and to raw feels cannot be eliminated from descriptions of perceptual phenomena in favor of terms referring to physical states. The phenomenal features enform an event occurring in a bodily organ and thus transform a mere *kinēsis* into an *energeia*, for example, the phenomenal features of a color transform a motion through a liquid into a seeing. Not only does the event occur in a bodily organ but it is simultaneously the actualization of a psychophysical capacity and the actualization of the perceptible qualities of a physical object. The psychophysical description fixes the denotation of the irreducible psychical element of that description, so at the ontological level, Aristotle's theory of perception is irreducibly psychophysical not dualistic.

However, one might question the coherence of Aristotle's psychophysical definitions by pointing out that at least some of the characteristics predicated of a particular psychophysical state under a psychological description cannot be intelligibly predicated of the state under a physical description.[89] For instance, anger under the description "desire for retaliation" can properly be described in terms of its intensity, although movements in the blood are not properly described as intense, whereas they are properly described as rapid, unlike desires. Aristotle does not speak to precisely this problem, but had he been pressed to do so, he might have appealed to the one-but-different-in-being (*einai*) principle. This principle is invoked to explain how a single event can be the actualization of a sense and the actualization of its object (*De An.* 426a9–19). To describe the event as the actualization of a sound, for instance, is to ascribe characteristics to it that are not ascribed by the description, "actualization of the capacity for hearing." Granted, Aristotle does not typically apply the same-but-different-in-*einai* principle to the relation between matter and form. Yet he invokes it to explain the sense organ's being a physical magnitude while the sense is not (*De An.* 424a25–28), and hence he might invoke it here as well. Or he might have modeled his answer on the recognition expressed in this principle—that different descriptions of the same object may license different inferences. As a final defense, Aristotle would probably claim, like many of his modern counterparts, that whether a particular psychological description is realized in a particular physiological process cannot be answered on linguistic grounds; rather it must be answered on empirical grounds. If in fact the state is realized physiologically, then to so describe it is unproblematic.[90]

A different challenge to the cogency of Aristotle's psychophysicalism has been raised by Hardie (1976, 402ff.). Terms such as *anger* or *desire* are typically used to refer to dispositions, but physiological descriptions of the sort employed by Aristotle seem to refer to occurrences. The physiological and psychological definitions of anger offered by Aristotle apparently denote entities falling under different logical categories. To resolve this difficulty we must establish that it is possible to state both formal and material definitions for dispositional and occurrent anger and that Aristotle's formal and material definitions are such that they might hold of the same type of anger. The Psychophysical Principle commits Aristotle to the occurrence and duration of some physiological change that serves as the substratum for the psychological disposition. "The boiling of blood" seems an improbable description of a dispositional state, but need we take these words so literally? Were we to take Aristotle's description as a stand-in for the physiological state, whatever it may be, that obtains from the onset of an anger until its termination, we could bypass Hardie's objection. As the disposition to experience an occurrent desire for retaliation, anger would be a tendency toward blood boiling. This leaves Aristotle's actual examples to serve as definitions of occurrent anger.[91] The physiological definition appears to be a definition of occurrent anger. The psychological definition can be used as a description of either occurrent or dispositional anger since desires may be either occurrent or dispositional.

5. Hylomorphism and Psychophysicalism

A final set of conceptual objections to Aristotle's psychophysicalism center on the extension of hylomorphism to the psychological sphere. Aristotle endorses the Normative Psychophysical Principle because he sees the deficiencies of reductive materialism and of dualism so clearly; for the same reason, he construes the relation between mind and body as an instance of the relation between form and matter. Several scholars have argued that this is a serious mistake.[92]

Ackrill was critical of making the body the matter of the biological individual.

> Aristotle's definitions of *psuchē* resist interpretation because (i) the contrast of form and matter in a composite makes ready sense only where the matter can be picked out in such a way that it could be conceived as existing without that form, but (ii) his account of the body and bodily organs makes unintelligible given the homonymy principle, the suggestion that this body or these organs might lack or have lacked *psuchē*. (1972–73, 126)

In the case of many artifacts, the matter can be picked out without difficulty because the matter of a particular artifact may be easily changed into the matter of another artifact. The bronze constituting a sphere may be melted down and molded into a rectangular object. In the case of a living thing, the matter, the body, is not easily transformed into the matter of something else. The body comes into existence with the ensouled individual, and so it could not have been the matter of any prior individual. It might, however, survive the death of the ensouled individual for a brief period. If it does, then Socrates' matter may be described in the same way as the bronze. Just as the bronze might have been something other than a sphere, Socrates' matter might have been, and someday will be, the matter of something other than Socrates, namely his corpse. To block this suggestion, Ackrill invokes the homonymy principle, namely, the doctrine that the parts of a biological individual are properly described as organs only as long as the individual is alive. "The eye is matter for sight, and if this is wanting it is no longer an eye, except homonymously, just as an eye in stone or a painted eye" (De An. 412b20–22).[93] Although Aristotle is hesitant about extending this principle to flesh and bone (cf. De Gen. et Corr. 321b28–32), he appears to do so in the De Generatione Animalium (734b24–31). If not even flesh and bone survive the death of the individual, then there seems to be no bodily stuff that serves as Socrates' matter and that might have been the matter of something else.

In the interest of clarity, the difficulty Ackrill raises will be broken down into two distinct objections: (1) it is not possible to refer to or otherwise pick out the matter of a biological individual; and (2) given the homonymy principle, bodily organs cannot serve as the matter of biological individuals. The first entails the rejection of the claim of such expressions as "the matter of Socrates" to genuinely refer to the matter of Socrates, presumably on the grounds that such expressions are vacuous unless we possess some description of the matter that fixes the referent of the expression. If we allow expressions such as "the constituent matter of A" to pick out the matter of A, the homonymy principle will be relatively unproblematic. Ackrill's difficulty arises when we insist that there be an independent description of the matter of A (M_A) available that makes no reference to A or to the form of A (F_A).

This is a stringent requirement that may not bear scrutiny.[94] In the first place, it is incompatible with the traditional doctrine of prime matter. The ascription of this doctrine to Aristotle is controversial today, but for our present purposes it will suffice to point out that the traditional doctrine of prime matter becomes unintelligible unless we allow expressions such as "the matter of A" to refer to matter that cannot be otherwise specified.[95] Moreover, this difficulty can be generalized to Aristotle's treatment of substantial change. The criterion Aristotle proposes for distinguishing between alteration (change in quality) and generation (change in substance) is the duration of the same matter through the change in the first instance and the transformation of the matter in the second instance (*De Gen. et Corr.* I, 4). If the notion of matter is coherent only when it is possible to describe M_A in a way such that the description would apply to M_B were A to change into B and would mention neither A nor B, as Ackrill believes, then Aristotle's account of substantial change is seriously flawed.

Fortunately, it is far from obvious that the contrast between matter and form requires an independent specification of the matter.[96] How one arrives at a notion of constitution or of constituent matter should be distinguished from the notions themselves. Aristotle makes use of artifacts to illustrate the notions of matter, form and composite, but once a general understanding of these notions is achieved, it is possible to apply them in contexts where the matter is not amenable to a precise specification. Aristotle's hylomorphic analysis places a weaker constraint than Ackrill suggests—independent descriptions are needed for two of the three, matter, form and composite. M_A would have a clear denotation if A did and if a precise description of F_A were available to make the distinction between A and M_A coherent. Then M_A might be described as the constituent stuff that F_A enforms to make A.

However, (2) is not so easily discounted. According to (2), an animal's organs cannot serve as its matter. Yet Aristotle seems to treat the body and bodily parts as the matter of the biological individual. Thus the homonymy principle returns to haunt us because the distinction between M_A and A collapses if F_A is already present in M_A. The only solution is to drive a wedge between the complex functional organs such as the heart and the hands and the proximate matter of the biological individual. This is not as impossible a task as it might at first appear for Aristotle recognizes different levels of matter corresponding to different levels of complexity. The structure and organization of the matter that is enformed by the capacity to see and thus constitutes a functional eye would of necessity be very complex.[97] A recently blinded eye, even though it lacks the form of the eye, namely, sight, might possess much of the structure of the functional eye, so much in fact that one might be inclined to use *ophthalmos* (eye) of it (*De An.* 412b20–22). Aristotle's example of the homonymous use of *ophthalmos* points the way to the distinction we were looking for—the difference between a highly complex eyelike material and the functional eye.

Contrary to (2), the homonymy principle supports the distinction between highly organized organic matter and functional organs. The homonymy principle recognizes the ambiguity of reference of the names of organs and allows for their (homonymous) use for items other than functional organs. Aristotle uses *ophthalmos* to refer to the matter of the eye at 412b20 and to refer to the functional eye at 412b18–19. The ambiguity of reference of the name of an organ would be problematic if there were no way to specify the different referents. However, as became apparent in the discussion of (1), a description of the organ and of the form is available; thus there is also available a derivative description of the matter of the organ, namely, "whatever stuff is enformed by the capacity to see to constitute the eye." On the assumption (now shown to be justified) that the distinction between an organ and its matter is unproblematic, Aristotle uses the same word to refer to both.

Strictly speaking, the matter of the organ is called by the name of the organ homonymously, but in this case, unlike the case of the nonfunctional organ, there is also a proper use of the name. The matter of the eye is potentially an *ophthalmos*, and in this description *ophthalmos* is used nonhomonymously (*De An.* 414a15–19; cf. *Met.* 1042b10). This may explain Aristotle's willingness to use *ophthalmos* without qualification for the matter as well as for the organ.

Therefore Aristotle has an answer to both (1) and (2), which are at the heart of Ackrill's objection to psychological hylomorphism. Contra (1), it is possible to refer to the matter of the living thing. Strictly speaking, (2) is true, but properly understood it is compatible with Aristotle's practice of using the names of organs to refer to the matter of the biological individual. Furthermore, it is now possible to make sense of the claim that the matter of a given biological individual might not be its matter. Immediately after dying the animal loses all the vital capacities that constitute its species-form and determine the character of its organs. It loses the capacities to see, to walk, to digest food, but the material structures that serve as the proximate matter for these capacities persist for a short period. In brief, it is possible to construct within the constraints of Aristotle's notions of form and matter and bodily organs a coherent account of the relation between mind and body that construes this relation as an instance of the relation between form and matter.

An important presupposition of this reply to Ackrill—that Aristotle's conception of psychological form is unproblematic—is indirectly challenged by Sorabji (1974). The identification of the soul with the form of the body is not the locus of Sorabji's worry; he is concerned with the extension of hylomorphism to the definition of psychological states, that is, with the hylomorphism expressed in the Normative Psychophysical Principle. Sorabji finds Aristotle's formal descriptions of psychological states unsatisfactory because they make implicit reference to physiological states. The formal definition of anger mentions desire, but desire like anger is a psychophysical state, so this definition also refers to matter. Sorabji proposes to construct an "Aristotelian" description of the formal cause of desire that is purified of the physiological connotations of Aristotle's examples but accords with Aristotle's general views on the subject. The "Aristotelian" formal description makes desire the efficient cause of action toward an end. This description meets Sorabji's immediate objective. There are, as Sorabji recognizes, however, several difficulties with his solution. It has limited application; not all cognitive or affective states are amenable to description as efficient causes of action. More important, Aristotle shows little interest in defining psychological states in terms of the behaviors they typically issue in (cf. Robinson 1978).

The solution lies instead in the recognition that Aristotle often uses the same term for the psychic form and the composite psychophysical state. Just as Aristotle uses *ophthalmos* for the matter of the eye and the functional eye, he uses *orgē* (anger) and *orexis* (desire) for the form and for the composite state. This practice would be bewildering, were it not the case that Aristotle accepts the designation of the term in ordinary speech as the primary sense—*ophthalmos* for eye, *orexis* for desire. In ordinary usage, terms such as *orexis* or *orgē* are used for psychological states. Aristotle assumes that in common parlance these terms have a purely psychical sense.[98] When *orexis* appears in the formal definition of *orgē*, it is being used in the popular psychical sense. However, when a philosophical analysis of *orexis* is undertaken by Aristotle, *orexis* turns out to be a psychophysical state.[99] The ordinary sense of *orexis* finds expression in the formal definition of *orexis*, which is now, from the standpoint of the theory, treated as the description of the formal (psychical) component of a psychophysical state.[100]

The most challenging problems other commentators have raised in connection with Aristotle's psychological hylomorphism have, I hope, been laid to rest in this section. Still a shadow of a doubt remains. My defense of Aristotle has been based on a somewhat disconcerting practice on his part—the use of the same term in a popular and a theory-laden sense. Although this practice is well documented in the Aristotelian corpus, it engenders confusions. It is often not immediately obvious in which sense Aristotle is employing a given term, and in many instances, the present included, a harsh critic may object to the charitable reading and choose a reading that makes Aristotle's position untenable. To such a critic, there is often no further answer except the advocacy of charity.

In subsequent chapters, Aristotle's psychological hylomorphism as expressed in the Psychophysical Principle in both its forms will be shown to be a powerful analytic tool in the construction of a theory of sense perception and perceptual consciousness, and this too counts in its favor.

3

The Five Senses and the Common Sense Perception and Apperception

Sense perception, namely, the employment of the five senses in connection with their proper, common and incidental objects, is the function of the perceptual faculty that Aristotle investigates at greatest length. The importance of sense perception derives from its status as the most fundamental operation of the perceptual faculty. Aristotle initially constructs a model to explain sense perception; he subsequently expands this model to include other perceptual capacities. Insofar as possible, Aristotle tries to increase the number of functions of the perceptual faculty without positing psychophysical structures in addition to the five senses.

To account for powers not identical to any of the special senses, Aristotle envisages a faculty, namely, the common sense, made up of all the senses. Each special sense is defined in relation to a particular type of sensible quality; the sense of sight is of color; the sense of hearing, of sound; the sense of smell, of odor; the sense of taste, of flavor; and the sense of touch, of the tactile qualities. The exercise of a sense requires the actualization of its proper object. To explain the perception by a sense of objects other than its proper object(s), Aristotle makes the proper object the vehicle for the perception of the other objects; common objects, such as shapes and motions, and incidental objects, such as people and buildings, are superimposed on proper objects. Because we see colors, we see colored shapes; because we see colored shapes, we see faces and tables. Not only is the Analytic Principle in evidence here but so is the Sensory Representation Principle. In making sensible qualities the vehicles for the perception of all other objects, Aristotle introduces a method of analysis that will culminate in making these same qualities the vehicles for imaginings, memories and dreams. Aristotle's objective is to bring a variety of perceptual and apperceptual phenomena under the purview of a theory of perception developed for the five senses. His device for doing this is the common sense, the faculty made up of the five senses, whose functions include reflexive awareness, complex perceptual judgments and memory.

However, our first task in this chapter is to complete the examination of Aristotle's account of the five senses. As we discovered in the last chapter, the cogency of Aristotle's psychophysical analysis of perception depends on the existence of a formal and a material description of the sense and its activity. Having discussed the physiological side of Aristotle's account in some detail, we should now take a look at the formal side. When Aristotle wants to capture the difference between the capacities of the sense organs and other physical potencies, he appeals to the notion of a *logos* (proportion) or *mesotēs* (mean).[1]

1. The *Logos* Doctrine

Each of the five senses is a *logos*; each is the capacity possessed by a bodily organ to respond to a range of sensible features, the range being determined by a pair of opposite qualities. The exercise of a sense is the actualization of the *logos* of opposite qualities that defines the sense object in question.

> For that which perceives is a magnitude while neither what it is to be percipient nor the sense are magnitudes, but a certain *logos* and power of the former. And it is clear from these considerations also why excess in the objects of sense destroys the sense organs; for if the movement is too strong for the organ, the *logos* is destroyed—and this is the sense— just as the consonance and the pitch are destroyed when the strings are struck violently. (*De An.* 424a26–32)

The *logos* doctrine, as I shall call it, is a difficult doctrine to grasp. What is the *logos* a *logos* of? Is it a *logos* of sensible qualities or of physiological characteristics?[2] Why does Aristotle appeal to this seemingly obscure notion to explain the elusive difference between sense organs and other organic bodies?

The *logos* doctrine is a direct consequence of the Actuality Principle. The sense is potentially what its object is actually. Each type of proper object is defined by a pair of opposite sensible qualities.[3] This insures the unity of the type of proper object and hence the unity of the sense. The pair of opposite qualities describes a continuum, and particular instances of the proper object fall along that continuum. When Aristotle says that a color is a *logos* of white to black, he means to call our attention to the individuating conditions for color in general. Nonetheless, the notion of a *logos* does double duty here for it also explains the unique character and unity of the particular color under consideration. We experience red, not so much white and so much black (cf. *De Sens.* 448a9–11). Just as an arithmetical *logos* assigns a single value to the relation between two numbers, a *logos* of sensible qualities determines the unitary character of the individual sense object.[4]

Aristotle's analysis of the proper objects is a further elaboration of a conception he finds in his predecessors. Several pre-Socratic accounts took the opposition of hot to cold or sweet to bitter to be fundamental to sense experience.[5] Even Parmenides, after banishing opposition from the noumenal world, reinstated a pair of opposites to explain our experience of the world (cf. *Met.* 986b27–34). Plato frequently describes sensible qualities in terms of pairs of opposites (*Theaet.* 184b; *Phil.* 17c). Aristotle systematizes this picture by using a single pair of opposites to define each type of sensible quality.

Not only were pairs of opposites mentioned in earlier perceptual theories, they also played a central role in many of the cosmological theories of Aristotle's predecessors (*Phy.* I, 5). Here again Aristotle agrees with the earlier approach and makes the basic principles in his physical theory two pairs of opposite features, the hot and the cold and the wet and the dry (*De Gen. et Corr.* II, 2–3). In combinations of two (one from each pair), these features determine the characters of the four elements.[6] Aristotle's cosmological theory reinforces the conception of tangible objects as *logoi*.[7] In the *De Generatione et Corruptione*, Aristotle reduces the several pairs of tangible opposites mentioned in the psychological treatises (namely, hard and soft, rough and smooth, hot and cold, and wet and dry) to the two physically significant pairs (329b16–330a29).

The proper objects, the objects whose actualizations are a necessary feature of any perception whatsoever, are constituted by the relation between two opposite qualities. As phenomenal objects, they are *logoi* of sensible qualities.[8] Acidic flavors, for instance, are *logoi* of the sweet and the bitter (*De Sens.* 442a18–20). Now, the exercise of a sense is the actualization of its proper object, that is, the actualization of a *logos* of sensible qualities. But since the active sense is one with its object, it too must be a *logos* when actualized. As an (unexercised) capacity, the sense is potentially a *logos*. This description of the sense makes no reference to the sense's embodiment. It is the purely formal description of the sense required by Aristotle's psychophysicalism. The actualization of the *logos* is the reception of the sensible form without its matter (*De An.* 424a18).[9]

With the help of the *logos* doctrine, Aristotle is better able to articulate the relationship between the physical substratum of a perception and the apprehension of sensible qualities that enforms the physiological process. By appealing to his version of the causal theory of perception and the *logos* doctrine, Aristotle tells a comprehensive and coherent story about how the external object of perception affects the medium and the percipient (see chap. 2, sec. 3). The physical structure of the external object is such that the object possesses two closely related dispositional properties—the power to bring about a temporary change in the medium and the organ and the power to bring about a perception in the percipient. The physical basis for these dispositions is a formal structure analogous to the form of the sense object. The physical structure that underlies the disposition to bring about changes in a transparent medium and in an eye is the limit of the transparent at the surface of a body (*De Sens.* 439a30–31).[10] The form of this characteristic is expressed as a *logos* of dark to light. This *logos* determines the formal aspect of the change transmitted through the medium to the eye. Unlike the medium, the eye sees; seeing is the actualization of a color, also a *logos* of dark to light.

Aristotle is not as clear as he might be about the relationship between the *logos* of dark to light, whose existence is not dependent upon being seen, and the *logos* of dark to light, which is actualized as the proper object of a seeing. He resolves the tension between his realism (colors exist in the world) and his representationalism (colors are actualized in the act of perceiving them) by invoking the distinction between potential sense objects and actual ones.[11] He may have intended to enforce this line of analysis by appealing to *logoi* in the discussion of the material substrata of perceptions. If so, what he should have said but did not is that the *logos* of dark to light possessed by the physical characteristic, which is the material cause of the perception of a color, is potentially the same *logos* as the one actualized in seeing. This would also solve another oft-told conundrum: How can a (red) physical object when not perceived be actually red as apparently required by the Actuality Principle and potentially red as Aristotle seems to claim? Aristotle's answer turns on the distinction between color and color-as-perceived (*De An.* 426a13–15). When no one is looking at it, the object is actually red in the first sense but only potentially red in the second sense; it possesses a *logos* of light to dark that is potentially the same *logos* as the one realized in the perception of red.

Despite the usefulness of the *logos* doctrine, recent Aristotelian scholarship abounds with interpretations that would restrict this doctrine in one way or another.[12] Some commentators would restrict it to certain physiological responses; others, to certain sense objects. On the former construal, "the literalist interpretation," the sense organ responds to a physical characteristic it shares with the external object by registering the difference between itself and the object with respect to this property. This model works best for the sense of touch and seems to fit Aristotle's description of touch at *De Anima* 424a2–7:

> And hence we do not perceive anything which is equally hot and cold or hard and soft but excesses of these, as the sense is a kind of mean [*mesotētos*] between the opposites in the objects of sense. And for this reason, it discerns sense objects, for the mean [*meson*] is capable of judging. It becomes with respect to one of the extremes the other.

The sensed temperature seems to be determined by the difference between the sense organ's temperature and the object's. On the literalist interpretation, to describe touch as a *mesotēs* is simply to identify the sensed temperature with this difference.

The initial plausibility of the literalist interpretation soon gives way to perplexity. Aristotle immediately extends this model to the other senses (424a7–10; cf. 431a19), but surely the eyes do not possess color or the ears sound in the same way that the sense organ of touch possesses temperature and solidity. Second, the model does not even work for touch. Were the literalist interpretation right, the organ of touch would literally become as hot as the object sensed or as solid, for the object is said to make the organ such as it is (424a2).[13] But this is absurd. Moreover, in the next chapter Aristotle distinguishes between taking on the temperature of a hot body and having the *mesotēs* constitutive of sensing heat.

> And this then is why plants do not perceive, although they have a part of the soul and are affected in some way by tangible objects; for even they are chilled and warmed. The reason is they have no mean [*mesotēta*] nor principle which is such as to receive the forms of sense objects, but they are affected with their matter. (424a32–b3).[14]

As a last resort, the proponent of the literalist interpretation of the *logos* doctrine might appeal to Aristotle's remark that that which sees is in a way colored (425b22).[15] But an argument from 425b22 alone to the literalist interpretation would be impossible to sustain, for this text is open to several different interpretations. If interpreted along the lines suggested by our initial discussion of the *logos* doctrine, the statement at 425b22 means only that the *logos* of black/dark and white/light, which is the color of the external object, is present in the watery eye jelly in the same sense in which it is present in the intervening air. Unlike the air, the eye is the locus of the actualization of the sense object (426a2–4; cf. 426a9–11, 425b22–23). Since the actualized sense object is a color, there is another way in which the eye may be said to possess color. The formal description of a seeing eye invokes the actualization of color, for the organ is potentially what its object is actually. However, the eye stands in a different relation to the color actualized in it than does the external object that is perceived as colored. An eye gazing at a red object is the locus of the event that is the actualization of red; the external object is the cause of this event, and through the event the object manifests the disposition to be perceived as red. Aristotle indicates this difference by using *hōs* (as if) to qualify "colored" in the case of the eye.

In short, the literalist interpretation is untenable. The *logos* doctrine should not be limited to physiological responses.

Let us turn to Barker's interpretation of *De Anima* 426a27–b3; it would limit the *logos* doctrine to special cases of sensing. Barker agrees that senses are *logoi*, but he denies that the exercise of a sense is always the actualization of a *logos*. According to him, Aristotle restricts the argument to show that sensing is a *logos* to specific cases, such as hearing a musical sound or tasting a "harmonious" flavor. The passage in question reads:

> And if voice is a kind of consonance, and the voice and hearing are in a way one and if the consonance is a *logos*, then necessarily hearing is also a *logos*. And for this reason the excess of either high or low pitch destroys the hearing; and in the same way in the case of flavors, excess destroys the sense of taste, in the case of colors also the too bright or dark destroys sight, and in the case of smell, a strong odor, either sweet or bitter, is destructive, as the sense is a kind of *logos*. (426a27–b3)

As traditionally interpreted, this argument involves an unwarranted generalization from hearing vocal sounds to hearing in general (cf. Hicks 1907, 441–42). Barker avoids this consequence by limiting the conclusion as well as the initial premise to a specific instance of hearing, the hearing of a musical sound.

The obstacles to adopting Barker's reading are several: On it, *phonē* at 426a27 means "a musical sound." This conflicts with Aristotle's usual use of *phonē*. Aristotle gives a detailed account of *phonē* in *De Anima* II, 8 and takes its primary sense to be the sound that an ensouled creature deliberately makes (420b5–14).[16] Were Aristotle giving *phonē* a different meaning in III, 2, he would most likely have commented on this fact.

If *phonē* means "voice" at 426a27, then the claim that voice is a consonance (*sumphonia*) need not mean that animal voices are typically or always musical but rather that they are constituted by high and low pitch (cf. Philoponus *De An. Comm.* 476, 15). This makes the generalization from hearing a voice to all cases of hearing more plausible (albeit without making the argument valid). Aristotle may have reasoned that if all the varieties of voice are *sumphoniai*, then surely all other sounds are; this conclusion might have seemed all the more compelling since it was thought to be true for all musical sounds.

At 426a31 Aristotle generalizes from the case of hearing to other sense modalities, to taste, sight and smell. This generalization is also limited by Barker to specific instances of tasting, seeing and smelling. Why Aristotle might have been motivated to extend a model based on hearing a musical sound to other sense modalities is far more perplexing than the generalization from one sense modality to another. So once more the traditional reading seems on somewhat firmer ground than Barker's reading.

The passage under consideration resembles no other passage so much as 424a25–32. There the sense is described as a *logos*; here the exercise of a sense is described as a *logos*. If we take both passages to be making general claims about the senses, then the connection between the two is readily explained by invoking the Actuality Principle: The object of sensing is a *logos*, hence the active sense is a *logos*. The sense as a power is simply the capacity to realize this sort of *logos*, so it too is described as a *logos*. Barker's reading of III, 2 obscures the connection between the two passages, for Barker claims that while the sense is always a *logos*, its exercise sometimes is a *logos* and sometimes is not.

On balance, these considerations far outweigh the reasons we might have for adopting Barker's interpretation of 426a27–b3, which would limit the description of hearing as a *logos* to specific instances of hearing. Unfortunately, the arguments marshaled against Barker do not resolve the original difficulty with the argument at 426a27–29, namely, Aristotle's hasty generalization from one case of hearing to all. I can see no way to make the argument both valid and consistent with other texts. If we wish to be charitable, we could entertain the hypothesis that at 426a27–29 Aristotle means to give an inductive rather than a deductive argument.[17] A particular kind of hearing is cited as an example in support of a claim about hearing in general, and hearing is cited as an example in support of a claim about sensing in general. As stated, the argument is not very persuasive, but Aristotle may assume that other examples, for instance, hearing a musical sound, are available for the attentive listener to supply.

To summarize, our initial impression that Aristotle intends the *logos* doctrine to apply to all the senses and to all instances of sensing has been borne out by an examination of the relevant texts. The *logos* doctrine enables Aristotle to give a uniform treatment of the senses in accordance with the Actuality and Analytic Principles; it also enables him to give a purely formal description of sensing as required by the Psychophysical Principle. This completes the picture of the five-sense model of perception presented in De Anima II and De Sensu 1–6. Let us now turn to Aristotle's account of the common sense.

2. Koinē Aisthēsis

The primary problem facing an interpreter of Aristotle's notion of the common sense is the diversity of its functions. These include the perception of the common sensibles, the reflexive awareness of perception, judgments about the unity of complex sense objects, and the discrimination of differences among proper objects.[18] How these cognitions differ is more obvious than how they resemble each other. If there are no underlying similarities, then Aristotle's conception of the common sense seems ad hoc at best and arbitrary at worst. I shall argue that Aristotle assigns all these activities to the same faculty because in every case the activity is the consequence of several senses acting as one (cf. De An. 425a31–b3). The common sense is, as Aristotle puts it, the point at which the special senses converge (426b17–427a14). This conception of the common sense enables Aristotle to complete the account of sense perception within the theoretical framework provided by his five methodological principles.

Aristotle introduces the common sense to explain the perception of the common objects. He introduces the latter notion in the initial description of sense objects in De Anima II, 6: "By common sensibles [koina] are meant motion, rest, number, figure, size; for such qualities are not the proper objects of any single sense but are common to all. And in fact, a particular motion can be perceived by touch as well as sight" (418a17–20; cf. 425a14–16). The distinctive features of the koina are (1) they are perceived by more than one sense and (2) they are perceived in themselves (kath' hauta). Aristotle does not defend either of these claims; he takes them as evident from observation. The first seems to be relatively unproblematic. The second seems to stand in need of further explication and justification, for the perception of a koinon kath' hauto differs in several respects from the perception of a proper object kath' hauto. Kath' hauta perceptibles act directly on the sense perceiving them. As a potential sense object, a kath' hauto perceptible exists as an independent, physical characteristic; as an actual sense object, a kath' hauto perceptible exists as the object of the perception it causes. The proper objects can be reduced to basic pairs of opposite sensible qualities, but the koina are not amenable to a similar reduction. A shape perceived through sight and touch cannot be represented either as a *logos* of dark to light or of hard to soft; yet its perception seems to be just as immediate as the perception of color or solidity. The feature(s) that bring about the perception of shape simultaneously through eye and hand must be in some sense independent of those bringing about the perception of color and solidity. And the feature(s) must be efficacious, that is, it (they) must act on the senses. Aristotle captures these characteristics by saying that the *koina* are perceived in themselves.

Yet Aristotle is unwilling to assign the same degree of autonomy to these features as to the proper objects. Only the latter are perceptible in the strictest sense (*kuriōs*) (418a24). Its own proper object brings about the exercise of a sense even when the sense is simultaneously exercised in connection with a common object. The proper object is the vehicle for the perception of the *koinon*. However, a different proper object may present the same *koinon* to a different sense, and this raises the question of the relation between a *koinon* and the various senses that apprehend it. Aristotle is well aware that the autonomy he ascribes to the *koina* threatens the unity of the individual senses. Since both shape and color are apparently perceived *kath' hauta* through the eyes, the sense of sight seems to bifurcate into a sense for color and one for shape. To avoid this outcome, Aristotle assigns the *kath' hauta* perception of the *koina* to the common sense (425a27).[19]

In *De Anima* III, 1, Aristotle argues that (1) there is no special sense for the *koina*, that is, the *koina* are not a sixth type of *idion* (proper object) and (2) there is a sense, namely the common sense, that perceives the *koina kath' hauta*. A difficult argument at 425a14–24 supports (1):[20]

> Nor indeed can there be a special organ for the common objects which we perceive incidentally through each sense, for instance, motion, rest, figure, magnitude, number, unity. For all these we perceive by motion, for instance, magnitude by motion (as a result, also figure, since figure is a kind of magnitude); also what is at rest is perceived by the absence of motion, and number by the negation of continuity, and by the special objects. For each sense perceives one kind of object so it is clear that it is impossible for there to be a special sense for any of these, for instance, for motion. For if so, it would be as we now perceive sweet by sight. This we do because we happen to have a perception of both and in this way we recognize them at the same time when they fall together.

This argument cites two differences between the perception of a proper object and the perception of a *koinon*.[21] First, unlike the objects proper to a special sense, the *koina* are not instances of a single quality. Motion does not underlie the perception of rest in the way in which color underlies all visual perceptions. Second, the perception of a *koinon* through a special sense differs from the perception through a special sense of another sense's proper object. Commentators are generally agreed that the second point is the crux of the argument, but there the agreement ends.

Is Aristotle implicitly appealing to the difference between the *kath' hauto* perception of a *koinon* by a special sense and the *kata sumbebēkos* (incidental) perception of the proper object of another sense by a special sense? This is unlikely. Aristotle does not mention the *kath' hauta* perception of the *koina* in the course of the argument. Having initially claimed that the *koina* are perceived *kata sumbebēkos* by the special senses (425a15), Aristotle cannot consistently base the subsequent argument on the tacit claim that the *koina* are perceived *kath' hauta* by the special senses.[22] Aristotle concludes the discussion of this topic by again acknowledging that the *kath' hauta* perception of the *koina* requires a faculty that is not identical to any of the special senses: "For the *koina*, we even now have a common sense not *kata sumbebēkos*."

On the most plausible reconstruction, the argument at 425a14–24 turns on the difference between the *kata sumbebēkos* perception of a *koinon* by a special sense and the *kata sumbebēkos* perception of another sense's proper object by a special sense, for example, the difference between the perception of shape by sight and the perception of sweet by sight. Thus, we need to account for the difference between these two types of *kata sumbebēkos* perception. What makes the difference in the two cases, Aristotle hints, is the role of learning. In the case of a special object we have a perception through several senses of one object, for example, honey-milk; as a result, we associate white with sweet. Later seeing a similar white object, we perceive it as sweet without tasting it. This *kata sumbebēkos* perception depends on previous perceptions, but the *kata sumbebēkos* perception of a *koinon* need not, indeed given the nature of the common sense cannot, require previous perceptions.[23]

The *koina* are perceived immediately (i.e., without previous learning) through the individual senses; however as long as the perception of a *koinon* is through a single sense, it remains *kata sumbebēkos* because the *koinon* is by itself causally efficacious only with respect to the power constituted by the joint activity of several senses. Sight perceives shape because the colors that act on the sense present shapes as well as hues. Sight and touch converging on a shape allow shape to emerge as an independent perceptual object (cf. 425b4–11). Although perceived through sight and touch, shape is perceived *kath' hauto* by the common sense. The emergence of a *koinon* as a *kath' hauto* object is also the emergence of a distinct perceptual capacity exercised through the peripheral sense organs and manifested when the activity of several senses converges to form a single perceptual act with a single object. Having shown that the *koina* are not a sixth type of proper object (*idion*), Aristotle is able to conclude at 425a27 that the *koina* are perceived *kath' hauta* through the common sense (*koinē aisthēsis*). The common sense is not a separate sense; it just is the capacity for the joint exercise of several senses. By this means Aristotle significantly expands the number of capacities of the perceptual system. Each special sense is limited to a narrow range of objects, but there are no similar limitations on the objects that can be apprehended through the common sense.

The common sense not only apprehends the common sensibles, it is also the faculty that enables a percipient to make various apperceptual judgments—to judge that one thing is both sweet and white or to judge that white and sweet are different kinds of sensible qualities (*De Som.* 455a15–20; cf. *De An.* 426b8–21).[24] In *De Anima* III, 2, also in *De Sensu* 7, Aristotle puzzles about the discrimination of sensible differences: "Since we judge both white and sweet and each of the objects of perception by reference to each other, by what do we perceive also that they are different? This must indeed be by a sense [*aisthēsis*]; for they are objects of perception [*aisthēta*]" (*De An.* 426b12–15).[25] Some one faculty must make the judgment, for it is not possible to make a unified judgment through several separate faculties (426b17–29). Moreover, the awareness that a proper object of one sense differs from a proper object of another (e.g., that sweet differs from white) seems as essential to and as typical of human perceptual experience as the perception of colors or shapes;[26] it too would be a case of *kath' hauto* perception.[27] If so, both proper objects must act directly upon a single sense faculty. Acting upon their respective senses, they would not bring about the perception that they are different types of sense objects.[28] Neither special sense can make the comparison because its perception of the other's object is *kata sumbebēkos* and hence dependent on the perception of its own object. Since the comparison requires the actual sensing of white and sweet, some one faculty, Aristotle argues, is affected by the objects of both senses and perceives their difference.

Judgments fitting this description are problematic for Aristotle from both the formal and the physiological perspective. Formally, each sense is responsive to a *logos* of opposite qualities. If the faculty making the discrimination responds to a *logos* of black/dark and white/light and hence is aware of color, how can it respond to a *logos* of sweet and bitter at the same time? But if it cannot respond to both objects at once, how can it judge that they are different? Physiologically, the organ undergoes a change that constitutes the awareness of a particular sensible. In the case at hand, the organ would seemingly undergo several different and presumably incompatible changes simultaneously.

In the *De Anima*, Aristotle's answer to this dilemma is in terms of metaphors. The sense in question is like a boundary (431a22) or a point (427a10–14). In these examples, a single entity (a point or a boundary) functions as more than one thing, for instance, as the point at the center of a circle functions as the terminus for all the radii (see Modrak 1981c, 417–19). The point belongs to many lines but retains its unitary character. Enormous difficulties beset an interpreter who tries to elicit from these geometrical examples an explanation of how it is possible for a sense to respond to radically different stimuli simultaneously or for an organ to be moved in opposite directions. Nonetheless, they provide further evidence that Aristotle conceives the common sense along the lines suggested above. Each sense is actualized in relation to its own proper object, sight in connection with white and taste in connection with sweet, and in this respect their operation is like two separate lines. The exercise of sight and the exercise of taste coincide in the judgment that white and sweet are different kinds of sensibles or the judgment that both are properties of honey-milk; this is analogous to the point where one line intersects another. As a single faculty made up of the five senses, the common sense is "one by number but different with respect to kinds and forms" (*De Sens.* 449a18). In the *De Somno*, Aristotle appeals to a common function of the special senses and a common part of their organs to explain these judgments.

Reflexive self-awareness is another component of perceptual experience that fascinates and provokes Aristotle. He wonders whether it is "by sight that one perceives that one sees or by another sense" (*De An.* 425b13). In *De Anima* III, 2, Aristotle seems inclined to make each sense aware of its own activity. To be aware of seeing is, Aristotle insists, to be aware of color since "the activity of the object of perception and of the sense is one and the same" (425b26).[29] The awareness of color is *ex hypothesi* seeing, so being reflexively aware of seeing is itself a kind of seeing (425b12–15). The *De Somno* finds Aristotle taking a somewhat different position: "But there is also a common faculty [*koinē dunamis*] associated with all [the senses], through which one is aware that one sees and hears; for it is not by sight that one is aware that one sees" (455a16–18). In the *De Anima*, Aristotle assigns reflexive awareness to each sense on the grounds that this is the simplest hypothesis (425b17).[30] In effect, Aristotle adds another function to the functions of the special senses, and this complicates the conception of a special sense, for a special sense can no longer be defined simply in terms of its proper object(s), as Aristotle recognizes (425b20). In the *De Somno*, this complication is avoided. The proper function of each sense is the awareness of a particular kind of object, as it is in *De Anima* II, 7–12. But apperceptual judgments of all sorts are assigned to a common faculty (*De Som.* 455a16–21).[31]

The *De Somno* account not only has these advantages, it also affords a unified treatment of reflexive awareness. In order to recognize that whiteness and sweetness are different types of sense objects, we must be reflexively aware of the perception of white and the perception of sweet. Aristotle could not assign this awareness to either sight or taste; it must be a function of the common sense. Assigning other cases of the reflexive awareness of seeing to sight complicates the picture unnecessarily.

The analysis Aristotle offers of the perception of the *koina*, apperceptual judgments, and reflexive self-awareness is one that (in accordance with the Analytic Principle) maximizes the role of the perceptual faculties in question while minimizing the number of faculties involved. The common sense is the capacity for unified activity on the part of the special senses. Invoking the common sense, Aristotle extends the range of the perceptual system as a whole far beyond the narrow confines advocated by Plato, who had restricted perceptual faculties to the apprehension of objects presented through a single sense modality (*Theaet.* 184–86).

The job of the *De Somno* passage cited above is to bring Aristotle's treatment of all the functions of the common sense together. This passage deserves to be quoted in full:

> Since each sense has a special function and a common function. The special function, for example, of sight is seeing, that of the auditory sense is hearing, and similarly with the other senses. But there is also a common faculty [*koinē dunamis*] associated with them all, through which one is aware that one sees and hears (for it is not by sight that one is aware that one sees; and one judges and is capable of judging that sweet is different from white not by taste, nor by sight, nor by a combination of the two, but by some part which is common to all the sense organs). (455a13–21)

By making the faculty for all types of apperceptual awareness a capacity possessed in common by all the senses, Aristotle provides a model of the perceptual faculty that accommodates the shared characteristics of the perceptual and apperceptual operations he assigns to the common sense. In *De Anima* III, 1, the *kath' hauta* perception of the *koina* is assigned to the common sense because the same *koinon* is perceived through several senses at once; in *De Anima* III, 2, the discrimination of sensible difference is assigned to a nonspecific perceptual faculty because its objects are diverse sense objects and for the same reason to a common capacity of the senses in *De Somno* 2. The senses acting together and "perceiving as one" possess powers they do not possess individually;[32] despite the emergence of these powers, the senses remain limited in number.

The physiological basis for the common sense duplicates the sense's psychological character. It too is simply a point of convergence; it is the physiological point at which the physical bases of the individual senses coincide. For each sense, the physiological basis consists of a peripheral sense organ, an internal organ and internal structures linking the two.[33] The internal organ or some portion of it is the same for all the individual perceptual systems. Thus, in accordance with the Psychophysical Principle, the common sense exists as the shared function(s) of the individual perceptual systems and as the form of the shared internal organ.

Up to this point we have assumed that all the passages referring to a common perceptual faculty describe the common sense. Hamlyn has challenged this assumption. In his commentary on the *De Anima* (1968a, 128–29), he urges a distinction between the common sense, the faculty for the apprehension of the common sensibles, and something he calls general sensibility, which is the source for apperceptual judgments.[34] There are many reasons for rejecting this view:[35] the most compelling is the lack of textual evidence for it.

In the *De Anima* and the *De Memoria,* Aristotle speaks of a common sense (*koinē aisthēsis*); in the *De Somno,* he speaks of a common capacity (*koinē dunamis*); in the *De Sensu,* of a nonspecific sense faculty (*aisthētikon pantōn*); and in the *De Memoria,* of a primary sense faculty (*proton aisthētikon*).[36] According to Hamlyn, *koinē aisthēsis* and *proton aisthētikon* name a perceptual faculty whose only function is the perception of the common sensibles, and *aisthētikon pantōn* and *koinē dunamis* name the faculty that discerns differences among sense objects (cf. Hamlyn 1968a, 128). Were it Aristotle's intent to distinguish between these two types of faculty, we would expect him to use similar names for the same faculty, that is, to use *koinē aisthēsis* and *koinē dunamis* for one faculty and *proton aisthētikon* and *aisthētikon pantōn* for the other. Rather than try to force a distinction on Aristotle that the text does not support, it is better to assume that he envisages only one central perceptual faculty, which, in keeping with his usual aversion to technical terms, he calls by a variety of names.

A final issue to decide is whether to follow tradition and include the perception of the incidental objects among the functions of the common sense (cf. Ross 1955, 35). Aristotle discusses the distinction between *kath' hauto* and *kata sumbebēkos* (incidental) objects of perception in more detail in the *De Anima* than in any other work.[37] He does not mention the common sense in this connection, so, should it seem advisable, we have the option of assigning some cases of incidental perception to the special senses. In order to decide this question, we need to get clearer about the nature of incidental sensibles.

Aristotle introduces the distinction between *kath' hauta* and *kata sumbebēkos* sensibles in *De Anima* II, 6. He explains what an incidental object is at 418a20–24: "An object of perception is called an incidental object, if, for example, the white thing were the son of Diares. For we perceive this incidentally, because that which we perceive is incidental to the white thing. And hence the object of perception as such does not affect us at all." The sensory basis for the perception of an incidental object does not fully determine the content of the perception. The physical characteristics of the son of Diares suffice to bring about a perception (in a healthy percipient under normal conditions) of a white thing having a certain shape and magnitude. However, only a percipient acquainted with the son of Diares would be able to peceive this white shape as the son of Diares. Similarly, only a person who has experienced flavors can perceive a white thing as sweet through sight. The object you perceive as the son of Diares, I may perceive as your obnoxious acquaintance, but unless one of us has a defective or diseased sense organ, under standard conditions we will both perceive a white object.[38] The percipient plays an active role in shaping the content of an incidental perception. If "son of X" is treated as a name and a rigid designator, to perceive X as the son of Y requires the recognition of this person as a particular individual. If "the son of X" functions as a definite description for Aristotle, then the percipient must have and apply the general concept "son of" to perceive the son of Diares.

Nonetheless, incidental objects turn up repeatedly on Aristotle's lists of sensibles. This fact alone defeats the attempt to reclassify incidental objects as objects of belief rather than perception.[39] Although commentators frequently remark that the perception of a *kata sumbebēkos* sensible is not a genuine case of perception, they seldom argue for this position.[40] If a reason is given at all, it usually turns on the allegedly inferential character of this type of perception. That the perception of a *kata sumbebēkos* sensible is the apprehension of an interpreted sensory object is beyond dispute. What is questionable is the assumption that Aristotle intends to limit the scope of perception to uninterpreted sensory contents, color patches and the like. The perception of an incidental object arises spontaneously in the percipient whose past and present experiences are conducive to the apprehension of the incidental object in question. When a white shape acts on sight under the appropriate (internal and external) conditions, it produces a perception of the son of Cleon. The incidental object is an object of perception for Aristotle because the apprehension of the complex of proper and common objects is sufficient in a particular context for the perception of the incidental object. Moreover, there is no textual evidence for attributing to Aristotle a narrow notion of perception that would exclude interpretation.

Aristotle's use of the terms *kath' hauta* and *kata sumbebēkos* to distinguish between types of sense objects provides further support for the thesis that the incidental sensibles are genuine objects of perception.[41] The distinction between *kath' hauta* and *kata sumbebēkos* properties is a familiar Aristotelian distinction.[42] In other contexts, it marks the distinction between the essential properties and the accidental properties of a composite substance. Being rational is one of Socrates' *kath' hauta* properties; having a snub nose is one of his *kata sumbebēkos* properties. Socrates' *kath' hauta* properties are a direct consequence of his having the substantial form he has. The relation of the *kath' hauta* perceptible features of a concrete particular to its *kata sumbebēkos* perceptible features is analogous to the relation between the *kath' hauta* properties of a substance and its *kata sumbebēkos* properties. In both cases, the *kath' hauta* properties are required for the very existence of the object qua object of perception or qua substance, whereas specific *kata sumbebēkos* properties are not required for the existence of the object qua object of perception or qua substance. Socrates might have had an aquiline nose, and a percipient might have perceived the white shape without having perceived the son of Diares. The *kath' hauta* perceptibles are the vehicles for the perception of the *kata sumbebēkos* perceptibles, and this is a somewhat peculiar feature of the application of the *kath' hauta/kata sumbebēkos* distinction to sensibles. But it is important to notice that the complex of *kath' hauta* sensibles constitutes the sensible form of the perceived object, and in this sense the complex of proper and common objects is more like the composite substance, which is the bearer of the *kata sumbebēkos* properties, than the form of the composite, which strictly speaking is not the bearer of these properties.

The temptation to assign all cases of incidental perception to the common sense is great. Doing so accommodates Aristotle's classification of incidental objects as sense objects and the fact that the complex of sensible qualities representing the incidental object do not fully determine its nature. There are, however, reasons for caution. *De Anima* III, 1 seems to assign two types of incidental perception to the individual senses, namely the perception of each other's proper objects (425a30; cf. 425a22–25) and the perception of the *koina* by a single sense (425a15). As we have seen, Aristotle is tempted in *De Anima* III, 2 to simplify the account of reflexive awareness by making each sense self-aware; although he abandons this view in the *Parva Naturalia*, the desire to assign as many perceptual functions as possible to the components of the perceptual system remains strong. This desire would motivate Aristotle to make the perception of a particular incidental object a function of a single sense when the vehicle for this perception acted on only a single sense. If the visual image of a white object produces the perception of the son of Cleon, the incidental perception is a function of sight; if hearing the sound of his voice, touching his soft hand and seeing his light skin produces a perception of him, then the perception belongs to the common sense. In the absence of textual evidence that Aristotle ultimately assigns all cases of incidental perception to the common sense, we should assign to the common sense only those cases that involve the convergence of several senses on a single object. This preserves the unity of Aristotle's account of the common sense without doing violence to his account of incidental perception.

3. The Physiological Basis of the Common Sense

In the preceding section we considered the structure of the common sense conceived functionally in terms of kinds of awareness. In this section we examine the physiology of the common sense. Not only is this an interesting topic in its own right, but it bears importantly on the question of Aristotle's commitment to psychophysicalism. In the preceding chapter we established that Aristotle's account of the five senses agrees with the Psychophysical Principle. In this chapter we must decide whether the account of the common sense is consistent with the Psychophysical Principle or whether it emphasizes the psychical at the expense of the physiological or vice versa. If Aristotle's commitment is fainthearted because he identifies complex perceptual capacities with forms of awareness *simpliciter*, we would expect him to pay little or no attention to the physiology of the common sense. If Aristotle's commitment to psychophysicalism weakens and he opts for a physicalist account of the common sense, we would expect him to work out in great detail the physiological model of the common sense.

Generally speaking, in the *De Anima* Aristotle pays relatively little attention to the physiology of the sense organs. In *De Anima* III, 1, Aristotle assigns a specific material to each of the peripheral organs. The eye, for instance, is made of water, the ear, of air. Aristotle makes some attempt to explain the causal mechanisms producing the physiological changes in the peripheral organs, but he makes no attempt at all to describe the changes occurring in any other part of the body. In *De Anima* III, 1, he also posits a common sense and by implication a common organ. Yet no bodily organ is named as the central organ, and no attempt is made to mark out the connections between the common organ and the peripheral organs.

The situation is slightly better in the *Parva Naturalia*. There Aristotle makes the heart the central organ in sanguineous animals, although he remains vague about the details.[43] The *De Somno* gives a physiological explanation of sleep that identifies the common organ with the heart.[44] Sleep is "a paralysis of the primary sense organ (*prōton aisthēterion*) to keep it from functioning" (458a29–30). Sleep comes about when the heavy, hot evaporation following the intake of food reaches the head and turns around and falls upon the heart, inhibiting its motions. The incapacitation of the common organ results in the inhibition of ordinary perceptual activity (455a28–b2). When the food has been digested, the evaporation dissipates and the animal awakens.

Both the *De Somno* and the *De Insomniis* mention movements in the blood to explain the transmission of sensory impulses to the common organ. Dreams occur because impulses not discharged in perception during the day reach the common organ.

> In animals having blood, when the blood settles down and separates, the movement preserves the sensory contents [*aisthēmata*] from each sense organ and the movement makes the dreams healthy and makes something appear and the dreamer believe through the things brought from sight that he sees and through the things brought from hearing that he hears. And the same is true of the movement from the other sense organs. (*De Ins.* 461a24–30)

In comparison to the movements produced by stimuli present to the senses, the residual movements are too weak to bring about sensory awareness while the animal is awake. During sleep, when the peripheral sense organs are inactive, the residual movements bring about dreams.

Turning to the biological treatises for more details, we find the same account of the central organ coupled with arguments against the Hippocratic identification of the central sense organ with the brain (*On Sacred Disease*, chaps. 17–20).[45] In the *De Partibus Animalium*, Aristotle argues on the basis of the heart's location (at the center of the body) and its structure (a uniform substance with an irregular shape) that the heart is the central organ.[46] The nature of touch, Aristotle argues, is such that its organ must be at the center of the body, and thus the common organ must be there as well. To be receptive to the characteristics of physical objects, each peripheral sense organ must be made up of a single element and the internal organ must be uniform and homogeneous (647a3–23). Actual sensory awareness, as distinguished from the transmission of sensory impulses, requires some structural irregularity; thus the heart is percipient but not the blood. The brain, on the other hand, is neither at the center of the body nor irregular in shape. Moreover, the heart develops before the brain in embryos and the perceptual faculty must be present from the start for it distinguishes animal life from plant life (666a19–23, 666a35–36). For these reasons, Aristotle concludes that the heart is the central organ.

The vehicle for the transmission of sensory impulses from the peripheral organs to the heart seems to be the blood.[47] The organ of touch connects directly with the vascular system.[48] The fluid organ of sight extends to the brain. The organs of hearing and smell connect with the blood vessels around the brain through passages (*poroi*) filled with air (*De Gen. An.* 744a1–2). Although the mechanism for sensory transmission is left unspecified in the case of the eyes, Aristotle assumes that the veins around the brain mediate the connections between the peripheral organs in the head and the vascular system as a whole (*De Gen. An.* 743b36–744a12).

An uninformed reading of the biological treatises and the *Parva Naturalia* would lead one to conclude that the blood is the internal medium of perception that communicates sensory impulses from the peripheral organs to the central organ. Nevertheless, commentators have hesitated to attribute this position to Aristotle. Their reasons are several. First, Aristotle does not have our conception of the circulatory system. The blood originates in the heart and flows outward, taking nutriment to the rest of the body.[49] If, as Aristotle believes, blood moves out from the center and sense impressions move in toward the center, sense impressions may need some other vehicle, one that moves in the proper direction.[50] Second, according to Aristotle, "every bloodless part as well as the blood itself is without sensation" (*De Part. An.* 666a17–18; cf. 656b19–22).[51]

Uncomfortable with making blood the sensory messenger, commentators have opted for *pneuma*.[52] The best case for this view is based largely on circumstantial evidence as the text offers scant direct evidence that *pneuma* communicates sensory impulses to the heart.[53] The persuasive arguments reduce to two: (1) Aristotle frequently invokes *pneuma* in physiological explanations so it is likely he meant to invoke it here as well. From respiration, where *pneuma* is inhaled air, to procreation, where it is the soul's vehicle in the semen, *pneuma* is essential to animal life, and *pneuma* is found in the passage connecting the organs of hearing and smell to the veins around the brain (*De Gen. An.* 744a2).[54] (2) The sophisticated theories of the nervous system propounded by Hellenistic medical writers made *pneuma* the agent for neural transmission of all sorts; since in other respects Aristotle's views influenced theirs, perhaps the later theories also borrow from his conception of sensory transmission.

The case for *pneuma* is largely based on generalization, generalization from Aristotle's own comprehensive use of this notion and from its employment by Hellenistic theorists.[55] The generalization from Aristotle's practice rests, I suspect, on the mistaken view that Aristotle's psychophysicalism commits him to a distinct material substratum for the soul; the importance of *pneuma* to a number of vital functions makes it the obvious candidate. But if we examine Aristotle's actual employment of the *pneuma* concept, we find he uses it to explain phenomena where the mechanisms involved suggest a vaporous substance.[56] Aristotle recognizes that muscles must contract and expand to bring about bodily movements; he hypothesizes that the presence of a vaporous substance (*pneuma*) in the muscles causes their expansion and contraction (cf. *De Motu An.* 703a19–28). Even in the case of semen, Aristotle appeals to the frothiness of semen as evidence that it contains *pneuma* (cf. *De Gen. An.* 736a14–21). The other major use of *pneuma* is to explain respiration and the role of inhaled air (*pneuma*) in cooling the body. In animals lacking lungs, the cooling function is taken over by innate *pneuma*.[57] The core notion of *pneuma* involved in all these discussions is that of an internal gaseous material that contributes in a rather straightforward way to the maintenance of life. The case of perception is different; with the exception of the initial reception of sounds and odors, there is nothing about the experience itself to suggest a vaporous agent.

In the case of the central organ, the observational evidence would not suggest *pneuma* as the agent. Aristotle locates the connections between the peripheral sense organs and the central organ in the system of blood vessels leading to the heart. Granted Aristotle mentions *pneuma* in connection with hearing and smell, whose organs consist of air (*De*

An. 425a6–7; *De Part. An.* 656b17).[58] However, even here he limits the role of *pneuma* to the initial reception of the sensory impulse, and he argues for this position on empirical grounds. Aristotle has no reason to extend the role of *pneuma* in perception beyond the role explicitly stated in the text.

As for the generalization from the use of this notion by later medical writers: with the exception of Praxagoras, these theorists made the brain the central organ.[59] Since they differ with Aristotle on this crucial issue, there is little reason to construe their conception of *pneuma* as the articulation of a view already found in Aristotle.[60]

For all that, one might believe, along with previous commentators, that the thesis that blood is without sensation counts in favor of the *pneuma* interpretation.[61] It does not. *Pneuma* like blood is a uniform substance. Moreover, unlike bodily organs, *pneuma* is not made up of blood, but according to Aristotle, only organs consisting of blood can serve as sense organs. Quite likely Aristotle attributed perception to the peripheral organs because they receive the sensory stimulation from outside the body, and to the central organ because the awareness of the external object occurs when the sensory impulse reaches it. If so, he would have viewed the substance(s) through which the sensory impulse travels to the heart simply as a medium and would not have attributed perception to it (them).[62]

The arguments for the *pneuma* interpretation have not borne up under examination, so we should trust our initial impression that on Aristotle's theory blood transmits sensory impulses to the heart. The textual evidence for this is greater. The circumstantial evidence for *pneuma* cannot bear the burden placed on it; it does not establish *pneuma*'s role as a sensory agent. If *pneuma* is not the vehicle for the transmission for sensory impulses, then blood is the only other candidate.

Aristotle does not spell out the details of the physiology of the perceptual system as a whole.[63] As in the case of the peripheral organs, Aristotle locates the central organ in a bodily structure, the heart. In the psychological treatises, he discusses sensory transmission only in problematic cases, cases where the transmission seems to be delayed, as in dreams or the recollections of the melancholic. To explain these cases, Aristotle alludes to movements that reach the central organ through the blood, on their own so to speak, propelled neither by the stimulation of a peripheral organ or by a conscious attempt to recall. In the biological works, Aristotle frequently mentions blood and movements in it to explain sensory phenomena, but he does not elaborate on this function of the blood. Nevertheless, since Aristotle's physiological sketch of the perceptual system identifies the physiological substratum of the common sense, it meets the requirements of the Psychophysical Principle.

4. Theory and the Common Sense

In chapter 2 I set out the descriptive and prescriptive principles that provide the theoretical framework in which Aristotle discusses the various functions of the perceptual faculty. The conception of the common sense that has emerged from our deliberations in this chapter provides further evidence of the importance of the foundational principles.

The Psychophysical Principle dictates that the full description of the common sense include a psychical component and a physiological component. The psychical structure, determined in accordance with the Actuality and Analytic Principles, is the capacity for perceptual activities that integrate information received through more than one sense; the physiological structure is constituted by a network of five peripheral organs and a central organ in which each of the peripheral organs terminates. The fit between psychological and physiological descriptions of the common sense could not be better. As forms of awareness, the senses converge to make up the common sense, while their physical embodiments coincide in a central organ.

As discussed in chapter 2, the Psychophysical Principle licenses shifts of perspective from psychology to physiology and conversely. This practice is also evident in Aristotle's approach to such issues as the existence of a special sense for the *koina* or the identity of the central organ. Aristotle treats the hypothetical identification of the common sense with a special sense as the same question as the hypothetical identification of the common sense organ with a special sense organ (*De An.* 425a14–21). To establish that the heart is the central organ, Aristotle invokes conceptual constraints deriving from the nature of the common sense, and he cites physiological evidence based on observable connections between bodily organs. The character of the common sense (as a form of awareness) is such that its organ must be at the center of the body. Appealing to anatomical details, Aristotle argues that the heart alone is connected to all the peripheral organs.

The Analytic Principle dictates the extension of the five-sense model of perception, found in *De Anima* II and *De Sensu* 1–6, to as many other perceptual functions as possible. *De Anima* III, 1 argues against a proliferation of sense faculties, against the existence of an additional special sense for a sixth type of proper object or for the common objects. The *De Somno* distinguishes between two types of capacity possessed by the individual senses—a specialized perceptual capacity and a common one. By making the special senses constituents of the common sense, Aristotle is able to expand the five-sense model to include perceptual and apperceptual functions that exceed the competence of any of the special senses.

The Actuality Principle provides a nonarbitrary reason for the structure of the common sense determined in accordance with the Analytic Principle. The Actuality Principle causes Aristotle to frame the questions leading him to posit a common sense in terms of the objects of the perceptual experience under consideration. Aristotle first recognizes the existence of the *koina* and then asks what faculty perceives them. Similarly, he begins with the recognition that white differs from sweet, and then he investigates the nature of the discriminating faculty. In both cases, the presentation of the object through several senses becomes the basis for attributing the object's apprehension to a faculty made up of several senses.

The Actuality Principle applied to the physical substratum of perception yields the distinction between *kath' hauta* and *kata sumbebēkos* objects. Certain features of the external object cause changes in the sense organ, producing the awareness of certain sense objects that are related to the causally efficacious features of the external objects as actual to potential sensibles. These features also produce the awareness of other concommitant sense objects. Because they play a direct causal role, the former are perceived *kath' hauta*; because they do not, the latter are perceived *kata sumbebēkos*.[64] The Actuality Principle also explains why, for Aristotle, the incidental object is a sense object. The person perceiving the son of Cleon is immediately aware of the approaching white thing as the son of Cleon. Since the act of perceptual awareness is one with its object, its object, namely the son of Cleon, must be a perceptual object.

The influence of the Sensory Representation Principle is also evident in the treatment that complex perceptual judgments receive in Aristotle's hands. It is his reason for arguing that the cognitive faculty that discriminates between white and sweet must be a perceptual faculty and for assigning reflexive awareness to a perceptual faculty. The Sensory Representation Principle also provides part of the motivation for making the incidental objects sense objects.

5. Epistemological Issues

The dependence of knowledge on perception is a familiar Aristotelian theme (*Pst. Anal.* I, 18; II, 19; *Met.* I, 1). In the *Posterior Analytics*,

Aristotle says that had we fewer senses than we in fact do have, we would know less than we in fact know and we would be unable to make up the deficit (81a37–40).[65] Knowledge evolves from sense perception by a process of generalization that converts the particular truths grasped in perception into the universal truths of art and science. How Aristotle thinks about sense perception is therefore of considerable importance to his epistemology. Since we have now reconstructed Aristotle's account of perception through the five senses and the common sense, let us briefly consider its epistemological implications.

The more reliable we believe perception to be, the less troubled we will be about basing knowledge on perception. In his epistemological writings, Aristotle assumes that we can rely on the senses for the information from which to derive the generalizations and abstractions that are required for knowledge. In his psychological writings, Aristotle gives us a theory of sense perception that ascribes different degrees of reliablity to different types of sense perception. Our question then concerns the fit between the two approaches—is the most reliable form of perception the most important one for securing the foundations of knowledge? As it turns out, this is a hard matter to settle. The most reliable form of perception is the perception of the proper objects. From the perspective of Aristotle's theory of perception, this is as it should be since the proper objects are the vehicles for the perception of the other types of sense objects. From the epistemological perspective, it is more problematic.

Aristotle's distinction between proper and common objects divides up perceptible qualities in much the same way as the more familiar distinction between secondary and primary qualities. Colors, sounds, flavors, odors and tactile qualities are proper objects for Aristotle, secondary qualities for us; motion, figure, extension and number are common objects for him and primary qualities for us.[66] Typically, proponents of the distinction between primary and secondary qualities have taken the fact that primary qualities can be measured and can play a role in scientific theories as evidence that primary qualities are features of the world, whereas secondary qualities are features the world has only in relation to creatures with certain types of perceptual equipment (Hirst 1967).

Aristotle considers and rejects a similar theory. Democritus had made the perception of colors and flavors and other proper objects the result of the shapes of the atoms impinging on the sense organ.[67] Aristotle charges that this approach, because it reduces all sense objects to common objects, collapses the distinctions among the special senses as well as eliminating the distinction between the special senses and the common sense (*De Sens.* 442b10–24). He makes the proper objects the bearers of the common objects and gives the proper objects an objective basis. Unlike the ancient atomist or the modern empiricist, Aristotle believes that the proper objects as such exist (potentially) in the world. The perception of red or of sweet is the actualization of a characteristic of the external object perceived as red or sweet. Moreover, the proper objects of the sense of touch are constitutive of the basic types of matter as described in Aristotle's cosmological theory (*De Gen. et Corr.* II, 2–5).

Not only are the proper objects more basic both in perception and in the world than the common or incidental objects, they are apprehended with considerably more accuracy. The senses seldom make mistakes about their proper objects (*De An.* 428b18–19). Aristotle sometimes makes the stronger claim that mistakes about proper objects never occur (*De An.* 418a12, 418a15, 427b11, 430b29; *De Sens.* 442b9). Since the perception of the proper objects provides the foundation for other types of perception and perception provides the basis for knowledge, the degree of reliability assigned to this type of perception on Aristotle's psychological theory is consistent with the role assigned perception in his epistemology.

Indeed, Aristotle may be motivated by his belief that the proper objects are perceived more accurately than others to make them the basic perceptual objects. Plato had drawn a sharp distinction between perception and knowledge, but he had not rejected perception's claim to adequately apprehend proper objects (*Theaet.* 184–86; Modrak 1981d). While disagreeing with Plato about the scope of perception, Aristotle may well have been influenced by Plato to the extent that he makes the proper objects the basis for the perception of everything else.

More serious difficulties arise at the next level with Aristotle's account of the perception of the common and the incidental objects. Although fundamental to our perception of the world, the common objects are apprehended with considerably less accuracy than either the proper objects or the incidental objects (*De An.* 428b24–25, 442b8–10). Aristotle does not ponder the apparent conflict between the immediacy and the accuracy with which the common objects are perceived. Had he been pressed for an explanation, he might have said something like this: The proper objects fully determine the faculty perceiving them, so there is little or no room for error. As *kath' hauta* objects, the common objects emerge when several senses converge in the apprehension of a single sensible characteristic. Since the cognitive process involved in their perception is more complex than in the case of the proper objects, error is more likely (cf. 442b8). Yet, with the exception of the tactile objects, the common objects are at least as important to the construction of scientific theories as the proper objects. Fewer mistakes are made about the incidental objects than the common objects because the *kath' hauta* objects that serve as the vehicle for the perception of an incidental object do not fully determine the content of the perception; thus the actual perception of an incidental object is likely to occur in circumstances that favor its correctness. By contrast, the common objects are given in the perception of the proper objects. The impossibility of perceiving a color, for instance, without also perceiving a shape means that even under conditions that do not favor a veridical perception of shape, a percipient having a visual experience will perceive shape as well as color. This increases the likelihood of mistakes about the common objects.[68]

Nevertheless, the fit between Aristotle's theory of perception and his epistemology is the least satisfactory in the case of the incidental objects. In *Posterior Analytics* II, 19, Aristotle describes a cognitive process that moves from the perception of concrete particulars to universal concepts, from the perception of an individual person to a universal concept of man. A human being is not a proper object of perception but an incidental one. Thus, knowledge seems to develop out of a form of perception that is susceptible to error and whose objects are not completely determined by the sensible characters causing the perception. Even the term *kata sumbebēkos* (incidental) suggests an absence of systematic connections between the *kata sumbebēkos* object and the underlying *kath' hauto* object(s).[69] But Aristotle's realist epistemology assumes systematic connections between the objects of perception and the concepts of natural kinds that are based on them. If we try to save Aristotle's epistemology by positing systematic connections between the perceptual stimulus and the *kata sumbebēkos* object, then we shall do violence to the distinction between *kath' hauto* and *kata sumbebēkos* sensibles. To preserve the distinction is to threaten the empirical basis of the concepts of natural kinds. At this stage of our inquiry, no solution suggests itself. In chapter 7 we return to Aristotle's epistemology and the relationship between knowledge, perception and thought.

4

Phantasia

The discussion of apperception in *De Anima* III, 2 concludes Aristotle's account of sense perception, and in the next chapter he turns to *phantasia* (imagination).[1] In certain respects Aristotle's notion of *phantasia* is broader than our notion of imagination.[2] *Phantasia* is invoked in explanations of sensory illusion, memory, dreaming, action and even discursive reasoning.[3] The cognitions grouped together under *phantasia* are all functions of the perceptual system. "The faculty of *phantasia* [*phantastikon*] is the same faculty as the perceptual faculty of the soul" (*De Ins.* 459a16). By making a number of different cognitive activities manifestations of *phantasia* and making *phantasia* a function of the perceptual faculty, Aristotle extends the range of the perceptual faculty significantly beyond sense perception and reflexive sensory awareness. Consequently, *phantasia* is a crucial concept in Aristotle's theory of the perceptual faculty. As often happens in the case of Aristotelian notions, the very characteristics that account for its importance also threaten the cohesiveness of Aristotle's concept of *phantasia*.[4] On the one hand, *phantasia* should share certain features with other functions of the perceptual faculty; otherwise the unity of the latter faculty will be compromised. On the other hand, *phantasia* should have certain distinctive characteristics and these characteristics should be shared by all cases of *phantasia*. But when we consider the multiplicity and diversity of the cognitions falling under *phantasia*, we are likely to despair of finding any common features.

As in the case of any other cognitive state, *phantasia*'s identity will depend in large part on its objects; however, as a component of the perceptual faculty, the capacity for *phantasia* is exercised in relation to the same type of objects as other perceptual faculties. Consequently, Aristotle cannot simply appeal to the object of *phantasia* to justify the inclusion of a number of diverse mental activities under the rubric *phantasia* instead of a different perceptual faculty, nor can he use its object to differentiate *phantasia* from other functions of the perceptual faculty. What Aristotle thinks the individuating features of *phantasia* are is a vexed question.

I shall argue that Aristotle includes in the full formal description of a sensory experience the conditions under which the experience occurs. Perception occurs under standard conditions.[5] *Phantasia* occurs under nonstandard conditions, that is, under conditions that are not conducive to veridical perception.[6] This approach gives Aristotle a great deal of flexibility. It enables him to include diverse types of sensory experience under *phantasia* and thus to extend the functions of the perceptual faculty within the conceptual framework elaborated in *De Anima* II, 5–III, 2.

1. What *Phantasia* Is

After a few preliminary remarks, Aristotle introduces his own analysis of *phantasia* by offering a nominal definition: "*Phantasia* is that in virtue of which we say a *phantasma* arises in us" (*De An.* 428a1–2). As ordinarily used, *phantasma* means an appearance, image or phantom.[7] A *phantasma* may be, but need not be, a purely mental presentation; for the word *phantasma* can be used to refer to the appearance produced in a percipient by an external object.[8] Typically, *phantasma* connotes a sensory presentation where the cognitive object has sensible features, such as color and shape or sound, odor or flavor.[9] In addition, *phantasma* often connotes a failure of verisimilitude.[10] The object as presented in a *phantasma* fails to correspond precisely to any object actually in the subject's perceptual field. Whether a *phantasma* is an actual object appearing in an uncharacteristic way or an image presenting an object not concurrently present to the senses, a *phantasma* is a sensory presentation of an object that cannot simply be identified with an object in the subject's immediate environment.

The nominal definition of *phantasia* is only the first bit of evidence that *phantasia* is the awareness of a sensory content under conditions that are not conducive to veridical perception (the Sensory Content Analysis). Although stated in the modern idiom, this paraphrase expresses the core notion that lies at the heart of Aristotle's multifaceted use of *phantasia*. Since I have argued for the Sensory Content Analysis elsewhere (Modrak 1986), I shall present it in summary form here. The Sensory Content Analysis consists in two key phrases, "awareness of a sensory content" and "conditions not conducive to veridical perception." Each will be taken up in turn.

Cognitive awareness for Aristotle is transparent; it is simply the actualization of the object of the experience.[11] (This is a consequence of the Actuality Principle.) In the case of all perceptual activities, the object of awareness is a sensory content as required by the Sensory

Representation Principle. A sensory content is a complex of sensible characters. In the case of perception and nonveridical appearance, these characters are properties that the external object possesses in relation to the percipient; in the absence of an external stimulus a sensory content is an internal representation of sensible characters.[12] There is ample textual evidence that the object of *phantasia* is a sensory content in our sense. The features of the *phantasma* mentioned above support the identification of a *phantasma* with a sensory content, as does Aristotle's statement in the *De Insomniis*, that the faculty of *phantasia* (*phantastikon*) and the perceptual faculty (*aisthētikon*) are the same faculty but differ in *einai* (*De Insom.* 459a16–17; cf. *De An.* 432a31–b2).[13] The *phantastikon* is exercised through the same organs as the *aisthētikon*.[14] *Phantasia* occurs in organisms that perceive and with respect to those things of which there is perception (*De An.* 428b12–13).

As described by Aristotle's theory of perception, there are three types of sensibles. At *De Anima* 425b25–30, Aristotle extends this analysis to *phantasia* and divides the objects of *phantasia* into proper, common and incidental objects. The ultimate bearers of perceptual information are the proper objects (cf. 418a24–25), and we would expect the same thing to hold true of *phantasia*. Aristotle's descriptions of both types of *phantasia*, namely nonveridical appearance and mental imagery, bear out this expectation. The object of perception is a complex of sensible characters that belong to an external object, as is the object of *phantasia* in the case of nonveridical appearances.[15] When an inanimate object seen at a distance appears to be a man (428a14), or when a stranger appears to be one's beloved (460b3–13), the object of the experience is presented sensorially; its vehicle is a complex of sensible characters.

In other cases of *phantasia*, such as dreaming or remembering, the object is a complex of sensible characters that represents an object not immediately present to the senses.[16] In the *De Insomniis*, Aristotle groups together rational faculties including *doxa* and contrasts them to faculties through which sensory characters are apprehended, namely, *aisthēsis* and *phantasia*, to argue that a dream (*enupnion*) is a kind of *phantasma* (458b10–459a22). Dreaming is not to be identified with opining because "we seem to see that the approaching object is white as well as a man [in a dream]" (458b15).

Memory is also a function of the *phantastikon*. Memory is "the disposition of a *phantasma* related as a likeness to that of which it is *phantasma* (*De Mem.* 451a15–16). Aristotle distinguishes between what is remembered *kath' hauto* and what is remembered *kata sumbebēkos*

(450a23–25). Concrete particulars that were seen, heard or otherwise experienced in the past are remembered *kath' hauta*. The vehicle for the memory is a *phantasma* representing the past experience. Abstract objects are remembered *kata sumbebēkos*. Here *phantasmata* function in memory as they function in contemplation. In these cases, the thinker uses a *phantasma* of a member of the class of objects he or she is considering in the same way that he or she would use a drawing to represent a geometrical object (cf. 450a1–6). A theorem, for instance, is remembered *kata sumbebēkos* because the associated image does not fully represent the theorem; instead the image serves as an illustration by presenting a case where the theorem applies.[17] We remember past sights, sounds and odors *kath' hauta* because these objects are represented sensorially and thus can be adequately represented by a *phantasma*.

Aristotle bridges the gap between perception and thought by appealing to *phantasmata*.[18] In *De Anima* III, 8, in support of the claim that all thought is grounded in sense perception, Aristotle asserts that all thinking requires *phantasmata*: "And for this reason if one did not perceive anything, one would not learn or understand anything, and when one contemplates one must simultaneously contemplate a *phantasma*; for *phantasmata* are like sensuous contents [*aisthēmata*]" (432a7–9). If *phantasmata* did not preserve the characteristics of the objects of perception, they could not function as *aisthēmata* (cf. 431a14–15), nor could they mediate between perception and thought.[19]

The sensory character of phantasmata is a constant theme in the *De Anima*, the *De Memoria* and the *De Insomniis*. This suffices to establish the appropriateness of calling *phantasia's* object a sensory content. Let us now turn to the second part of the Sensory Content Analysis: "under conditions not conducive to veridical perception." As noted earlier, *phantasma* is ordinarily used to describe the object of a sensory experience that fails to correspond to objective reality.[20] We can divide the cases of *phantasia* Aristotle discusses into two groups: (1) cases where the *phantasma*, although occasioned by an object in the subject's perceptual field, does not correctly represent the object, and (2) cases where the *phantasma* does not at all represent an object in the subject's perceptual field.[21] Aristotle's examples of cases of type (1) turn out to be cases where some feature of the total situation, for instance, distance from the object, adversely affects the perception or where the perceiver's perceptual apparatus is not functioning properly.[22] Not only does the Sensory Content Analysis fit cases of both types, but one of its advantages over competing interpretations is that it explains why Aristotle treats cases of nonveridical appearance and cases of imagery as manifestations of the same cognitive capacity.[23] Both are types of sensory experience occurring under conditions not conducive to veridical perception.

Aristotle appeals to the conditions under which *phantasia* and *aisthēsis* occur to distinguish between the two:[24] "then when we are exercising our senses accurately with regard to objects of perception, we do not say that this appears [*phainetai*] to us to be a man" (*De An.* 428a12–14). Whether Aristotle describes a particular sensory apprehension as an instance of *aisthēsis* or of *phantasia* depends upon features of the total situation in which the object is apprehended; these include states of the percipient and states of the external environment. Aristotle makes the choice depend upon the accuracy with which the external object is apprehended or, more precisely, the likelihood of its being accurately perceived. Sometimes what appears in the distance to be a woman actually is a woman; sometimes it is not. In either circumstance, the experience is an instance of *phantasia* because it occurred under conditions not conducive to veridical perception. The contrast between standard and nonstandard conditions that Aristotle exploits here can be counted among the ramifications of the Psychophysical Principle. An adequate account of a perceptual activity must describe the physiological substratum fully up to and including the external conditions that play a causal role in determining the state of the substratum. Hence factors such as the distance between the percipient and the object are taken into account.

For the most part, in psychological contexts, Aristotle uses *aisthēsis* and its cognates for cases of veridical perception.[25] To describe cases where the stimulation of a peripheral sense organ results in a distorted representation of the external object, Aristotle qualifies the use of perception words. If he uses a perception verb, he uses *dokein* (seems to) as well, or he uses a verb derived from the relevant perception verb by adding the prefix *para-* (mis-). Or he uses *phainesthai* (to appear). Sensory experiences described in any of these ways are cases of *phantasia*.[26]

The kind of *phantasia* in question is determined by additional criteria.

> Nor is every *phantasma* that occurs in sleep a dream. For in the first place, it happens that some people even perceive in a way sounds, light, flavor and touch, but faintly and as if far away; for people looking up while asleep have seen dimly the light of the lamp, as they supposed, which later, upon awakening, they immediately recognized to be really the light of the lamp, and others hearing faintly the crowing of cocks or barking of dogs clearly recognized them when they awoke. (*De Ins.* 462a19–26).

Until the sleeper awakens, the conditions for veridical perception are not met; however, nor are the conditions for dreaming met in the case described because the *phantasma* is an appearance of an external sensory stimulus.[27] A dream is a sensory representation of an object not concurrently acting on the senses.

There is a certain tendency, frequently found among commentators, to equate the thesis that *phantasia* is unreliable with the fact that *phantasia* occurs under conditions not conducive to veridical perception. Having expressed the important insight that *phantasia* is nonparadigmatic sensory experience, Schofield went on to argue that whenever a sensory experience is classified as a case of *phantasia* there is good reason to be skeptical about the information it conveys. This is a mistake, for the former does not entail the latter. For all practical purposes, the distinction collapses when the object of *phantasia* is an object in the subject's perceptual field; for when standard conditions do not obtain, the deliverances of our senses are much less reliable. In other cases the Sensory Content Analysis is satisfied because the object represented by the *phantasma* is not present in the subject's perceptual field. Thus, the Sensory Content Analysis of *phantasia* applies to cases where the *phantasma* correctly represents an actual object or a past or present state of affairs as well as cases of misrepresentation.

The proper object of memory is a *phantasma*. Nonetheless, memory plays a crucial role in guiding the behavior of animals, including human beings. In that capacity, memory must provide reasonably reliable information. Memory is also a crucial link in the cognitive chain leading from perception to knowledge. Here again it must be trustworthy. Clearly, Aristotle's appeal to *phantasia* in the explanation of memory rests on the assumption that the feature that makes *phantasia* unreliable in some circumstances does not make it unreliable in all circumstances.

Our brief survey of the relevant texts has secured the Sensory Content Analysis. We have determined that the immediate object of *phantasia* is always a sensory content, a complex of sensible characters, and that *phantasia* occurs under conditions not conducive to veridical perception. Equipped with this conception of *phantasia*, Aristotle is able to extend the functions of the perceptual faculty to include memory, dreaming, and complex sensory representations.

The conception of *phantasia* summarized in the Sensory Content Analysis is integrally bound up with the conception of the perceptual faculty expressed in the foundational principles. This is especially true of the Actuality, Sensory Representation and Analytic Principles. The

Psychophysical Principle does not bear directly on the Sensory Content Analysis, which articulates the formal definition of *phantasia*.

On the Sensory Content Analysis, the focal object of *phantasia* is a complex of sensible characters, as is the focal object of perception; in accordance with the Actuality Principle, Aristotle makes both of them functions of the perceptual faculty of the soul. Nonetheless, the *aisthēton* is not identical to the *phantasma*, and thus *aisthēsis* and *phantasia* are different in essence.[28]

The Sensory Representation Principle explains why Aristotle assigns so many different cognitive activities to the perceptual faculty. Aristotle's conception of sensory representation finds expression in his conception of *phantasia*. *Phantasmata* are the vehicles for sensory representation, and Aristotle's concept of *phantasia* is in part the concept of a form of internal representation that employs sensory characters.

The Analytic Principle motivates Aristotle to increase the number of the functions of the perceptual faculty rather than postulate other, unrelated faculties. *Phantasia* is his device for bringing fantasy, imaging, dreaming, remembering and animal "practical reasonings" under the purview of the perceptual faculty of the soul. The Sensory Content Analysis explicates this role of *phantasia* by displaying the common character of all manifestations of *phantasia*.

2. *Mnēmē, Anamnēsis* and Dreaming

Phantasia, as Aristotle conceives it, functions as a form of internal representation.[29] By appealing to the notion of internal sensory representation in the *De Memoria*, Aristotle is able to include memory among the functions of the perceptual faculty. Memory (*mnēmē*) is by definition "a *hexis* of a *phantasma*, as a likeness [*eikōn*] to that of which it is a *phantasma*" and it is a function of that faculty in us "by which we perceive time" (451a15–18). This definition makes three claims: (1) the focal object of memory is a *phantasma*; (2) the *phantasma* represents in virtue of being an *eikōn*; and (3) to remember is to distinguish between past and present experience. (cf. *De Mem.* 450b23, 451a2, 451a11–12, 452b23–24). On the one hand, we may be impressed by the sophistication of Aristotle's analysis. The first condition allows Aristotle to treat memory as an extension of *phantasia* and to attribute memory to many animals besides human beings. The second condition gives him a device for securing the referent of the memory-*phantasma*. The third condition maintains the crucial difference between having the same type of experience more than once and remembering. To visualize a face is not to remember it, unless the visual image is associated with a face seen in the past (450b12–451a8).[30]

On the other hand, not one of the three conditions is wholly unproblematic. The first makes sensory representation the vehicle of memory; yet it seems unreasonable to suppose that memory always employs imagery.[31] Worse still, the second condition seems to limit the vehicle of representation in memory still further, namely, to representation through resemblance.[32] The third condition seems too stringent; many animals, according to Aristotle, have memory, but are they also aware of the passage of time? The best way to approach these issues is to see how well Aristotle's theory of *mnēmē* accounts for various cases of remembering.

In the case of human beings, several different types of experience would appear to fall under *mnēmē*. There are cases where we remember the content of a past perception; we remember the glowing sunset or the cock's crowing. There are other cases where we remember facts; we remember that when equal magnitudes are added to equal magnitudes, the sums are equal. In the first instance, sensible characters were the vehicle for the original experience. On Aristotle's theory of perception, I cannot be aware of any feature of a visual perception, either of the object or of the act of perception itself, without simultaneously being aware of a color; a consequence of this doctrine is that I cannot remember an object I saw in the past or remember a past seeing unless I am aware of a complex of colored shapes.[33] When Aristotle claims that to remember a past experience is to be immediately aware of a *phantasma*, he is simply extending the explanatory framework developed in connection with sense perception to *mnēmē*, another exercise of the perceptual faculty.

By his own lights, Aristotle is on solid conceptual ground here. From the modern standpoint, the issue is not whether memory objects per se are adequately represented by sensible characters but whether any relatively complex object can be represented in this way. If we are willing to grant this possibility and to countenance imagery and sensory representation, we will have little reason to reject Aristotle's account of remembering a past experience. If we are not, we will have good reason to reject Aristotle's account; however, this rejection rests on a view about mental representation, not shared by Aristotle, that rules out the representation of complex objects by sensory means, so it raises a difficulty not specific to his account of memory.

We seem to remember abstract objects as well as concrete particulars. Aristotle is hard pressed to account for these memories since the vehicle for a memory of this sort does not seem to be a sensory content. Nor does Aristotle claim that we remember abstract objects in the same way that we remember past experience. "Nothing prevents our remembering *kata sumbebēkos* some object of which we have knowledge" (*De Mem.* 451a28–29; cf. 450a13–14).[34] Aristotle does not explain why objects of knowledge are remembered *kata sumbebēkos* except to say that such memories are not possible without *phantasmata*—a description he repeatedly applies to the relationship between thinking and the *phantasmata* employed in thinking (*De Mem.* 449b31; *De An.* 431a16, 432a8, 432a13).[35] The point seems to be that these memories, like the thoughts of which they are memories, cannot be reduced to the *phantasmata* they employ (cf. *De An.* 432a13, 431b2).[36] The immediate object of memory is a *phantasma*, so abstract objects are not remembered *kath' hauta*.

This difficulty is compounded by the second condition. The memory image is an *eikōn* (*De Mem.* 450b23, 451a2, 451a11–12, 451a14, 451a16).[37] The standard reading of *eikōn* is "likeness," so memory seems not only to depend upon *phantasmata*, but upon *phantasmata* that resemble the object remembered. But there is no good reason to believe that when we remember some piece of information rather than something we perceived in the past, we employ *phantasmata* that resemble the fact we remember.[38] Let us suppose that a student remembers that the sum of the interior angles of a triangle is equal to two right angles and remembers having heard her teacher utter this theorem. Even if we accept the first condition on *mnēmē* and agree with Aristotle that the vehicle for the memory is an auditory image, we are unlikely to believe that the auditory image resembles the fact expressed in the theorem.

Trying on Aristotle's behalf to resolve the difficulty, we might redefine *eikōn* and say that an *eikōn* need not resemble what it represents, but there is little textual support for this solution. A more promising approach grants that, if *A* is an *eikōn* of *B*, *A* must resemble *B* in some respect, but limits the resemblance of the memory *eikōn* to some feature of the past experience being remembered, a feature that need not be the intentional object of the memory. This approach recognizes that one gives different answers to the questions, How do you know you are remembering that? and What are you remembering? To answer the first question, on Aristotle's account, is to say that the memory image resembles in some respect a sensory content that was apprehended in the past. To answer the second, one need not mention the memory image. Whether this is actually Aristotle's solution remains to be seen.

Despite its disadvantages, the *eikōn*-condition on *mnēmē* serves Aristotle well. There is a prima facie conflict between the kinds of creatures possessing *mnēmē* and the third condition on *mnēmē*—that a creature remembers only insofar as it is aware of the past. To limit memory to objects that the subject consciously relates to the past would conflict with our use of the word *memory*. When we say that a computer has a memory, we mean that it is able to retrieve and utilize information stored in the past. Aristotle, by contrast, says that to remember X one must be antecedently aware (*proaisthanetai*) of having experienced X in the past (450a19–23). Aristotle's concept of *mnēmē* need not cover computers, but since we humans are not alone in possessing *mnēmē*, Aristotle's concept of *mnēmē* should be broad enough to apply to other animals (450a15–16). When we say that an animal remembers, we often intend to say nothing more than that the animal's behavior seems to be based upon information acquired in the past. However, Aristotle at times speaks as if, in the case of *mnēmē*, an articulated awareness of the past were at issue: "For always when one is exercising memory, one says in one's soul that one heard or perceived or thought this before" (*De Mem.* 449b23–24). Taking the phrase "saying in one's soul" too literally will make the attribution of memory to animals quite bewildering. Aristotle's thesis must be that when a creature remembers, it is somehow aware of the object in relation to a past experience. But what can it mean to say that an animal is aware of a *phantasma* in relation to the past?

The *eikōn*-condition provides Aristotle with a way out of this difficulty. The vehicle for a memory is a *phantasma* originating in a previous experience. The subject may recognize that the *phantasma* of X, which she is now having, originated in a perception of X yesterday. However, this feature of the *phantasma* may escape her notice, in which case memory proper is not exercised. "Sometimes we are in doubt whether it is memory or not. But sometimes it happens that we reflect and recollect that we heard something or saw it before" (*De Mem.* 451a5–7). The *eikōn*-condition works to secure the referent of the *phantasma* in a way that makes the awareness of the *phantasma* an act of memory.[39] The *phantasma* presents an object apprehended in the past; because the *phantasma* resembles the original object, the subject is apt to take the *phantasma* to refer to the past experience. To apprehend the *phantasma* as an *eikōn* is to recognize the relation between one's present experience and one's past experience. "Insofar as it [the *phantasma*] is regarded in itself, it is only an object of contemplation or an image; but when considered in relation to something else, for instance, as its likeness [*eikōn*] it is also a mnemonic image [*mnēmoneuma*]" (*De Mem.* 450b25–27). To discriminate between past and present, one need only recognize that his present cognitive state differs from his past cognitive state (cf. *Phys.* 219a23–29). An animal would have the requisite awareness of time, were she to recognize the difference between having previously seen a watering hole at a particular location and visualizing the location now as she travels toward it. Her cognitive experience would meet the third condition. In short, the three conditions fit together to provide a coherent picture of memory through sensory representation that allows Aristotle to differentiate between memory and other cases of *phantasia* (by appealing to the perception of time) and to attribute memory to many different kinds of animals.

This of course does not speak to the poor fit between the *eikōn*-condition and the assumption that it is possible to remember abstract objects. But Aristotle may not accept the latter supposition. More precisely, he may believe that abstract objects are remembered only insofar as they are remembered as part of a past perceptual experience.[40] That is, I may remember hearing a geometry teacher utter the Pythagorean Theorem and in this sense remember it; insofar as I simply concentrate on the Pythagorean Theorem, I may not be remembering it at all. "Nor do we remember a theoretical object [*theōroumenon*] when we are actively contemplating it or thinking about it" (*De Mem.* 449b17–18). This gives us a new handle on Aristotle's claim that theoretical objects are remembered *kata sumbebēkos*. Just as the *kata sumbebēkos* object of perception "rides piggyback" on a complex of proper and common objects, the abstract object qua object of memory is superimposed on the complex of sensible characters that tie it to a previous experience. In and of itself an abstract object, a geometrical theorem, for instance, does not change from one apprehension to another; as Aristotle puts it, it is simply an object of knowledge, not an object of memory (*De Mem.* 449b18).

Taken in context with the Actuality Principle, Aristotle's position is less perplexing than it might otherwise be. To give an analysis of memory, for Aristotle, is to give an analysis of an occurrent cognitive state that has the feature of referring its object to a past experience. The character of a memory, like that of any other second actuality state, is determined by its object. The object is a *phantasma*, a complex of sensible characters, that resembles the sensible characters constituting (part of) the original perceptual experience. If the remembered object is a concrete particular, the sensible characters presenting it in memory duplicate characters it had when it was perceived and it is remembered *kath' hauto*;[41] if the object is an abstract object, the sensible characters duplicate characters of the perception(s) that served as a vehicle for the acquisition of this bit of information and the object is remembered *kata sumbebēkos*.

Aristotle supplements the account of *mnēmē* with an account of a peculiarly human form of memory, namely *anamnēsis* or recollection.[42] *Anamnēsis* is the activity of recovering (*analambanein*) the object of a past perception or knowing (451b3–5). Recollecting differs from remembering in that it is a conscious undertaking, a deliberate seeking for an object previously perceived or learned. Associations of one sort or another are the stepping stones leading in the case of a successful recollection to the retrieval of the sought-after cognitive object. *Anamnēsis* is the cognitive process that a human being employs to effect the change from dispositional memory to actual remembering (451b3–6). The basis for dispositional memory is a *pathos* (passive state) brought about in the subject by the original experience.[43] The *pathos* makes remembering possible (cf. 451b22–31). Just as an external object is a potential sense object, the *pathos* is a potential *phantasma*. Just as a potential sense object becomes an actual sense object when perceived, the potential *phantasma* becomes an actual *phantasma* and memory image when remembered. Remembering is the object of *anamnēsis*: "*anamnēsis* is a search for a *phantasma* in a bodily *pathos*" (453a15–16).[44] *Mnēmē* is the state of remembering; *anamnēsis* is an inferential process aimed at producing *mnēmē*.

At the beginning of the *De Memoria*, Aristotle asks, "to which part of the soul does *anamnēsis* belong?" He answers the equivalent question for *mnēmē*: *mnēmē* is a function of the perceptual faculty. In the case of *anamnēsis*, Aristotle fails to answer this question. As an inferential process no other animal is capable of, *anamnēsis* seems an unlikely candidate for an assignment to the perceptual faculty. Plato had made *anamnēsis* a function of the soul alone, in contrast to perception which he assigned to the joint activity of body and soul (*Phil.* 34b). Aristotle seems to accept a psychic origin for *anamnēsis* (*De An.* 408b17). These considerations would lead us to expect Aristotle to assign *anamnēsis* to the rational faculty as would the peculiarly human character of *anamnēsis* as a kind of reasoning (453a8–12). Yet *anamnēsis* culminates in a "perceptual" activity, a remembering. More significantly, the series of impulses (*kinēseis*) constituting a process of recollection are bodily movements (*De Mem.* 453a15–31; cf. *De An.* 408b15–18). *Anamnēsis* is a psychophysical phenomenon described in the same terms as other activities of the perceptual faculty.[45]

The relationship between *anamnēsis* and *mnēmē* and the psychophysical character of *anamnēsis* suggest that Aristotle's silence may be an oversight—perhaps he intended to assign *anamnēsis* to the perceptual faculty. On the other hand, to do so would be to assign a unique function to the perceptual faculty in the case of human beings (something Aristotle is quite reluctant to do.)[46] But there is an alternative open to him. *Anamnēsis* might be an emergent property of the human perceptual faculty—a property we possess because we are rational animals.[47] *Anamnēsis* would then be a capacity possessed by creatures having memory and having recourse to some nonsensory form of internal representation. For our present purposes, it is not necessary to decide on Aristotle's behalf between making *anamnēsis* a function of the perceptual faculty or treating it as an emergent property of the perceptual faculty; for our future purposes, it is important to note that *anamnēsis* depends upon a kind of conceptualization not possessed by other animals. For the present, the crucial point is that *anamnēsis* terminates with the conscious awareness of a *phantasma* that represents an object as an object of a past cognition.

Dreaming is another psychological activity that Aristotle's conception of *phantasia* enables him to include under the perceptual faculty. Two short treatises are devoted to this topic—the *De Insomniis* and the *De Divinatione per Somnum*.[48] As in other cases, Aristotle bases his analysis of dreaming on what he takes to be the uncontroversial features of dreams. In the first place, "a dream seems to be a kind of *phantasma* . . . and it is apparent that dreaming belongs to the perceptual faculty but belongs to it qua *phantastikon*" (*De Ins.* 459a18–22). Dreams are sensory representations. The sensible characters making up a dream are internal representations of perceptible properties (cf. *De Ins.* 459a1–8). Moreover, incidental objects of perception and states of affairs as presented in dreams often bear little resemblance to actual objects and states of affairs. On the basis of these differences, it is possible to distinguish between dream-*phantasmata* and ordinary perceptions.

Second, Aristotle's explanation of dreaming is primarily etiological and tends to be stated in physiological terms. When the peripheral organs are acted upon by external objects, certain changes are brought about in the organs, that persist after the stimulation of the organ ceases. During sleep, when the peripheral sense organs are inactive, movements that were too weak to reach the central organ during the day act on it, causing dreams (*De Ins.* 460b28–461a8). In addition, as Aristotle notes, the sensory content of a perception sometimes outlasts the stimulation of the peripheral organ. After looking at a bright color for a long time or at a rapidly moving object, a percipient will continue to see the color or the motion, even though the stimulation has ceased (*De Ins.* 459b11–20; cf. 460b2–3). The cognitive experiences we have during the day also "pave the way for" (*prohodopoiein*) our dreams (*De Div.* 463a25–30).

Third, dreams are "deceptive." While asleep, we accept the sensory experience of dreaming as if it were veridical perceptual experience. Aristotle explains this "deception" by pointing out that the sensory representations constituting dreams bear some (albeit often a slight) resemblance to the object represented in the dream (cf. *De Ins.* 461a7–30). He also appeals to the fact that sleep is the partial paralysis of the common sense that normally coordinates the sensible characters apprehended through the special senses (*De Ins.* 460b16–23).[49] Without the inhibiting activity of the common sense or the competition of the continuous stream of sensory impulses received through the special senses during the day, the physiological traces of daytime perceptions give rise to all sorts of sensory representations during sleep.

Aristotle not only gives a physiological explanation for the origin of dreams but he also appeals to physiology to explain the distorted form in which waking perceptual experiences resurface in dreams.[50] If the blood is turbulent, other movements in the blood will interfere with the transmission of the sensory impulses from the peripheral organs; thus the sensory message that reaches the heart is garbled, and the dream that results bears little resemblance to its external progenitors (*De Ins.* 461a8–25). This also explains, according to Aristotle, why some people do not dream; their internal movements completely overwhelm the residual sensory impulses before they reach the central organ (*De Ins.* 462b4–8). Just as the melancholic is unable to abandon the effort to recollect after initiating the series of physiological changes involved in recollection (*De Mem.* 453a14–19), the melancholic is also more prone to free association in dreams, for one movement follows another with great rapidity (*De Div.* 464a32–b5).

Dreaming and remembering are alike in that both employ sensory representation and both originate in actual perceptions. There the similarities end, for dreams more often than not deceive us whereas memory by definition correctly represents past events. Yet both satisfy the Sensory Content Analysis, and the discussion of both proceeds in accordance with the foundational principles. Since their focal objects are *phantasmata*, both are attributed to the *phantastikon* as the Actuality Principle dictates and hence to the perceptual faculty in accordance with the Sensory Representation Principle. The Analytic Principle also favors the inclusion of dreaming and memory among the functions of the perceptual faculty.[51] The requirements of the Psychophysical Principle are met by the physiological account of dreaming and to a lesser extent by the physiological description of memory and recollection.

3. *Phantasia* and Voluntary Movement

Phantasia plays a key role in Aristotle's account of animal motion.[52] "In general, then, as has been said, in so far as the animal is capable of desire, it is capable of moving itself; and it is not capable of desire without *phantasia*" (*De An.* 433b27–28; cf. 434a3–5; *De Motu. An.* 702a15–19). Aristotle clearly assigns *phantasia* a unique and important position with respect to the arousal of desire; desire is the efficient cause of voluntary animal motion, and its object is the final cause of the motion (*De Motu An.* 7; *De An.* III, 10). The text is less clear about the contours of *phantasia*'s role in this connection. Moreover, although Aristotle makes desire depend upon *phantasia*, it is not clear whether this dependence should be interpreted generally or specifically.[53] A general connection between the two would be compatible with the occasional occurrence of a desire without a concomitant occurrence of *phantasia*; a specific connection would not be. To decide these questions, we must look at Aristotle's conception of desire and of voluntary movement as well as at the notion of *phantasia* he invokes in explanations of desire and animal motion.[54] Desire is actualized in relation to particular objects. Because desire is a psychophysical state, an occurrent and unopposed desire focused on a particular object will set the animal in motion. Aristotle recognizes that desires sometimes fail to issue in action; one desire may offset another so that the animal does not act on either, or an animal may fail to act on a desire because it does not find an appropriate object in its present situation (*Met.* 1048a10–24).

There is a gap between desiring food and eating a particular piece of fruit. The logical structure of a decision to act, as sketched in the *De Motu Animalium* consists in the subsumption of a particular under a general description expressing a desire. This description may state a preference, for instance, "I want something to eat" (cf. 701a32); or it may assert a moral or prudential judgment, for example, "everyone should eat dry food." Aristotle believes that the task confronting the philosopher who would propound a theory of action is to explain how a desire for a certain type of object fixes upon a particular object and how, when fixed, a desire causes the body to move. The latter, for Aristotle, is a matter of body mechanics: the desire once aroused causes a change in the internal temperature, which in turn causes changes in the muscles and so the animal moves. The psychological question concerns the arousal of a desire in connection with a particular object. In the first place, the agent must be actively aware of the object. The apprehension of the desired object might occur through perception, *phantasia* or thought.[55] The hungry bird sees a succulent berry that inspires desire, and the desire causes the bird's body to move toward a clump of berries. The thought that fruit is good for human beings and the belief that there is a fruit tree over the knoll provokes the desire that moves the human's body in the direction of the tree.

Aristotle often speaks as if the recognition that strategy A would bring about a desired end is sufficient to cause the agent to act in accordance with A. "I want a covering, a cloak is a covering; I want a cloak. What I want, I ought to make; I want a cloak; I ought to make a cloak. . . . If there will be a cloak, this is necessary first, if this, that; and straightway one does this" (701a18–22). The first type of covering that comes to mind seems to be the one the agent chooses. Similarly, the pattern of reasoning known as the practical syllogism seems to ignore the complexity characteristic of deliberations leading up to an action. The "sweet food syllogism" is a typical example. The premises expressing the agent's beliefs, namely, "everything sweet is pleasant" and "this is sweet," immediately produce an actualized desire for the sweet in question, and unless the agent is prevented, he will eat the sweet (*E.N.* 1147a28–31). This scheme fails as an analysis of motivation because it cannot accommodate the agent's selectivity with respect to an object of satisfaction.[56]

However, Aristotle's description of practical reasoning might be intended merely as a sketch and a deliberate simplification of the actual cognitive process involved.[57] If so, the presentation of a potential object of desire need not in his view result in an actualized desire for the object, and the presentation of an object through *aisthēsis, phantasia* or thought would be a necessary but not a sufficient condition for the arousal of desire in connection with that object. To explain why the agent decides on a cloak rather than another kind of garment, some other cognitive factor must be mentioned. In short, there are two possible ways of construing the texts that describe the relationship between envisaging a particular outcome and actually desiring it. On the one hand, the presentation of the object is a necessary condition for the desire; on the other, it is a sufficient condition. But the former is more plausible, and it leaves room for a special role for *phantasia*, as suggested by *De Anima* 433b27–28.

Phantasia seems to focus desire on a particular object in a way in which neither perception nor thought does. *Phantasia* provides the "something else" that explains the agent's choice. Suppose a hungry animal is looking for food and discovers two edible fruits, either of which, if eaten, would satisfy her desire. She chooses one of them and eats it. While it is certainly true that she would not have eaten the fruit had she not seen it or had she not been hungry, the piece of fruit she chooses is not uniquely determined by these factors. For some reason, a particular piece of fruit appealed to her more than any other. Perhaps certain features of its appearance called up especially pleasurable sensations; perhaps its scent produced an intrinsically pleasant perception of sweet nectar (cf. E.N. 1174b15–1175a1).

To explain the association of gustatory pleasure with an object presented through other sense modalities, we must appeal to information not immediately present to the senses; the most likely source of this information would be past experience.[58] In bringing past experience to bear on present perceptions, *phantasia* would play the role of memory in the modern sense, namely, the utilization of previously acquired information.[59] In some cases, where the subject is conscious of the past origin of the association, *phantasia* would be involved qua *mnēmē*. In either case, the animal's desire is focused on a specific object through the association of pleasure with that object. The mechanism involved presumably would be a *phantasma* that was accompanied by a feeling of pleasure and hence mediated the connection between the present experience and the past. Cases of avoidance would be explained in the same way; the desire to flee is inspired by the association of pain with a situation presented to the agent through some cognitive faculty. As the vehicle for pleasant and painful associations based on past experience, *phantasia* transforms an object without affective connotations into an object of approach or avoidance. "On account of this, at the same time, so to speak, that one thinks one ought to go, one also goes, unless something else hinders him. For the affections [*pathē*] fittingly prepare the organic parts, and desire prepares the affections, and *phantasia* prepares desire, and *phantasia* arises through thought or through perception" (*De Motu An.* 702a16–19). The passage describes a two-part cognitive process. *Aisthēsis* or *noēsis* presents the object, and *phantasia* elaborates upon the object, reinterpreting it in light of anticipated pleasures and pains. This description secures a place for *phantasia* even in cases where a different cognitive faculty presents the object.[60] This is not to say that there need be subjectively distinguishable stages involved; that is, there need not be, from the agent's perspective, one stage where he apprehends the object, another where he construes it as an object of approach or avoidance, and a final stage where he reacts to it. From the animal's perspective, the desire for an immediately accessible bit of food, recognized through one sense modality or another, may constitute the whole of the conscious experience accompanying his exertions to obtain the food.

Aristotle assigns *phantasia* a unique role in action contexts because he recognizes the psychological complexity of choosing between potential objects of approach or avoidance.[61] This complexity is not captured by the logical scheme he sets out for practical reasoning nor by appeal to nonevaluative perceptions or thoughts. As the vehicle for pleasant and painful associations, *phantasia* brings about the transformation of potential objects of desire into actual objects of desire.

Nussbaum (1978) has given a different account of the role of *phantasia* in motivating action. She has argued that *phantasia* interprets the impress of the external object, enabling a percipient to perceive an object as a particular thing and to perceive it as desirable.[62] For the most part, Nussbaum treats *aisthēsis* as a purely passive faculty that receives the impress of external objects (pp. 257–59).[63] *Aisthēmata* are uninterpreted sensations; perceptions are interpreted sensory objects. *Phantasia* transforms *aisthēmata* into perceptions in our sense. If we follow this line of analysis to its logical conclusion, we must assign the perception of incidental *aisthēta* to *phantasia* (cf. p. 259). To paraphrase Nussbaum, *phantasia* allows the animal to see X as Y, for example, to see a white shape as Socrates. This would mean that *phantasia* is always involved in the apprehension of an incidental sensible. But Aristotle makes no such claim. At *De Anima* 428b18–30, Aristotle contrasts the *aisthēsis* of an incidental object to the *phantasia* of an incidental object.[64] Elsewhere he describes incidental perceptibles without making reference to *phantasia*. Moreover, according to Aristotle, *aisthēsis* is a critical faculty (*kritikon*); were *aisthēsis* as passive a faculty as Nussbaum claims, then *aisthēsis* would not be *kritikē*.[65] In short, Nussbaum assigns *phantasia* too broad a role in the interpretation of sensory information.[66] A percipient apprehends interpreted sensory wholes as well as proper objects through *aisthēsis*.

On the other hand, Aristotle needs a way to explain the attachment of pleasant or painful sensations to certain cognitive objects but not to others. According to Nussbaum, *phantasia* enables the agent to experience a particular object as desirable. This is correct, as *phantasia* is involved in the actualization of particular desires. The Sensory Content Analysis of *phantasia* makes it clear why Aristotle assigns *phantasia* the role of serving as the cognitive bridge between the object of a current perception or *noēsis* and a past experience of pleasure or pain. The actualization of a desire depends upon the actualization of an object of desire.[67] This in turn depends upon the presentation of a state of affairs that might be an object of approach or avoidance as (subjectively) pleasant or painful.

The complexity of the cognitive activity involved in voluntary motion attests to a broad conception of the powers of the perceptual faculty. The animal sees the berry as pleasant-for-him-at-this-moment; this complex cognition takes account of his present situation (that he is hungry) and his past experience with berries of this sort. Always in the case of animals and frequently in the case of humans, such complex cognitions are a function of the perceptual faculty. Had Aristotle a different, narrower notion of the perceptual faculty, then he would be unable to justify assigning complex psychological activities to it. As it stands, his conception of the perceptual faculty as exercised through the five senses, singly and jointly, and as exercised through *phantasia* provides an adequate theoretical underpinning for his account of motivation.

4. Sensory Representation

The importance of *phantasia* to Aristotle's account of the cognitive states of humans and other animals should by now be firmly established. As we have seen, Aristotle invokes *phantasia* to explain all sorts of cognitive phenomena from sensory illusions to practical decision-making. To do the work Aristotle requires of it, *phantasia* must be understood in terms of a broad notion of sensory representation. (As used here, *sensory representation* means the depiction of objects and states of affairs by means of sensible characters.)[68] The details of Aristotle's notion of sensory representation remain to be discussed. Aristotle exhibits the characteristics of *phantasia* by contrasting it to other cognitive states and by describing its object. This procedure gives us some information about his conception of sensory representation. It establishes that complexes of sensible characters are the vehicles for both perception and *phantasia*. In the former instance, the sensible characters are properties of the external objects of perception. In the latter, they are often internal objects whose causal antecedents were previous perceptions.

Perceptions can be highly complex cognitive structures, on Aristotle's account, and this fact attests to a rich notion of sensory representation, which, for that very reason, is also a controversial notion. *Aisthēsis*, it is often said, is ambiguous with respect to the modern distinction between *sensation* and *perception*. The difference is one of logical complexity and representational capacity: sensation is simply the apprehension of sensible qualities such as colors or sounds; perception involves the interpretation of sensory data—it is the apprehension of concrete particulars, such as people, trees and trains, and of concrete situations such as the train pulling out of the station. Few, if any, modern philosophers would limit the objects of perception to sensory contents; some other form of representation must be involved, it is argued, because complex perceptual objects are not easily reduced to sensible features.[69] Taking a similar line, Plato argued that the only objects the soul apprehends through the senses are sensible qualities (*Theaet.* 184–86). Aristotle, on the other hand, allows the senses to grasp complex states of affairs; the only limitation he recognizes is our inability to grasp universals or to manipulate concepts through perception.[70] Incidental objects of perception are interpreted sensory wholes— to perceive the approaching object as the son of Cleon is to engage in a cognitively complex operation. Previous learning informs the sensory base to yield the object represented by the immediately perceived sensory features (the proper and common objects); in this way complex objects are represented by sensible characters. Since in the case of human beings and other higher animals an enormous amount of information is received through the senses, Aristotle assumes that clusters of sensible characters can adequately represent complex, concrete situations.

The work that *phantasia* does for nonhuman animals is similar to the cognitive work *doxa* does for us, and thus Aristotle describes *phantasia* as a kind of thinking (*De An.* 433a10; cf. 427b28). According to *De Anima* III, 3, both *doxa* and *phantasia* are critical faculties (428a3–5) and both are subject to error (428a19). They differ in that *phantasia* is up to us, while *doxa* is not (427b17–20), and that *doxa* carries conviction (*pistis*), while *phantasia* does not (428a20–22). At 428a18–25 Aristotle argues that *phantasia* and *doxa* must be different faculties because animals possess *phantasia*, but (lacking reason and, hence, lacking conviction) must lack *doxa*. Since animals exhibit beliefs (where belief is defined operationally in terms of nonverbal behavior), conviction and *doxa* must involve some cognitive operation that animals cannot perform.[71] What animals lack would seem to be the ability to manipulate concepts of a logically complex sort or, as Aristotle puts it, to reason discursively (434a5–11; cf. *De Mem.* 453a10ff.).

This also explains why Aristotle rejects *phantasia's* claim to be a kind of *hupolēpsis* (supposal), the species of which are knowledge, *doxa*, understanding and their opposites (427b24–26). The difference between *phantasia* and perception, on the one hand, and *hupolēpsis* and *doxa*, on the other, is the difference between the employment of sensory representation alone and the employment of some mode of representation that can handle logically complex notions.[72] *Doxa* enables us to go beyond concrete representations using sensible characters and to reflect on these representations, to evaluate them and whenever appropriate to reject the information they convey. Despite appearances, we need not believe that the sun is only a foot across (*De An.* 428b3–4; *De Ins.* 458b29, 460b18–19).

Further evidence that the distinction between *doxa* and *phantasia* rests on a distinction between cognitive faculties that are not limited to sensory representation and those that are is provided by the *De Insomniis*, where Aristotle again contrasts *doxa* and other exercises of the rational faculty to *aisthēsis* and *phantasia* (*De Ins.* 458b10–459a22).[73] Dreams consist of *phantasmata*, and thoughts occurring during sleep that are contrary to the *phantasmata* occurring then are not part of the dream (*De Ins.* 462a29).[74] Not only do these distinctions establish the sensory character of the *phantasmata* constituting dreams, they also establish *phantasmata* as representational entities. Were a *phantasma* not a representation, no conflict could arise between it and a thought, which is a representation.

Our ability to simultaneously represent the same object in two incompatible ways depends, as Aristotle recognizes, on our ability to have two distinct apprehensions of the object.[75] Each representation makes a claim about the object (cf. *De Ins.* 460b13–20). A nightmare portrays a raging boar charging at the dreamer; the accompanying thought tells him that the animal is only a dream image. The dream presents the animal as posing an actual threat; the thought presents it as an imaginary and hence harmless creature. Having explained such experiences by appealing to distinct mental acts, Aristotle must find a way to individuate each type. Since both acts are representations of the same object, the same animal, Aristotle opts for differences in modes of representation. In the dream, the animal is represented by a colored shape, certain sounds or odors, perhaps. The thought, while about the same thing, represents the animal in a way that is incompatible with its representation in the dream.

Aristotle's practice of ascribing truth values to perceptions and *phantasiai* is another indication that sensory contents are representational. Aristotle recognizes that only thoughts or sentences that make assertions are properly described as true or false. "Truth and falsity imply combination and separation" (*De Int.* 16a11; cf. *Met.* 1051b1; *De An.* 430a26–28). By describing an instance of *aisthēsis* or *phantasia* as true or false, Aristotle is tacitly attributing a propositional structure to its object. He assumes that some sensory contents exhibit states of affairs and that these sensory contents function as propositions in the cognitive processes employing them.

It might be objected that Aristotle's practice of assigning truth values to perceptions and *phantasiai* is open to more than one interpretation.

An influential modern alternative distinguishes between the sensible features that are the bearers of perceptual information and the mental representation of that information, and it makes the latter representation the basis for assigning a truth value (cf. Anderson 1978). While the form of the original presentation was sensory, the form of the subsequent representation is symbolic. On this view, sensory contents play no role in mental representation, so the issue of the cogency of treating sensory contents as representational does not arise.

Modern philosophers have tended to group propositional objects and symbolic representation together and to contrast this group with raw feels and mental objects represented by sensible qualities.[76] Questions of truth arise only in connection with the first group; they do not arise in connection with the second. Whatever intrinsic merit this scheme has, the fact is that Aristotle does not divide cognitive objects up in this way, and if we interpret his notion of truth in accordance with our scheme, we will fail to come to terms with his conception of truth as it applies to *aisthēsis* and *phantasia*.[77] For Aristotle, perceptions of all sorts are true just in case things are as they appear to be in the perception, and *phantasiai* are true just in case the objects represented in the *phantasmata* are as they would be presented in a true perception (cf. chap. 3, sec. 5, and Modrak 1986).

Despite the many passages that speak of true and false *phantasiai*, Aristotle expresses a different and seemingly contrary sentiment at *De Anima* 432a10–11: "But *phantasia* is different from assertion and denial; for what is true or false involves a combination of thoughts." Aristotle might mean either (a) *phantasiai* never have truth values or (b) they sometimes do not. If (a), then Aristotle is here asserting a view that he repeatedly contradicts elsewhere; this is a prima facie reason to attribute (b) to him. More significantly, the next lines provide evidence that Aristotle has a certain kind of *phantasia* in mind. "For what distinguishes the first thoughts from *phantasmata*?" Aristotle asks. The *phantasma* in question is one corresponding to an isolated term or thought that is a constituent of a larger cognitive whole; in the case in point, the whole is the complex thought constituting a bit of knowledge. The apprehension of a complex cognitive object of this sort involves the apprehension of one or more *phantasmata*, but the cognitive object cannot be reduced to the *phantasmata*. A complex judgment about the nature of water is not adequately represented by a *phantasma* of a stream. However, in many other cases, for instance when a (nonhuman) animal envisages a course of action or a human dreams, the object of *phantasia* is a sensorial representation of a state of affairs. In these cases, Aristotle is quite happy to ascribe truth values to *phantasiai*. One way of understanding all of this—in fact the way the Stoics "cleaned up" Aristotle's account—is to say that in certain cases the *phantasma* is implicitly propositional. Then truth values can be assigned to *phantasiai* on the basis of the assignment of truth values to the propositions that correspond to their sensory contents.

Although Aristotle sometimes finds it convenient to talk as if the object of *phantasia* were a proposition, its propositional content is expressed sensorially. There are not two kinds of *phantasia*—one having a propositional content and the other a sensory content (pace Rees 1971, 500). Nonetheless, some sensory contents are more easily expressed in propositions than others because sensory contents may fall anywhere along a continuum—from the sensorial representation of complex states of affairs to sensory fragments. For instance, a memory image might consist in a composite of visual and auditory features representing a group of people engaged in conversation. This image would represent a quite complex state of affairs. By contrast, another image might simply present a single musical note. In one context, this image might exhibit a state of affairs corresponding to the proposition "this is shrill"; in another context, as a component of a larger sensory whole, the image might function very much as a single word functions in a statement.

In short, Aristotle construes sensory contents as representational entities, and he allows them to represent complex states of affairs as well as isolated sensible qualities. This conception of sensory representation enables him to make the perceptual faculty do an enormous amount of cognitive work. Since the operations of the perceptual faculty involve a versatile form of representation, to include memory and the "thought" processes of animals among the functions of the perceptual faculty is relatively unproblematic. Despite its advantages, Aristotle's conception of sensory representation may yet turn out to be flawed.

How does representation by sensible features work? Aristotle's notion of sensory representation might resemble the following conception in crucial respects: the existence of a pictorial mode of representation ultimately depends upon the existence of a nonpictorial, discursive mode of representation that interprets the pictorial representations. The underlying representational structures enable the mind to generate images and arrange perceptual objects (cf. Kosslyn 1983, chap. 6; Fodor 1974, 80–81). This model of mental representation, which has modern proponents, will not meet Aristotle's needs since he distinguishes between the perceptual and rational faculties on the basis of modes of representation. In the case of the perceptual faculty, the mode of representation at all levels must be by sensible characters.[78] To represent a concrete particular or a more complex state of affairs, a sensory content must successfully refer to an extramental object; the sensory content refers to the object as it exists in the world or to the object as it would exist in the world, were it to exist. Securing this reference without appealing to any other mode of representation may be difficult. The standard philosophical line on representation by imagery makes reference depend on resemblance; the image represents an object by resembling it.[79] Photographs, paintings and maps represent by virtue of structural similarities to the objects represented. If images represent, they too must represent by similarity.[80] This means that images will be very limited in their representational function or without any at all, or so it is argued.

Aristotle seems to believe that (at least in some cases) *phantasmata* represent by resemblance. His account of *mnēmē* makes the memory image an *eikōn*. Of the interpretations of this claim that we canvassed, one would make the memory image resemble the content of the memory, the other would make it resemble the original experience, which may, but need not be, the intentional object of the memory. Both construed the relation between an *eikōn* and its exemplar as similarity. The latter interpretation allowed for the employment of an image to represent something other than the perceptual situation of which it is an *eikōn*. However, there is some reason to suppose that this use of memory images is peculiar to human beings (see chap. 5, sec. 2). If so, then according to Aristotle *phantasmata* play the role they standardly play in memory because they resemble the objects remembered. For all of that the case of memory is peculiar in that the memory image not only must represent some state of affairs but must do so in a way that associates the representation with the past (cf. sec. 2). In contexts other than remembering and dreaming, Aristotle is silent about whether the *phantasma* is an *eikōn* of its referent or not.[81]

If we grant that resemblance is a sufficient condition for sensory representation of the sort Aristotle invokes, then the question becomes Is it also a necessary condition? We might believe that to make it a necessary condition would immediately open the analysis up to counterexamples. I might use a visual image of my house to decide what color paint to buy. Let us suppose that the color of the image resembles the color of the paint, not the actual color of the house; in this example certain features of the house as imagined resemble features of the house as perceived, although the color does not. But I might use a *phantasma* of a house to imagine the house I plan to build or would like to build. In this case the *phantasma* need not resemble any actually existing house, and yet it might represent a particular house, the house I want. It is arguable that the house as imagined resembles a possible house, the house it represents, in which case the example does not force us to abandon the view that sensory contents represent by resembling.

This brings us back to the original question: Is the representational capacity of a sensory content always dependent upon resemblance? Aristotle divides the objects of perception into *kath' hauta* sensibles and *kata sumbebēkos* sensibles. The proper and common objects do not resemble features of physical objects, for these sense objects exist potentially in external objects and are actualized in relation to percipients. To treat the relation between potentiality and actuality as one of resemblance would be a serious misreading of Aristotle. There is, however, *phantasia* of the proper and common sensibles. In many cases of *phantasia*, the proper and common objects are not actualized sensible features of physical objects in the subject's immediate environment; they are internal representations of the perceptible features of external objects. Presumably, if queried, Aristotle would say that these *phantasmata* resemble the proper and common perceptible features of physical objects.

An incidental object of perception is neither identical to the complex of proper and common objects that is the vehicle for its perception nor identical to the external object it represents. Typically, the perception of a particular incidental object depends upon the past experiences of the percipient. Certain characteristics not immediately given in the sensible characters perceived *kath' hauta* have become associated with these characters. The incidental perception of a bitter flavor through sight, for instance, occurs because a color such as yellow comes to be associated with a bitter flavor as a result of the simultaneous perception of bitter and yellow through taste and sight respectively (cf. *De An.* 425a30–b4). The capacity yellow has to represent bitterness seems to depend upon the resemblance between the yellow object currently seen and a yellow and bitter object perceived in the past. (In this case, resemblance is invoked to explain how one quality comes to represent another and not how one quality comes to be referred to another.)[82]

The standard case of incidental perception is the perception of a concrete particular represented by a complex of proper and common objects. We see the son of Cleon because we see his shape and color, and this complex of sensible characters provokes certain associations and thus represents the son of Cleon to us. Do we refer the incidental object to the physical object because the representation resembles the object? One might argue that we could never know whether the object as perceived resembled the actual object since we cannot know what the object is in and of itself as distinguished from the object as perceived by creatures like us. If we appeal to past experience, the critic will point out that we have only established that one perception resembles another. The object as perceived now and the object as perceived in the past might very well resemble each other without either one of them bearing any resemblance to the actual object. This skeptical critique does not fit very well with Aristotle's realism. Aristotle does not question the percipient's ability to refer the incidental object to an external object, so he does not explicitly appeal to resemblance or any other relation to explain the reference.[83] Nonetheless, had he been pressed, Aristotle probably would have decided in favor of resemblance. If incidental objects of perception resemble the extramental objects to which they are referred, there would seem to be some epistemic justification for our practice of basing generalizations about the nature of the world on perceptions of this sort. As a premise of Aristotle's realist epistemology, the correspondence between generalizations based on objects as perceived and objects as they are cannot be dispensed with.[84] This correspondence might be guaranteed in some other way, but positing perceptions that resemble the objects they represent is the most obvious solution.[85] This is a further reason to assume that sensory representation relies on resemblance since even in the *De Anima* Aristotle is seldom oblivious to the epistemological implications of his position.

On Aristotle's theory of perception and *phantasia*, we conclude, resemblance often secures the reference of a sensory content. Does this feature have untoward philosophical consequences for Aristotle's conception of sensory representation? We might think so for the following reasons: (1) It is not the bare fact that the *phantasma* resembles the object represented which secures the reference; the subject must recognize the resemblance, and it is arguable that the recognition of resemblance would not be part of the original representation (cf. Nussbaum 1978, 224–26). (2) There is a conceptual gap between the content of the representation and the sensory content used to represent it.

The first objection would not impress Aristotle. In the first place, the same difficulty can be raised in connection with any mode of representation. In the second place, Aristotle would point out that the motivation leading us to posit a second representation to secure the reference of the first would lead us to posit a third representation to explain the representational capacity of the second and so forth ad infinitum. The appeal to a more abstract form of representation has undeniable advantages from our perspective. It has few from Aristotle's. Not only does Aristotle want to limit other animals to sensory representation, he wants, whenever possible, to avoid the proliferation of cognitive abilities and faculties.[86] To explain one form of representation in terms of another would be to initiate a regress that can only be stopped by positing a form of representation that is self-contained (cf. *De An.* 425b16). Aristotle stops with the original sensory representation and thus blocks the regress before it begins.

The second objection poses a more serious problem. The complexity of the behaviors that Aristotle invokes the perceptual faculty to explain and the range of objects he assigns to *phantasia* and perception would be incompatible with a circumscribed notion of sensory representation. A gustatory *phantasma* of wine may resemble the flavor of the wine I hope to drink tonight, but the object of the cognition might be a state of affairs, my drinking wine tonight. Aristotle introduces the distinction between *kath' hauta* and *kata sumbebēkos* sensibles to take account of the differences between immediately given and interpreted sense objects. He assumes that interpreted sensory contents are apprehended in perception and *phantasia*, and he does not think it necessary to invoke cognitive capacities other than the five senses to explain this phenomenon. Whether this is a mistake or not is far from clear. Today there is some empirical evidence that interpretation is built in at the basic level of perceptual response (cf. Gregory 1970; Gibson 1966). As far as purely conceptual considerations are concerned, the distinction between proper and common objects, on the one hand, and incidental objects, on the other, seems well advised. Positing a different mode or level of representation that converts complexes of proper and common objects into interpreted sensory wholes seems to raise as many questions as it answers, and this hypothesis is less parsimonious than the assumption that the incidental objects are represented by complexes of proper and common objects. But if sensory contents represent objects more complex than sensible qualities, sensory representation cannot be limited to resemblance; associations and previous learning must also shape these cognitions. Aristotle assumes that this happens, but he does not explain how.

5. *Phantasia* and the Foundational Principles

The Psychophysical Principle is at work in Aristotle's account of *phantasia* in the *De Anima*, the *De Insomniis* and the *De Memoria*. The paraphrase of the formal definition of *phantasia*, expressed in the Sensory Content Analysis, has been discussed at length, but we have largely ignored the physiological side of *phantasia*. When Aristotle summarizes his findings concerning *phantasia* at the end of *De Anima* III, 3, he identifies the material substratum of *phantasia* with a physiological change brought about by the stimulation of a peripheral sense organ.[87] To explain the phenomenon of dreaming, Aristotle cites movements in the sense organs and in the blood. For one reason or another, during waking hours certain sensory impulses from the peripheral sense organs do not reach the central organ or, if they reach it, they are too weak to affect it; during sleep these impulses act on the central organ, causing dreams (*De Ins.* 461b7–31). Aristotle appeals to physical conditions to explain natural variations in the capacity for memory. Rapid growth, for instance, has an adverse affect on memory (*De Mem.* 450b1–10). Melancholics, because they have too much moisture around their hearts, persist in trying to recollect, even when they wish to abandon the effort because they recognize its futility (*De Mem.* 453a16–20). In short, we can find numerous references to physiology in Aristotle's description of *phantasia* and of the other cognitive states centering on *phantasmata*. As in the case of perception, there is no detailed physiological treatment of *phantasia*. We are told only about its origin in a movement of a peripheral sense organ, about the transmission of potential *phantasmata* in the blood, and about the ultimate realization of *phantasia* in a movement in the central organ.

The Psychophysical Principle brings Aristotle's concepts of matter and form to bear on psychological phenomena. One of the tenets of hylomorphism is the primacy of form; not surprisingly, the material descriptions Aristotle gives of *phantasia*, memory and dreaming would not in themselves suffice to distinguish one type of sensory experience from another. The physical substrata for aisthēsis, *phantasia* proper, and other cognitions centered on *phantasmata* are very similar. When an external object brings about an occurrence of *phantasia* rather than aisthēsis (when, for example, the square tower in the distance brings about the awareness of a round tower), the physiological basis for *phantasia* would become in practice, and perhaps in principle, indistinguishable from the physiological basis of aisthēsis. In both cases, certain events occurring outside or on the surface of the percipient's body cause changes in the peripheral organ, which in turn cause changes in the central organ. To distinguish the physiological substratum for *phantasia* from that of aisthēsis in cases where *phantasia* arises "autonomously" would be unproblematic, but in these cases to maintain the distinction on physiological grounds between *phantasia* proper and other cognitions employing *phantasmata* is not always easy. In each case, a chain of physical causes links the present experience to an original stimulation of a peripheral organ.[88] In some cases, there are distinctive physiological factors at work; sleep involves the partial paralysis of the central organ, so it should be possible to differentiate dreaming from other types of sensory activity on physiological grounds. In other cases, the physiological boundaries would be hard to draw. For example, Aristotle does not give us a clue as to what physiological differences, if any, distinguish *phantasia* proper from memory.

The Actuality Principle provides Aristotle's justification for distinguishing between perception and *phantasia* and for distinguishing among the various forms of *phantasia*. The object of *aisthēsis* is a sensory content, as are the objects of *phantasia*, memory and dreaming. The *aisthēton*, however, is the object of an apprehension of an external object under conditions conducive to veridical perception, while the *phantasma* is the object of an apprehension of a complex of sensible characters under conditions not conducive to veridical perception. There are different kinds of *phantasmata* corresponding to different manifestations of *phantasia*. A *mnēmoneuma* is a *phantasma* that refers to the past. The Actuality Principle enables Aristotle to differentiate among the components of the perceptual faculty without undermining its cohesiveness. Each perceptual capacity is defined in relation to a sensory content with type-specific features. The unity and breadth of the perceptual faculty is insured by the Sensory Representation Principle. Because *phantasmata* are sensory contents, Aristotle is able to include dreaming, memory and imagining among the functions of the perceptual faculty and to develop a sophisticated notion of sensory representation.[89]

The Analytic Principle spawns the desire to extend the model of cognition developed for sense perception to *phantasia* and other cognitions centering on *phantasmata*. Aristotle begins with a psychic capacity exercised in connection with the sensible qualities of physical objects; he then conceives *phantasia* in a way that allows internalized sensible characters to be used to represent objects not present to the senses; finally he uses the notion of sensory representation elaborated under the rubric *phantasia* to explain memory, dreaming and goal-directed behavior and to justify the inclusion of these cognitive activities under the perceptual faculty.

Thus, Aristotle's treatment of *phantasia* is structured in accordance with the same substantive assumptions and prescriptive principles as the other parts of his theory of the perceptual system. The inclusion of *phantasia* under the purview of this theory is a significant achievement. As the form of representation employed in a number of different mental operations, *phantasia* plays a central role in the cognitive life of human beings and other animals. Having a unified theory of the functions of the perceptual faculty, including *phantasia*, at his disposal, Aristotle is able to explain the complex cognitive capacities possessed by many nonrational animals without recourse to an immaterial *psuchē* or to any cognitive faculty other than the perceptual faculty. This is a highly desirable result from Aristotle's point of view—and from our point of view as well insofar as the theory Aristotle propounds is simple, unified and comprehensive.

II

THOUGHT AND CONSCIOUSNESS

5

Thinking and Perceiving

Discursive thought is not a function of the perceptual faculty. Yet our account of the perceptual faculty would be incomplete if we did not consider Aristotle's conception of thinking.[1] Thought and perception are closely related. Aristotle uses a simile to describe their relation: thought is related to perception as a bent line is related to itself when straightened out (*De An.* 429b16–17).[2] Thinking consists in the apprehension and manipulation of concepts based upon past and present perceptions. Gaps in our conceptual powers would produce corresponding gaps in our knowledge (*Pst. Anal.* 81a38–39). Moreover, thinking requires the simultaneous awareness of a *phantasma*, so every act of thought is accompanied by an act of the perceptual faculty. In short, Aristotle's psychology and his epistemology envisage an intimate relationship between the perceptual and noetic faculties; this has important consequences for the unity of the human *psuchē* and the nature of human knowledge.

Determining the precise configuration of the relationship between the perceptual faculty and the noetic faculty is a large task that is here divided into parts. As a first step, we investigate the nature of the noetic faculty. What are its functions? What are the distinctive features of *noēta* (intelligible objects)? Having answered these questions, we examine the analogy Aristotle draws between noetic and perceptual capacities that suggests a unified conception of cognitive capacities and the doctrine of active nous, which seems to argue against this conception. Then since Aristotle contrasts thinking to sensory representation, we take a second look at his notion of mental representation. The chapter concludes with a discussion of the impact of the fundamental principles on Aristotle's theory of the noetic faculty.

1. The Nature of the *Noētikon*

When Aristotle turns his attention to the noetic faculty in *De Anima* III, 4, he describes the subject of the investigation in epistemic terms: "Concerning that part of the soul by which the soul both knows (*gi-*

nōskei) and understands (*phronei*), whether it is separable or not separable spatially but only in definition, we must inquire what distinguishing feature it has and how then thinking comes about" (429a10–13). As used by Aristotle the verbs *gignōskein* and *phronein* often carry the connotation of getting it right. Does Aristotle mean to restrict the thinking faculty to judging rightly? Just as Aristotle only uses *aisthēsis* for veridical perception, he might only use *nous* and its cognates to describe the apprehension of truths.[3] In the case of perception, Aristotle appeals to another notion, *phantasia*, to cover those cases where the object of the experience is a perceptible object, but the conditions surrounding its apprehension are such that it is unlikely to be accurately apprehended through the senses. *Phantasia* is included under the perceptual faculty, so we would expect Aristotle to include under the noetic faculty cognitive states that misrepresent the relation of one *noēton* to another or that are complex, intelligible structures built up incorrectly out of simpler *noēta*.[4]

The definition of *nous* at 429a23 establishes that the conception of noetic activity at work in the *De Anima* is broader than the circumscribed epistemic conception, sometimes found in the *Posterior Analytics*, that limits *nous* to the apprehension of truths. "I mean by *nous* that by which the soul thinks (*dianoeitai*) and hypothesizes (*hupolambanei*)." In the preceding chapter, Aristotle remarks that thinking (*dianoeisthai*) may err (427b13). There he uses the noun form of *hupolambanein*, *hupolēpsis* (belief) as the generic term for the rational capacities he contrasts with perception and *phantasia*. He mentions three types of *hupolēpsis*—knowledge (*epistēmē*), opinion (*doxa*) and understanding (*phronēsis*) and their opposites (427b25–26). Clearly the phrase "their opposites" is intended to cover cases where the mind is occupied with objects such as the objects of knowledge, (right) opinion, and understanding, but makes a mistake of one sort or another. No doubt Aristotle finds the operations of the noetic faculty that constitute states of knowing and understanding more interesting than others, but he means to include under this faculty all cognitive operations involving intelligible objects. Elsewhere in the *De Anima* Aristotle uses the term *dianoētikon* to refer to the faculty for thought.[5] Since *dianoia* (thought) does not have the epistemic connotations of *nous*, this provides a final bit of evidence that the faculty referred to as the *noētikon* in *De Anima* III, 4 is the general capacity for intellectual activity possessed by a human being.

Unlike perceiving, the activity of thinking (i.e., the second actuality of the noetic faculty) has no physiological substratum. Something happens in the eye when we see colors; there is no similar change in a bodily organ in the case of thinking. Thinking is not "mixed with the body," as Aristotle puts it (*De An.* 429a24–25). This conclusion is based on the characteristics of the objects of thought, the indefatigability of thought, and the absence of a bodily organ for thought. Aristotle takes the last feature for granted (429a24). We might wonder why he does not place thinking in the heart, which is the central sense organ. After all, in *De Anima* I he seems to allow bodily movements to accompany thinking; there he only denies that the movements involved belong to the soul as such (*De An.* 408b5–16).[6] Presumably, it is the distinctly human character of thinking that in the end deters Aristotle from locating thought in a bodily organ such as the heart, which is common to all sorts of creatures.

Aristotle argues for the asomatic character of thinking from the differences between objects of thought and objects of perception (429a18–b5). The physical constitution of a bodily structure restricts it to a certain range of objects. (Ears are so constituted as to receive sound but not flavor.) A bodily substratum for thought would similarly limit the range of the intelligible, but the mind is able to comprehend every conceivable type of object. The capacity to perceive a particular kind of object is susceptible to destruction by peculiarly intense objects of the same type; thus loud sounds produce deafness. However, nothing of this sort occurs in the case of intelligible objects. Aristotle takes this to be an indication that no physiological change occurs when we think and hence there is no possibility of physiological damage as a result of encountering intensely intelligible objects.

In *De Anima* I, Aristotle endorses the position that the human being, not an immaterial soul, is the subject of all mental attributes: "For it would perhaps be better not to say that the soul pities or learns or thinks, but that the man does these with his soul" (408b13–15; cf. 403a5–10). This conception of the psychological subject dominates Aristotle's thinking throughout the *De Anima*. It explains the emphasis he places on the similarities between thought and perception, and it explains why he envisages an intimate relationship between the perceptual and noetic faculties.[7] Because the noetic faculty does not enform any particular organ or system of organs, it menaces the psychophysical unity of the human being. The strategy Aristotle considers in *De Anima* I makes the noetic faculty dependent upon another psychic capacity, *phantasia*, which in turn is dependent upon a bodily system: "but thinking especially seems to be peculiar to the soul. But if this too is a kind of *phantasia* or is not possible without *phantasia*, it would not be possible for this to exist without the body" (403a8–10). *Phantasia* requires the physical substratum of the perceptual system as a whole.[8]

Thus the noetic faculty is dependent upon the body in a weak sense, and as a result the noetic faculty can be viewed as a dispositional property of a psychophysical subject, the human being. Therefore, we need not posit a psychic substance as the subject of noetic activity.

Thinking is a property of a psychophysical organism, a human being—even on the account given in *De Anima* III. However, it can be argued that in *De Anima* III, 5, with the doctrine of active *nous*, we find an unqualified commitment to dualism.[9] Should this argument prove correct, it would only show that there is a pronounced dualist strain in Aristotle's thinking about active *nous*; it would not show that the account of noetic activity found elsewhere in the *De Anima* should be rejected in favor of the highly controversial and fragmentary discussion of active *nous* in III, 5.[10] The task of reconciling these two seemingly quite different conceptions of *nous* will be undertaken in section 3. For the moment, let it suffice to say that Aristotle's final position is the same as his original one: noetic activity is a property of the human being (431b18–19, 432a3–14). The capacity for thought is not the form of a particular body organ, but it is a capacity possessed by a psychophysical being of a certain sort.[11]

The noetic faculty stands in the same relation to intelligible objects as the perceptual faculty stands to sensible objects (*De An.* 429b13; cf. 407a7); in both cases, the second actuality of the faculty is the actualization of an appropriate object. The characteristics of the object determine the characteristics of the state, so the crucial question is: What are the distinctive features of noetic objects? Aristotle has less to say on this subject than we might expect; the definitive characteristics of intelligible objects must be gleaned from his examples and descriptions of the capacities making up the noetic faculty. Aristotle's explicit descriptions of *noēta* make two claims: The *noēton* is the object of *nous*, and it exists potentially in perceptible objects. Aristotle also uses *noema* for the object of *nous* (*De An.* 407a7, 430a28, 431b7, 432a12). Insofar as he uses *noēton* or *noēma* for the object of occurrent *nous*, he treats them as synonyms. If Aristotle recognizes a difference between the *noēton* and the *noēma*, it is that the latter exists in us qua disposition as well as qua actualized object of *nous*, whereas the former exists potentially in external objects and actually in us as an actualized object of *nous*.[12] Aristotle's description of the *noēton* and the *noēma* set certain conceptual constraints on the noetic object but provide little by way of a positive characterization.

In *De Anima* III, 4, the examples of *noēta* are essences; for instance, what it is to be water or what it is to be straight. The objects exhibiting these essences are not as accessible through thought as their essences, either because they are concrete and hence perceptible or because they are less abstract and hence less intelligible. We perceive water and we conceive the geometrical line as straightness juxtaposed on continuity (cf. 429b10–20); in each case, the essence is more intelligible than its exemplification. In *De Anima* III, 8, Aristotle uses the term *epistēta* (objects of knowledge) as if it were synonymous with *noēta* (431b22–23). This also suggests that universality, if not an essential feature of the *noēton*, is at least characteristic of the paradigm cases of *noēta*.[13] A *noēton* par excellence is an abstract universal exemplified by particulars but fully expressed only in thought. As we shall see, this conception of *noēta* has important consequences for Aristotle's treatment of the relation between the noetic and the perceptual faculty and for his conception of mental representation.

To sum up, the *noētikon* is the psychic faculty exercised in the apprehension of the *noēta*; the *noēta* are too abstract for the perceptual faculty; they cannot be fully represented by sensory contents. The nature of the *noēton* and of noetic activity is such that it precludes the embodiment of the noetic faculty. This presents Aristotle with a conceptual problem of the first order—how to avoid Platonic dualism. In large measure his answer turns on the relation he envisages between noetic activity and the perceptual faculties.

2. The *Noētikon* and the *Aisthētikon*

At first glance, the most surprising feature of Aristotle's treatment of the *noētikon* is its brevity. Only four chapters of the *De Anima* are devoted to this topic, and it is given little attention elsewhere.[14] The explanation lies in part in Aristotle's conception of the relationship between the noetic and the perceptual faculties. Aristotle groups these two faculties together under the broader notion of cognition or the power to discriminate.[15] "The soul of animals has been defined by two faculties, the faculty of discrimination (*kritikon*), which is the function of thought and perception, and the faculty that originates movement with respect to place" (432a15–16; cf. 427a17–22). In other words, Aristotle takes animal life to be characterized by two basic abilities, the ability to discern features of the environment and the ability to respond accordingly. To be able to discern the warmth of fire and to move closer to the flame or away from it distinguishes an animal's way of being in the world from a plant's. Having marked off the capacities of animals in this way, Aristotle investigates at great length perception, the form of discrimination possessed by all animals.

When he turns to the rational capacities that separate human life from other forms of animal life, Aristotle emphasizes the similarities of the two types of discrimination. He extends the Actuality Principle to noetic activity. Thinking is the actualization of a *noeton;* perceiving is the actualization of an *aistheton.* Aristotle describes both faculties as impassive (*De An.* 429a29–30) and then makes each passive in relation to its object. Thinking, like perceiving, is a response to a particular kind of object. Perception occurs when perceptible objects act on the sense organs; thought occurs when intelligible objects act on the mind. To describe the same faculty simultaneously as impassive and responsive to certain objects seems paradoxical. Thus, it is all the more significant that Aristotle describes both the perceptual and noetic faculties in this way.[16] Although he cites a variety of differences between the perceptual and noetic faculties in *De Anima* III, 4, Aristotle persists in analyzing them within the same theoretical framework because, for him, they are the same sort of faculty.[17]

This leads him to entertain the hypothesis that the exercise of the one is simply the exercise of the other with a new twist:

> Since a magnitude and what it is to be a magnitude are different, also water and what it is to be water are different . . . , one discerns (*krinei*) what it is to be flesh and flesh either by means of a different faculty or the same faculty differently disposed. (429b10–14)

This description is repeated almost verbatim a few lines below, but this time Aristotle is describing the relationship between the cognition of an ideal straight line and the cognition of the essence of straightness.

> Again in the case of abstract objects, the straight is like the snub, for it involves continuity. But the essence is different, if what it is to be straight and the straight are different; let it be duality. One discerns (*krinei*) it then by something different or by the same thing differently disposed. (429b18–21)

By describing the differences between one exercise of the noetic faculty and another in the same terms as he describes the difference between an exercise of the noetic faculty and an exercise of the perceptual faculty, Aristotle again chooses to emphasize the similarities rather than the differences between these faculties.[18]

The difference between perception and thought is due to a difference in degree of abstractness, but, as Aristotle is quick to point out, there are similar differences among thoughts. Just as one and the same faculty apprehends geometrical and arithmetical objects even though the latter are more abstract, the same faculty might apprehend both a concrete particular and its essence. To apprehend a perception of water in relation to the essence of water might involve precisely the same sort of cognitive shift as the shift from a geometrical presentation of a straight line to an arithmetical representation of the essence of a straight line.[19]

The suggestion that cognitive objects form a continuum from concrete particulars to maximally general universals finds support elsewhere in the Aristotelian corpus. In *Posterior Analytics* II, 19, Aristotle describes an innate, critical capacity (*dunamis kritikē*) (99b35) that enables us to apprehend universals instantiated in objects of perception.[20] He describes a series of cognitions that yield increasingly general objects. A number of similar perceptions are collected together to form a single memory; a number of similar memories become a single experience; particular features are stripped away from the experience to produce a true universal (cf. *Met.* 980a26–981a7). This universal becomes in turn the object of a process of further abstraction. At each stage, the process leads to objects that are more abstract and possess greater generality than the objects apprehended at the preceding stage.

From the perception of Socrates to the recognition of the natural kind, *anthropos*, to the apprehension of the genus, living thing, the cognitive movement is from the more particular to the more abstract and the process of abstraction is the same in kind. This picture of a cognitive process beginning in perception and continuously stripping away the particularizing features of cognitive objects to arrive at maximally general objects explains why Aristotle wonders whether it is the same faculty differently disposed that apprehends the sensible particular and its essence. There is a single continuum of cognitive activity, and the line between perception and intellection is difficult to fix.

Human beings are able to manipulate percepts so as to produce insights into the natures of the objects perceived. The most fundamental type of insight comprehends what makes a thing the sort of thing it is. Having apprehended percepts of concrete instances of water in a particular way, we come to understand what water is. Since, for Aristotle, the objects in the world belong to natural kinds, the apprehension of the essence of water is ipso facto the apprehension of an abstract object applying generally to all genuine instances of water. On this picture, the noetic faculty might just be the outcome of a special and peculiarly human employment of the perceptual faculty.[21]

If the assumption that mental states are states of the central nervous system is right—and this assumption guides much of the research being done today in neurophysiology and psychology—then surely something like the cognitive continuum envisaged by Aristotle must obtain.[22] There is little room on this model for a sharp cleavage between perceptual and intellectual states of the sort championed by dualists such as Descartes or Plato. Not only do modern materialists favor a continuum view, but so did ancient materialists, who, according to Aristotle, identified thought with perception and posited a single faculty for both.

> The ancients indeed said that thinking and perceiving were the same; just as Empedocles said, "Wisdom increases for men according to what is present to them." . . . For all these consider thinking to be something bodily, just as perception is, and both perceiving and thinking to be of like by like. (*De An.* 427a21–28)

Motivated by the Psychophysical Principle and recognizing that perceptual and noetic activities share certain characteristics, Aristotle might have adopted the position he attributes to his pre-Socratic predecessors, that is, he might have chosen to include rational and perceptual capacities under a general faculty for discrimination. On this account, human beings would possess more powers than any other animal having this faculty, but the difference between human and other animals would presumably be no greater than the difference between the higher animals possessing all five senses and the simple animals possessing only the sense of touch (*De An.* 433b31–434a5). The latter difference is accommodated by Aristotle's theory of the perceptual faculty, so the mere fact that human beings possess rational capacities not possessed by other animals does not explain why Aristotle posits two distinct cognitive faculties.[23]

The Actuality Principle, however, does explain it, for Aristotle believes that *aisthēta* and *noēta* are different kinds of cognitive objects. *Aisthēta* are sensory contents. While it is possible to apprehend a sensory content in a number of different modes as long as the sensory content remains the focal object, these differences simply lead to the differentiation of subfaculties within the perceptual faculty. *Noēta* are not sensory contents. Hence Aristotle posits a separate noetic faculty. He supports the distinction between *noēta* and *aisthēta* by appealing to introspectible differences between the two types of object and to logical and conceptual differences between the two.

Sensory contents in the form of *phantasmata* play an integral role in thinking, yet Aristotle is careful to distinguish between thoughts and the correlative *phantasmata*. "Surely neither these nor other [thoughts] are *phantasmata*, but they are not possible without *phantasmata*" (*De An.* 432a13–14). Aristotle frequently points out that an object as represented through the noetic faculty may have characteristics incompatible with those it has as represented through perception or *phantasia*, even when the representations are simultaneous. When we think that the sun is larger than the inhabited world, we employ a *phantasma* that represents the sun as quite small (cf. *De An.* 428b2–9; *De Ins.* 458b28–29). When we think about geometrical objects, the *phantasma* we use has a certain magnitude, but the cognitive object as such does not have this feature nor do we so construe it (*De Mem.* 450a1–9). The thought "I'm dreaming," occurring in the midst of a dream, is true in contrast to the imagery of the dream (*De Ins.* 462a3–8).[24]

Aristotle makes the potential for representing universals the grounds for differentiating between sensible and noetic representations. We apprehend universals through the noetic faculty. Through perception and *phantasia* we apprehend objects that are instances of universals, and for this reason a perception can provide the information needed for the abstraction of a universal concept or principle. The geometer contemplates a particular triangle represented in a diagram or in a *phantasma*, but reasons about the universal concept, triangle. The difference in logical type is to Aristotle's mind the most significant difference between the two types of representations. Cognitive objects fall along a continuum from the most concrete to the most universal. By imposing the distinction between universal and particular on this continuum, Aristotle ends up with a category of intelligible objects, universals, that are not accessible through the perceptual faculty.[25] Following Plato, Aristotle limits the objects of art and science to universals. Art and science are the highest expression of our intellectual ability; the apprehension of universals is distinctive of human cognition. Since the representation of universals is not possible through perception or *phantasia*, our ability to apprehend universals separates us from other animals and enables us to possess knowledge. Necessarily this ability is realized through the noetic faculty alone.

It is one thing to say that universals are only apprehended through the noetic faculty and quite another to say that all *noēta* are universals and (potential) objects of knowledge. Plato may have taken the latter position, but Aristotle should have taken the former. There are passages, however, where Aristotle seems to equate being intelligible with being knowable (*epistētos*) (cf. *De An.* 431b21–22). Here Plato's influence is very evident. Throughout his philosophical career, Plato tended to divide cognitive objects up into perceptibles and intelligibles; the latter are universals and the proper objects of knowledge. This tendency finds its most eloquent expression in the writings of Plato's middle period. The *Republic* uses a line divided into segments as a metaphor for the relation between intellect and perception; the major divide is between the intelligibles (*noēta*) and the sensibles (*aisthēta*) and the faculties proper to each. Intelligible objects are knowable; perceptible ones are not (*Rep.* 509d–511e).[26]

In the *Posterior Analytics,* Aristotle espouses a similar doctrine: there is no knowledge of particulars; all knowledge is of universals; propositions expressing maximally general relations between classes are the objects of knowledge par excellence. The more universal the proposition, the more intelligible it is. Aristotle ranks sciences according to the scope of their first principles.[27] Sciences with more comprehensive first principles are epistemically superior to those whose first principles have a more limited range of applications. Not surprisingly, in the *Posterior Analytics* the distinction between an *aisthēton* and a *noēton* is assimilated to the distinction between a sensible particular and an abstract universal; hence the distinction between *aisthēta* and *noēta* becomes a distinction between objects that strictly speaking cannot be objects of knowledge and those that can be.[28] This picture is muted in the psychological writings but still present. "For existing things are either perceptible or intelligible, and knowledge (*epistēmē*) is in a way the objects of knowledge and perception (is in a way) the perceptibles" (*De An.* 431b22–24). The tacit identification of *noēta* with *epistēta* explains Aristotle's choice of examples of *noēta* (an essence has the requisite universality) and his use of epistemic characteristics to describe the *noētikon*.

At this point, we are confronted with two apparently incompatible strands in Aristotle's thinking about the noetic faculty. According to one strand, the noetic faculty is the perceptual faculty differently disposed and noetic activity is amenable to the same model of analysis as perceptual activity. According to the other, *aisthēta* and *noēta* are quite different objects, which seems to entail that the perceptual and noetic faculties are distinctly different faculties. Plato accepted this consequence; indeed he invokes his version of the Actuality Principle to argue from the difference between *aisthēta* and *noēta* for a rigid dichotomy between perception and intellection (*Rep.* 477d). Aristotle, on the other hand, tries to accommodate a "Platonic" conception of *noēta* within an integrated model of perceptual and noetic capacities.

The strategy Aristotle adopts is to locate the noetic object in a sensible presentation (*De An.* 431a17, 431b2, 432a5). The *phantasma* depicts an object of a certain type; the intelligible form is the essence of that object. A sample of bronze, for instance, apprehended in one way is a brown, hard mass; apprehended in another, it exemplifies what it is to be bronze. The *phantasma* is nested in the thought; thus, formally and materially, thinking is dependent upon *phantasia*. The dependence of thought on a *phantasma* and hence on changes in the perceptual system is analogous to the dependence of perception on physical causes. In the latter case, an object having certain physical characteristics is potentially perceptible; it is actually perceived when it brings about certain changes in a medium and in a functioning sense organ. The sense object exists potentially in the external object and as a result of a series of physical changes is actualized in the act of perception. The *noēton* exists potentially in the *phantasma*, and a series of bodily changes (the material substratum for the apprehension of the *phantasma*), like the changes in the medium, are necessary but not sufficient for the actualization of the *noēton*. The formal cause of the perception is the complex of sensible characters constituting the perceptual object; the formal cause of the thought is the complex of intelligible characters constituting the *noēton*. In each case, the material substratum is a vehicle for the formal cause. Thinking is the actualization of a *noēton*, the material substratum of which is a *phantasma*. In accordance with the Actuality Principle, the relation between the faculties would mirror the relation between their objects. While formally distinct from the perceptual faculty, the noetic faculty is the perceptual faculty differently disposed in the sense that the latter is its material cause.[29]

Remarkably, the psychological dependence of thought on perceptual activity exceeds the epistemically motivated concern to base knowledge on perception. A weak empiricist theory might make the perceptual faculty the source of information about the external world and hence indispensible for reasonings about matters of fact. A less weak one might strengthen the connection between the two faculties by making the perceptual faculty the source of all of our concepts on the grounds that all concepts are abstracted from or built up by generalization from the data of sense. As an epistemologist, Aristotle seems to adopt precisely this position.[30] In the *Posterior Analytics* and the *Metaphysics*, sense perception is the ultimate source of all concepts (*Pst. Anal.* I, 18; II, 19; *Met.* I, 1). The question, whether we have access through thought alone to previously acquired knowledge, is not addressed in these treatises, although nothing is said that would rule out this possibility, although it is ruled out by the *De Anima's* account of thinking. The issue of psychological dependence, however, is relevant to the issue of epistemological dependence only insofar as the hypothesized dependence is conceptual.

At this point, the Platonist might charge that by postulating simultaneous episodes of thinking and *phantasia*, Aristotle has not succeeded in integrating the activities of the noetic and perceptual faculties because he has not explicated the conceptual connection between the *phantasma* and the thought. Either the object of the thought and the *phantasma* are distinct mental objects, and hence, according to the Actuality Principle, the thought and the apprehension of the *phantasma* are different cognitions, or they are the same, and the distinction between the thought and the *phantasma* collapses and with it the distinction between the noetic and perceptual faculties. To think about the essence of water is either distinguishable from apprehending an image of water or it is not. Does Aristotle have the resources to meet this challenge? His choice of examples in *De Anima* III, 4 as well as the genetic account of *Posterior Analytics*, II, 19 suggest a way out. He would agree with the Platonist that the cognitions are quite different, yet he need not bow to the Platonist's conclusion. If, as these texts indicate, the mind employs *phantasmata* qua arbitrarily selected instances of the type under consideration, the object represented in the *phantasma* is arguably a universal exemplar from one perspective and from another a sensible particular.[31] From one perspective, the *phantasma* employed by the thinker apprehending the essence of water would be an arbitrary exemplification of water in general; from another, it might be a particular bluish puddle (cf. Grene 1963, 108–9). Both the *phantasma* and the thought represent the same object, the water; the former represents it as a sensible particular; the latter represents it abstractly in terms of its essence.

Aristotle succeeds, at least up to a point, in incorporating a Platonic conception of *noēta* into the integrated model of noetic and perceptual activity. The *noēton* is a particular way of apprehending a *phantasma* that yields a universal. The only question that remains is how to explain the actualization of the *noēton*; since the *phantasma* in its own right is an object of awareness, the very fact that the mind apprehends a particular *phantasma* does not guarantee that the corresponding *noēton* will be actualized. Presumably, such considerations prompted Aristotle to formulate the difficult doctrine of active *nous*.

3. The Autonomy of Thought

In accordance with the Actuality Principle, the object of thought, like the object of perception, is ontologically prior to the exercise of the faculty (*De An.* 429a15–17, 429b30, 431a1). In the case of perception, the object exists in the world; color is a property of physical surfaces, while color-as-actualized comes into existence as the object of actual perceivings. Even when the perceptual faculty is exercised in relation to an internal object, that object is a complex of sensible characters. The ultimate source of *phantasiai* are the objects in the world that act on the senses and bring about sense perceptions and the residual changes in the sense organs that constitute dispositional *phantasiai*. Up to a point, a similar story can be told about the noetic object; it too involves the apprehension of a *phantasma* whose history can be traced back to the sense perception(s) giving rise to it (cf. *Pst. Anal.* II, 19; *Met.* I, 1). Then the stories diverge and must diverge, for otherwise the distinction between the noetic and perceptual faculties would collapse.

The uniqueness of the noetic act resides in the uniqueness of its object. The noetic object is obtained by ignoring the particularizing and concretizing features of sensible objects and thus arriving at a representation that treats the sensible object as a token of a natural kind or an instance of a general rule.[32] The problem, as Aristotle sees it, is to explain where the noetic representation comes from. Elsewhere he waves this problem aside with the remark that our minds are so constituted as to be able to recognize the universal in the particular and to recognize natural kinds in their instances (*Pst. Anal.* 100a13–14). In the *De Anima*, the analysis of cognitive capacities in terms of first and second actualities forces him to say more.

What explains the shift from perceiving a cool, green fluid or contemplating the corresponding *phantasmata* to apprehending the essence of water? Confronting this issue presumably led Aristotle to assert the doctrine of active *nous* found in *De Anima* III, 5.[33] Aristotle compares active *nous* to light, which is a necessary condition for the perception of color.[34] Light is the state of a transparent medium that enables the (potential) color to act on the sense organ to bring about their mutual realizations in an actual seeing of color. The case of the potential noetic object and the noetic faculty strikes Aristotle as similar, and so he posits a pervasive state of noetic activity, "active *nous*" as a necessary condition for intellection. The potential *noēton* is present in the *phantasma* and the thinker has the potential for thinking about it, but active *nous* is required for the realization of these potencies in an actual act of thinking.

Appeal to the notion of active *nous* enables Aristotle to maintain the parallel between perceptual and noetic activity without compromising the distinction between their objects. It seems, however, to have several untoward consequences. First, on the integrated model of noetic and perceptual activity, thinking cannot occur without perceptual activity, for the *noēton* is a representation of an occurrent *phantasma*. Yet because it is a continuous and content-free state of intellectual activity, active *nous* is not dependent upon the presentation of *phantasmata*. Second, the noetic faculty, insofar as it is the capacity for ordinary thought, can only be exercised by a creature possessing sense organs.

But active *nous*, because it is independent of the perceptual faculty, is also independent of the body.

The literature abounds with interpretations of *De Anima* III, 5 and speculations about the character of active *nous*.[35] Since our primary concern is Aristotle's theory of the perceptual faculty and since this concern motivates our interest in the noetic faculty, we can put to one side many of the exegetical and conceptual questions about active *nous* that have occupied other philosophers. We should limit our investigation to examining Aristotle's motivation for introducing the doctrine of active *nous* and to deciding whether this doctrine is problematic from the standpoint of the integrated model of perceptual and noetic activity.[36]

Aristotle might have stipulated that the joint exercise of the perceptual and noetic faculties was sufficient to bring about the actualization of the *noēton*. On this account, thinking would simply be a peculiarly human way of representing an object presented in a *phantasma*. Nothing would be acquired for (actual) intelligibility apart from the exercise of the noetic faculty in connection with an object presented in a *phantasma* or a perception. In the case of previously acquired information, Aristotle is happy to adopt this position: "When the intellect has become each thing in this way . . . then it is also potential in a sense but not in the same way as before it learns and discovers. Then it is also able to think by itself" (*De An.* 429b5–9).[37] Once the universal is learned by an individual mind, then the mind is able to recognize the universal in the appropriate *phantasmata* and active *nous* need not be invoked to explain the cognition. Yet Aristotle stops short of claiming that the exercise of the noetic faculty in relation to a *phantasma* brings about the original actualization of the *noēton*.

The Actuality Principle in conjunction with Aristotle's conception of *noēta* motivates the doctrine of active *nous*. The act of thinking requires an actually intelligible object; the *phantasma* presents a potentially intelligible object. The problem is to explain how the sensible instance of a universal displayed in a *phantasma* is transformed into the universal that is the object of the thought. In the *Posterior Analytics*, Aristotle appeals to induction (*epagōgē*) and *nous* to explain the articulation of the universal.[38] In the *De Anima*, Aristotle posits a state of continuous noetic activity as a necessary condition for the actualization of the *noēton*. Like light in the case of color, active *nous* makes the actualization of the potentially intelligible object possible. Active *nous* is not a cognitive state, for it does not present the thinker with a cognitive object.[39]

Although the doctrine of active *nous* is not inconsistent with the integrated model of perceptual and noetic activity, it does postulate the existence of a type of intellectual activity wholly independent of the perceptual faculty. As a result, the ontological status of active *nous* is problematic. The ancient commentators tended to place it outside the individual mind.[40] This approach has certain advantages; for example, it does not entail a dualist conception of the individual human being. The major disadvantage of this view is that the relation between the universal active *nous* and the individual thinker is obscure, and it is no easy task to tell a coherent story about the connection between the two. On the other hand, if (as seems more likely) active *nous* is an internal state of continuous intellectual activity, but not the state of any bodily organ, then dualism becomes an issue.

Apart from positing its existence, Aristotle appears to have very little to say about active *nous*. However, since the text of *De Anima* III, 5 may be corrupt, appearances might be deceptive.[41] Yet I am inclined to believe that Aristotle in fact shied away from a detailed treatment of active *nous*; forced by his general theory of cognition to posit a state of continuous intellectual activity, Aristotle may have realized that this postulate could easily be exploited by dualists—an intuition the subsequent history of philosophy was to bear out.[42]

4. Mental Representation

Phantasia (as we have seen) is Aristotle's device for internal sensory representation. From sensible qualities to complex states of affairs, objects are represented by sensible characters, and thus animals are able to "reason" about situations, to pursue pleasure and avoid pain, to remember past events and anticipate future ones. Armed with a conception of internal (sensory) representation, Aristotle is able to explain the observable behavior of other animals and much of the cognitive life of human beings without appealing to any faculty other than the perceptual faculty. Certain features of human cognition, however, seem to exceed the scope of sensory representation, and they provide the impetus for positing a separate noetic faculty and with it a different mode of representation.[43] The representation of universals cannot be reduced to the mere apprehension of a sensory content. Only if a *phantasma* is taken as a token of the type that is the proper object of the noetic act can sensory representation play a role in the representation of universals. Hence Aristotle is concerned in *De Anima* III, 8 to distinguish between simple *noēmata* and *phantasmata*: "But what will distinguish the first thoughts (*noēmata*) from images (*phantasmata*)? Neither these nor even any other thoughts are images, but they do not occur without images" (*De An.* 432a12–14; cf. *De Mem.* 450a13).

As described, the *noēma* and the *phantasma* are conceptually simple, and the mind refers both of them to the same object. The only possible difference between them is the mode of representation employed. Just as the same rose smells sweet and looks red, the same water has certain sensible characteristics and a particular essence. Just as the distinction between the sense of smell and sight is maintained by the difference between odor and color, the distinction between the perceptual faculty and the noetic faculty is maintained by the difference between sensible characters and noetic representations.

Not only does the capacity to represent universals provide a basis for differentiating between sensory and noetic modes of representation, but Aristotle's description of the relation between *doxa* and *phantasia* also supports this distinction. Were sensory and noetic representation not distinct forms of representation, it would not be possible for a person to use one mode to represent the other. When our beliefs contradict illusory appearance, hallucinations, or dreams, we are simultaneously representing the same object in two incompatible ways.[44]

Just as there is considerable evidence that Aristotle envisages two different types of representation, there is, in addition, evidence that the mode of representation employed by the noetic faculty is properly described as symbolic. Even images are employed symbolically in thinking about abstract objects.[45] Aristotle remarks that in this case the *phantasma* is used in the same way that a geometer uses a drawing (*De Mem.* 450a1–9). The geometer ignores particularizing features such as size in order to treat the drawing as an arbitrarily selected instance of its class. Similarly, an image when used to facilitate reasoning about a type is treated as a representation of a token of the type under consideration, and the thinker ignores the features that are peculiar to it. The symbolic employment of a *phantasma* is already a distinct mode of representation. Moreover, there is some reason to believe that Aristotle envisages a kind of internal language as the vehicle for noetic representation. According to the *De Interpretatione*, "Spoken words are symbols of affections in the soul and written words are symbols of spoken words" (16a3–6). The attribution of a quasi-linguistic character to noetic representation would also explain the persistent association of noetic capacities with ratiocination.

The ability to draw inferences ranks with the ability to apprehend universals; it too is an essential mark of human rationality. Aristotle makes no attempt to derive the first ability from the second. He always construes reasoning as an activity of the noetic faculty and thus a uniquely human phenomenon; he does this even in contexts where it issues in a fallible judgment or a decision about a particular case.

And this is the reason why ⟨an animal⟩ is not thought to have belief (*doxa*), because it does not have belief based on inference (*ek sullogismou*). (*De An.* 434a10–11).[46]

While many of the other animals possess memory, none of the known animals so to speak possess recollection except man. The reason is that recollection is as it were a sort of inference (*sullogismos tis*). (*De Mem.* 453a7–11).[47]

These passages attest to the importance Aristotle attaches to the ability to reason discursively. Belief is one of the functions of the noetic faculty that can be false; nevertheless, to have a belief is to hold a position on the basis of evidence of one sort or another.[48] Only human beings are able to recognize and articulate the connection between a proposition and the evidential basis for that proposition. The crucial feature is not truth, but the cognitive process itself, which enables us to recognize the logical and conceptual relations obtaining among ideas. A system of representation that is more versatile than mere sensory representation is required for mental operations of this sort.

Other inferential processes, namely recollecting and deliberating about practical matters, ultimately issue in cognitions that typically are functions of the perceptual faculty. Recollection, a deliberate search for information acquired in the past, proceeds through associations to its object.[49] The process of recollection, when successful, terminates in the activity of remembering; unlike the former, the latter is a proper function of the perceptual faculty, for the object of memory is a past experience represented sensorially.[50] Similarly, deliberation about practical matters, which is an inferential process and a function of the noetic faculty, often terminates in a decision to perform a particular action. The decision might be expressed by a sensory representation of the anticipated outcome of the action or a representation of oneself acting in a particular way.

Even when the final result of deliberating or recollecting is expressed sensorially, the deliberative process, according to Aristotle, involves the manipulation of *phantasmata* and the deliberate construction of one *phantasma* out of many (*De An.* 434a7–10; cf. 431b6–8). The thinker must stand back from his or her immediate sensory representations and manipulate them in accordance with some general strategy aimed at bringing about the desired result. Other animals are trapped by the immediacy of perceptions, imaginings and desires; they are not able to deliberate about courses of action or to attempt to recollect a forgotten bit of information because they cannot distance themselves from their occurrent sensory representations. The difference between the human's grasp of the reasons for eating a certain food and the animal's *phantasmata* of pleasant sensations in connection with a particular food must ultimately rest on the difference between the way the object is represented by the noetic faculty and the way it is represented by the perceptual faculty.[51] In both cases, associations of various sorts play a role, and in both cases a sensory representation might be the sole vehicle for the final cognition expressing the agent's decision to act.[52] The cases differ in that the mere association of pleasure with the fruit is possible through sensory means, but something more is required in order to represent the rational basis for the belief that the fruit is desirable. To deliberate, to reason about *phantasmata*, to construct cognitive objects, to apprehend universals, to achieve insights; these are activities that exceed the cognitive powers of creatures possessing only the perceptual faculty because their execution requires the representation of complex states of affairs.

The relation Aristotle envisages between sensory representation and noetic representation coheres with the integrated model of perception and thought. The apprehension of a *phantasma* is an integral part of the cognitive activity of intellection. Noetic activity employs symbolic representation aimed at the manipulation of *phantasmata* and reflection about the objects presented in *phantasmata*. The perceptual faculty is the source of the *phantasmata*. Not only are both faculties involved (directly or indirectly) in the cognitive activity of thinking, but the very possibility of their joint activity depends upon the existence of two modes of representation. The *phantasma* is a sensory representation; the *noēton* is a simultaneous discursive representation of the object represented in the *phantasma*.

5. The Noetic Faculty and the Foundational Principles

In conclusion, let us consider the role of the foundational principles in shaping Aristotle's account of the noetic faculty. These principles, which (as we have discovered) are at the heart of Aristotle's theory of perception, are not limited to the perceptual faculty—with the obvious exception of the Sensory Representation Principle. Since Aristotle asserts them as general psychological principles, we would expect him to theorize about noetic activity accordingly, and this expectation is borne out by the text. Even when Aristotle is unwilling simply to apply a particular principle to the noetic faculty, the principle still influences his account. For example, the Psychophysical Principle as such does not apply to the noetic faculty. Aristotle's conception of noetic objects and the Actuality Principle lead him to conclude that there is no immediate physiological substratum for thinking. Nonetheless, Aristotle is unwilling to completely jettison psychophysicalism in the case of the noetic faculty; witness the fact that he opts for an attenuated connection between thinking and embodiment, which is mediated through *phantasia*. As a component of the perceptual faculty, *phantasia* has an identifiable physical substratum, the organs making up the perceptual system.[53] *Phantasia's* physiological component is thus a necessary condition for the exercise of the noetic faculty, even though the noetic activity as such is not an exercise of a bodily organ.[54]

The Actuality Principle does apply to the noetic faculty.[55] Each of its component faculties is distinguished from a function of the perceptual faculty by the capacity for the symbolic use of *phantasmata* and the apprehension of universals. Each noetic capacity is differentiated from the others by intrinsic or relational features of its object: some representations must be true, some must be of universals, and so forth (cf. *Pst. Anal.* 89a33–38). The object of *doxa* may fail to represent correctly the extramental state of affairs to which it refers; the object of *epistēmē* cannot. The object of *phronēsis* may be a particular; the object of *epistēmē* must be a universal. Moreover, the Actuality Principle provides Aristotle's ultimate justification for rejecting a single faculty for cognition in favor of two cognitive faculties. The noetic faculty is a distinct faculty because its object cannot be adequately represented by sensible characters alone. Sensible forms serve as the substrata for intelligible forms, but the latter cannot be reduced to the former.

The influence of the Sensory Representation Principle is also evident. It forces a distinction between two modes of apprehending a sensory content: A sensory content may be the focal object of the cognitive act, in which case the activity is assigned to the perceptual faculty. Or a sensory content may be employed symbolically to represent a universal that is the focal object of the cognition; in this case the mental activity is a function of the noetic faculty.

Finally, the Analytic Principle leads to the integrated model of the perceptual and noetic faculties. A single model of cognitive activity applied to both perceptual and noetic capacities is much more elegant and comprehensive than several models would have been. Moreover, as a result of the Analytic Principle, the perceptual faculty is expanded to include as many cognitive activities as possible without violating either the Actuality Principle or the Sensory Representation Principle. This leaves relatively few cognitions to be assigned to the noetic faculty, and the ones that are derive their objects from the *phantasmata* serving as the matter for noetic objects.

Our examination of Aristotle's theory of the perceptual faculty in the preceding chapters has established the strengths of Aristotle's approach—its underlying unity, coherence and explanatory power. The five methodological principles that provide the theoretical foundation for the theory of perception also shape, in one way or another, the account of the noetic faculty. It should now be clear that Aristotle invokes a unified theory of cognition in the *De Anima* and the *Parva Naturalia* to explain the central cases of cognitive activity.

In the final two chapters of this volume, we shall investigate some of the consequences of the theory of cognition we have discovered in Aristotle's psychological writings. First we shall take up the issue of consciousness. The other issue we shall consider is the relation between Aristotle's epistemology and his psychology. We shall find that the integrated model of perceptual and noetic activity gives us a handle on the perennial problems surrounding Aristotle's treatment of these topics.

6

Consciousness

Some modern philosophers (for instance, Rorty 1979, 38–61; Matthews 1977, 25) have congratulated Aristotle for formulating a psychology that is free from the unfortunate Cartesian notion of consciousness (cf. Matson 1966). The "mental" life of a human being or of some other creature is simply a way of life; it is how a particular organism relates to its environment (cf. Grene 1963, 244). The human or the animal is not "aware" of external stimuli and internal states; it recognizes an obstacle in its path or an emptiness in its stomach. But a consensus seems to be emerging among specialists in ancient philosophy that Aristotle has a theory of consciousness and that the key concept for understanding his theory is the concept of the common sense.[1] Kahn (1966, 79–80) originally stated the argument. He concluded that direct self-consciousness of thinking as well as perception is the work of the sense faculty (i.e., of the common sense). Hardie (1976) distinguished between general consciousness and reflexive consciousness, the two components of the Cartesian concept of consciousness, and he found both notions in Aristotle's conception of human consciousness. Filling out the composite picture supplied by Kahn's and Hardie's analyses of Aristotle's notion of consciousness, I demonstrated that Aristotle's conception of the common sense was his device for accounting for the central features of human consciousness as we understand it. I set out four features of consciousness that modern authors have taken to be definitive of consciousness, namely, unity, reflexive awareness, intentionality and apperceptual relations, and I found that Aristotle invoked the common sense to explain all four (Modrak 1981a).

We are now in an excellent position to evaluate these earlier efforts (mine included) and expand upon them because we have examined Aristotle's theory of cognition from every angle. We have reviewed his handling of sense perception, of apperception, and of thought. To say that Aristotle has a theory of consciousness is to say that when the pieces are brought together he has such a theory.[2] He presents this theory in parts; the parts are the descriptions of the various functions of the perceptual faculty and of the relationship between the functions of the noetic faculty and the functions of the perceptual faculty. In deference to Aristotle's analytic mode of exposition, we have looked at each of these in turn. It is time to attempt a synthesis of the sort characteristic of modern treatments of consciousness.

Aristotle's notion of consciousness centers on the common sense. Before discussing consciousness, we should review chapter 3's findings concerning the nature of the common sense. Aristotle groups together under the label *koinē aisthēsis* (common sense) all the functions of the perceptual faculty as a whole. The perceptual faculty is made up of the five senses. Insofar as the senses are exercised in relation to their own proper objects, they are distinct subfaculties of the perceptual faculty; insofar as they are exercised jointly in the simultaneous apprehension of the same object, they are components of a single perceptual capacity, the common sense.[3] Any cognitive activity employing only sensory representation and involving any sort of synthesis is a function of the common sense. The perception of the common sensibles, apperceptual judgments, *phantasia*, the reflexive awareness of perceptual activity, waking consciousness and memory are all exercises of the common sense. The common sense's versatility and its capacity for synthesis are such that it can do the work of consciousness, and Aristotle appeals to the common sense to explain those features of experience that modern philosophers have dealt with under the rubric of consciousness.

I propose to look at Aristotle's conception of the common sense in relation to the four features of mental life that are central to the modern conception of consciousness. They are as mentioned earlier: (1) unity of experience, (2) reflexive awareness, (3) intentionality and (4) interrelatedness of cognitive states. In the first two sections of this chapter, I argue that Aristotle recognizes all of these features of experience and that his conception of the common sense is such that it can accommodate these features. Nonetheless, as we shall discover in the third section, it would be a mistake to assimilate Aristotle's position to the modern conception of consciousness. The concluding section analyzes the relation between the foundational principles of the theory of perception and Aristotle's ability to explain the phenomenon of consciousness.

1. The Common Sense and the Unity of Experience

One of the central features, if not the central feature, of consciousness is the unity of experience. Any adequate account of consciousness must address this issue. There are two ways of analyzing the unity of experience. The one that has been characteristic of post-Kantian philosophers is to stress the unity of the subject; the "I" of consciousness imposes a perspectival and temporal unity on its experiences. The other way is to look for unity in the content of the experience. The former, "subjective" notion of the unity of experience is scarcely found in Aristotle's writings. The "I" for Aristotle is, like a state of awareness, transparent. The Actuality Principle makes the unity of the cognitive state depend on the unity of its object. The "objective" notion of the unity of experience, on the other hand, can be found in Aristotle.

In a number of different contexts, Aristotle takes note of or appeals to the objective unity of experience. These contexts include the puzzles about apperception, the explanation of sleep, the analysis of perceptual mistakes, the description of desire and the account of thinking. However, to establish that Aristotle recognizes the unity of experience is not to show that he has a satisfactory account of it. If the experience consists in a number of different cognitive and affective states occurring simultaneously, then the objective unity of the experience would be a function either of the convergence of the psychological activities or the cohesiveness of their objects.[4] We would expect Aristotle to emphasize the second alternative since the Actuality Principle would allow him to derive the first alternative from the second. But in cases where this strategy would be problematic, the Psychophysical Principle can be invoked in support of the convergence thesis.

The question remains whether Aristotle has the theoretical resources to explain the unity of experience by appeal to the common sense, and this question has several facets. In the first place, Aristotle's conception of the common sense seems to accommodate the unity of perceptual experience more easily than the unity of consciousness, when the subject's experience also includes affective states and noetic states. In the second place, we need to determine whether the common sense is completely passive or whether it includes the capacity to shape experience albeit to a limited extent.

Aristotle's sequential approach to the functions of the perceptual faculty tends to preclude the discussion of such issues as those of a unified consciousness or of the reflexive awareness of self. When we read the *De Anima* and the *Parva Naturalia* with the topic of consciousness in mind, however, we find that, far from being insensitive to such issues, Aristotle is concerned to address them. One place where this concern is manifested is in Aristotle's fascination with certain types of apperceptual judgments.

When Aristotle ponders the status of apperceptual judgments that involve the simultaneous awareness of the special objects of different senses, he is grappling with the problem of the unity of experience considered from the point of view of the perceptual object.[5] Ordinarily, the perceptual experience of a human being or of any other animal possessing five senses involves the simultaneous apprehension, integration and differentiation of many sensible qualities. (For instance, the sound of a Mozart string quartet against the background sounds of the neighbor's lawn mower and children, the dark-blue ink, the light-blue carpet, the smooth pen, the hard desk are only a part of the perceptual whole that confronts me as I write this.) In several different treatises, Aristotle attempts to explain this phenomenon.

In the *De Sensu*, Aristotle considers and rejects one way of waving the problem aside: "For perhaps some might say even now concerning this [the simultaneous perception of different sensible qualities] that one seems to see and hear at the same time, because the time between is not noticed" (448a23–24). Aristotle argues that no interval of time is perceptible, that we are continuously aware of ourselves and our perceptions. The "apparently" simultaneous apprehension of a complex of sensible qualities through several sense modalities is actually simultaneous. Just as objects in the world are white and sweet, and loud and hard at the same time, we perceive all of these features at the same time (cf. *De An.* 425a30–b3, *De Sens.* 449a13–16). Moreover, apperceptual discriminations often accompany the apprehension of different sensible qualities. We recognize that white is a different sensible quality from sweet at the same time that we perceive the white and sweet dessert.

Explaining the unity of perceptual experience is not an easy job since the basic theory of sense perception found in *De Anima* II, 6–12 and *De Sensu* 1–5 treats each sense as if the sense functioned in a vacuum.[6] Because Aristotle recognizes the tension between the initial, simplified account of perceiving and the complexities of actual perceptions, he turns immediately to problems concerning apperception and the joint activity of the senses in *De Anima* III, 1–2 and *De Sensu* 6–7. (The same issues are raised again, albeit summarily, in *De Anima* III, 7 and in the *De Somno*.)

In the *De Anima*, Aristotle decides that apperceptual discriminations of unity and difference require several senses to act as one. In the *De Sensu*, he assigns these judgments to the *aisthētikon pantōn*, literally, the sense faculty for all objects, namely the common sense (449a14–20). In both places, Aristotle appears to reason as follows: the judgment that white and sweet are different must be made by one faculty because the act of judging brings together different sensible qualities in a single cognition. The faculty making the judgment is one as is the judgment itself (*De An.* 426b17–21, 427a14). The special senses converge in the activity of the common sense, and their objects become components of its object.

This picture of unified perceptual activity through the common sense is also found in the *De Somno* and the *De Insomniis*. In these treatises, the physiological convergence of the special organs in a central organ is made the basis for explaining the objective unity of perceptual experience. Sensory impulses that fail to reach the central organ or, for some other reason, fail to be realized in an exercise of the common sense are not perceived at all (cf. Neuhaeuser 1878, 60–70): "and in each case when a sensation either internal or external, arises, a movement occurs in the primary sense organ [*prōtōi aisthētēriōi*]" (*De Som.* 456a21–22).

Sleep is the partial paralysis of the central sense organ, "but just as we have now said, [sleep is] an incapacitation with respect to use of the primary sense organ, the organ by which one perceives all things. For when this is incapacitated necessarily one is unable to perceive with any of the organs" (*De Som.* 455b8–13). All the senses are inhibited when we sleep; when we are awake (under normal circumstances) all are active, and sensible qualities of all types are simultaneously apprehended in a continuous flow.

A similar account of the role of the common sense and the central organ is found in the *De Insomniis*, where Aristotle gives a physiological explanation of dreaming (cf. Lulofs 1947, xxvii–xlii). During waking hours, the sensory impulses that arrive at and affect the central organ become the physical substrata for actual perceivings; others are less successful and remain in the peripheral organs, the blood, or even the common organ (*De Div.* 463a8–10; cf. chap. 4, sec. 2). During sleep, these residual sensory impulses act on the central organ, causing dreams. Central to this account is a particular conception of sentience as the continuous actualization of a stream of sensible characters that takes place at a central location in the perceptual system. Under normal conditions, the senses converge to form a single system and the sensible characters that are apprehended at the same time constitute a single, coherent experience (cf. *De Ins.* 460b16–22). Of the potential sense objects, which ones are perceived at a given time is partly a function of the whole field of incoming sensory impulses and not simply a function of the stimulation of the peripheral organs.

Typically, the presentation of an external object through one sense coheres with its presentation through another, and the common sense is simply the vehicle for the apprehension of the object through several different senses. But in some cases the presentation of an object through one sense modality is inconsistent with its presentation through another, and the common sense becomes the vehicle for the integration of the characteristics apprehended through the individual senses and hence the vehicle for the suppression of inconsistent reports (*De Ins.* 460b16–22). Yesterday the cracks on the wall did not frighten Coriscus; today when he is quite feverish they do; today the cracks create the impression of a raging boar. This perception is at odds with other features of Coriscus' perceptual experience, which indicate that he is within the walls of his house and protected from wild animals. The perceptual whole confronting Coriscus is fundamentally incoherent.

According to Aristotle, "The reason why these things occur is that the controlling faculty [*to kurion*] does not judge through the same power as that through which the appearances [*phantasmata*] arise" (460b16–18). The context determines the referent of *to kurion* (cf. 461b3–5). In the example Aristotle gives to elucidate its usage, reason overrides vision, correcting the impression of the sun's size, and vision overrides touch, correcting the impression of the number of objects between two crossed fingers (460b18–22). In the case of delirium, the controlling faculty would be the common sense since the objects judged are sensible objects and it is a question of deciding the coherence of sensory experience.[7] Similarly, the dreamer is deceived and takes the residual image of Coriscus for the man himself because the authoritative sense, namely the common sense, is not functioning properly due to sleep (461b5–461b31). In the course of explaining these phenomena, Aristotle assigns the common sense a limited role in shaping experience insofar as it is able to correct misleading impressions.

Further evidence of the cohesiveness of experience is provided by Aristotle's description (in the *De Sensu*) of cognitive interference: "hence when things are put before our eyes, we do not perceive them if we are deep in thought or are fearful or are hearing a loud sound" (447a15–17). The very possibility of competition among cognitive and affective states presupposes a notion of the unity of experience. Significantly, Aristotle treats thinking on a par with perceiving. One perception can interfere with another, and so too can a thought interfere with a perception and conversely. Aristotle might have subscribed to a segregationist view of experience where mental activities are compartmentalized and thoughts and perceptions occur completely independently. Experience would consist in the simultaneous actualization of discrete and unconnected mental objects. While this is clearly not the case, it is less clear whether Aristotle means to derive the unity of experience from the hypothesis that simultaneous psychological acts simply converge or from the hypothesis that the momentary object of experience is a coherent whole. Aristotle's approach to cognitive states, however, is such that he would have been hard-pressed to explain their convergence qua forms of awareness if he did not make their objects constituents of an integrated object.[8] Aristotle, who argues from the unity of a judgment about different sense objects to the unity of the subject making the judgment (*De An.* 426b8-23), could not merely assume (as we might) that the fact of cognitive interference is to be explained by appealing directly to a unified cognitive activity. Actual and potential thoughts and actual and potential perceptions can interfere with one another because the ones that are realized simultaneously make up a unified object, that is, different (potential) cognitive objects compete for a place in the composite cognition, which is the object of consciousness.

However, Aristotle prefaces the description of cognitive interference with the words "if indeed the stronger impulse [*kinēsis*] always repulses the weaker" (447a15). This seems to suggest that the ultimate composition of the object of awareness is merely a matter of mechanics; the strongest impulses prevail and are realized in actual perceptions and thoughts. But when we remember that thinking supervenes on certain perceptual activities and is not itself manifest in a movement of a bodily organ, we realize that the referent of *kinēsis* is a psychological activity. The strength of a psychological movement is in part a function of the subject's antecedent psychological states, including his or her desires and interests. If one is totally focused on a thought, she cannot attend to the perceptual features of her environment without destroying the coherence of the thought. Up to a point, our choices determine which potential perceptual and intelligible objects will be at the center of the object of experience; the central objects determine which of the other possible sensory and intelligible features are taken account of.

Not only are perceptions and thoughts included in the momentary object of experience, but memories and *phantasiai* are also included. Since both memory and *phantasia* are functions of the common sense, their involvement in a complex cognition is ipso facto the involvement of the common sense (*De Mem.* 450a12, 450a14, 451a17).[9] Past associations as well as memory proper (*mnēmē*) have an important role to play in cognition. Associations of all sorts, ranging from previously acquired concepts to anticipated pleasures and pains, shape our perceptions of incidental sensibles. *Phantasmata* are often the vehicles for such associations, and thus *phantasia* and the common sense are involved in these perceptions. Memory proper, *mnēmē* in Aristotle's sense, requires the explicit awareness of the past origin of the present mental object. Both in the modern sense of stored information and in Aristotle's technical sense, memory is a source of unity and coherence; the cognitive pieces fit together as they do because complexes of proper and common objects are taken to represent concrete objects and states of affairs. The perceptual whole is an integrated presentation of immediately given sensible characters, *phantasiai*, explicit memories and implicit associations. The common sense is peculiarly equipped to effect this integration, for it includes all the senses and is the faculty for *phantasia* and memory. The unified and coherent object of experience has a counterpart in the unified activity of the common sense.

Aristotle's notion of the common sense enables him to explain the observation that the momentary object of perceptual experience consists in a large number of different sensible characters organized so as to constitute a single, coherent whole. Ordinarily, however, perceptions and other sensory representations are only a part of the cognitive whole apprehended by a sentient being. The awareness of emotions, desires and (in the case of human beings) thoughts is also a part of conscious experience. Aristotle recognizes the existence of drives, passions and reasonings as well as their importance; can his account of consciousness handle them?

Not only does Aristotle recognize the phenomenon of cognitive interference in the case of perceptual and noetic states, he also acknowledges that the percipient's emotions can cause him to make mistakes about the perceptual object: "we are easily deceived about our perceptions when we are in emotional states . . . for instance, the coward in his fear, the lover in his love, so that from a slight resemblance, the former seems to see the enemy, and the latter his beloved" (*De Ins.* 460b3–8). This passage testifies to the interrelatedness of affective and cognitive states. The incidental objects apprehended through perception and *phantasia* reflect the emotional state of the percipient, and thus we can hope that Aristotle's theory of perception is equipped to deal with this feature of experience.

The conception of desire found in the *De Anima* is broad enough to cover all affective states; emotions and passions are species of desire. Desire (*orexis*) takes three forms, namely, appetite (*epithumia*), passion (*thumos*) and rational desire (*boulēsis*). An emotion is a pleasure or a pain experienced with respect to a particular type of object under particular circumstances. Each type of emotion is defined in relation to its object and the circumstances of its occurrence.[10] Anger is pain occasioned by a conspicuous slight; pity is pain occasioned by the undeserved suffering of others (*Rhet.* 1378a31–b2, 1385b13–19). Unfortunately, Aristotle's treatment of affective states is much less extensive than his analysis of perceptual ones. For the most part, desires are discussed in connexion with the theory of action, and emotions are discussed in connexion with rhetorical persuasion (cf. Fortenbaugh 1970, 40–41). Aristotle's strategy for dealing with emotions and desires of all sorts is to reduce them to the experience of pleasure or pain in relation to a particular object or situation and to treat the awareness of pleasure and pain as a kind of perceptual activity (cf. *De An.* 431a12– 14).

Since, if his notion of the common sense is such that it can encompass affective states in addition to perceptual ones, Aristotle is well on his way to having a satisfactory account of consciousness, we should attempt to discover whether, despite the brief treatment accorded affective states, there is any evidence for attributing the awareness of them to the common sense. The *De Motu Animalium* lends some support to the thesis that emotional states are included among the objects of the common sense. While the explanation of how desire moves the animal is relatively mechanistic, Aristotle's explanation of how desire arises emphasizes the presentation of the object that provokes the desire. Desire is the outcome of apprehending an object as immediately pleasant or painful; the presentation of a particular object or situation as pleasant or painful is typically a function of *phantasia* (see chap. 4, sec. 3). On an etiological account, the perceptual presentation precedes the desire. But since the object as presented is a component of the desire (there is no desiring without an object), the desire is itself a particular way of apprehending an object as well as an impulse to pursue or avoid that object.[11] To treat desire as a species of perception involving the association of pleasant or painful sensations with particular objects or states of affairs would be consistent with the description of the appetitive faculty in the *De Anima*.

> For both avoidance and desire [*orexis*] as actual are the same and the faculty for desire [*orektikon*] and the faculty for flight [*pheuktikon*] are not different, either from each other or from the perceptual faculty [*aisthētikon*]; but they are different in being [*einai*]. (431a12–14)

Immediately before this, Aristotle remarks:

> To perceive then is like simply asserting or thinking; when something is sweet or painful, sense pursues or avoids the object as if affirming or negating it. Being pleased and being pained is to be active with the perceptual mean [*aisthētikēi mesotēti*] with respect to the good and bad as such. (431a8–11).[12]

To feel pleasures and pains, to experience emotions and desires, is just another way of relating to objects in the world and thus is a form of perception.[13]

Whenever possible, Aristotle assigns the awareness of a psychological state to the same faculty as the state. Since the faculty of desire is a disposition of the perceptual faculty, Aristotle could include the awareness of affective states under the common sense without doing violence to other aspects of his theory. A single faculty employed in connection with the apprehension and representation of objects in the world and the internalized apprehensions and representations of such objects is the psychological ground for the complex cognitions consisting in perceptions and affective states that are characteristic of (human) consciousness.[14]

However, we have up to now largely ignored one aspect of human consciousness—the consciousness of thoughts. How, one might ask, can the common sense play a role in this form of consciousness? Yet, if the common sense is not involved in the consciousness of thinking and if Aristotle does not have any other device for explaining the awareness of noetic activity, then noetic activity will fall outside the purview of his account of consciousness. In the case of an adult human being, the momentary object of experience would usually (perhaps always) include thoughts; hence Aristotle's methodology should compel him to posit a faculty that is able to apprehend, in addition to perceptual and affective states, the thoughts that are also components of the total object of experience. Moreover, the existence of such a faculty is presupposed by Aristotle's description of cognitive interference (*De Sens.* 447a13–18). Unfortunately, Aristotle does not tell us which psychic faculty (the perceptual? the noetic?) apprehends the unified object of experience in such cases.

The perceptual faculty and the noetic faculty would seem to be the only two candidates. These faculties might act individually or jointly. If individually, the perceptual faculty seems the more likely choice, for the noetic faculty is very limited in its capacity to apprehend sensory contents. Assigning the awareness of thoughts embedded in a larger cognitive whole to the perceptual faculty would not be without precedent in the Aristotelian corpus. Aristotle (as we discovered in chap. 4) takes this approach to memory; thoughts are remembered *kata sumbebēkos* through the perceptual faculty. On the other hand, Aristotle might make the simultaneous awareness of thoughts and perceptions a function of the joint activity of the perceptual and noetic faculties.

We can invoke the integrated model of thought and perception (found in the *De Anima* and discussed in chap. 5) in support of the hypothesis that the awareness of a thought—at least insofar as the thought is embedded in a larger cognitive whole—can be a function of the perceptual faculty acting either individually or jointly with the noetic faculty. Aristotle's query whether the faculty for thinking is merely the perceptual faculty otherwise disposed is answered by the relationship envisaged between the object the thought is about and the *phantasma* employed in thinking about that object. The *phantasma* is a sensible particular, for instance, a representation of a pond; the same object is represented abstractly through the noetic faculty, which treats the pond as an arbitrary instance of the essence of water. The total cognition is such that the universal, what it is to be water, and the sensible particular are simultaneously present to consciousness. Although the sensory representation of a body of water is possible without the abstract representation of its essence, the converse is not possible on Aristotle's psychology.[15] For every act of thinking there is a simultaneous act of the perceptual faculty and a single state of awareness of a single object represented sensorially and abstractly. Although the integrated model does not entail that the apprehension of the total object of experience comprehending both perceptions and thoughts occurs through the joint activity of the two faculties, it does lend credence to this interpretation. Moreover, Aristotle likes to assign reflexive awareness to the faculty that originally apprehended the object. This preference, combined with the integrated model of perceptual and noetic activity, would incline him to assign the apprehension of the momentary object of experience to the joint activity of the two faculties when it includes thoughts.

The case is not yet settled in favor of the joint activity hypothesis, however, because other features of Aristotle's account of cognition suggest that the awareness of the momentary object of experience, even when thoughts are included, would always be a function of the common sense acting alone.[16] Aristotle's silence on this point in *De Sensu* 7 may simply have been an oversight; after all, the discussion that begins with the case of thought interfering with perception concludes with the assertion that the simultaneous awareness of sensible qualities is possible through the common sense. Aristotle often invokes a distinction between the simple awareness of a cognitive object and the awareness of the larger cognitive whole that includes the object. The simple awareness of color, for instance, is a function of sight, but the awareness of color embedded in the judgment that white and sweet are different sensible qualities is a function of the common sense. The simple apprehension of a *phantasma* is a function of *phantasia;* the apprehension of a *phantasma* embedded in the abstract representation of the object is a function of the noetic faculty acting in conjunction with the perceptual faculty. Were he to make a similar distinction between the first- and second-order awareness of thoughts, Aristotle could hold, without being inconsistent, that the apprehension of an intelligible object in and of itself is a function of the noetic faculty, whereas the apprehension of the complex cognition consisting of the thought and any perceptions occurring at the same time is through the common sense.

Since sensory representation is the vehicle for the common sense, the common sense would apprehend thoughts *kata sumbebēkos*. This is the device Aristotle uses to include thoughts among the objects of memory. A thought is remembered *kata sumbebēkos* because the vehicle for the memory is a *phantasma*. When the momentary object of experience includes thoughts as well as perceptions, the thoughts might be apprehended *kata sumbebēkos* by the common sense, even though the *kath' hauto* apprehension of an intelligible object is an exercise of the noetic faculty.

To decide between these two interpretations is not easy. It is clear that when the total cognitive state of a human being includes thoughts and perceptions, the common sense would be actively involved in the apprehension of the composite mental object. Whether in this instance the common sense is exercised alone or in conjunction with the noetic faculty cannot be decided on the basis of the textual evidence. Were we to decide the question on conceptual grounds, we would probably decide in favor of the joint activity model. To explain human consciousness by appeal to the perceptive faculty alone seems to exclude too much of human cognitive life. To explain the phenomenon of human consciousness by appeal to the joint activity of the perceptual and noetic faculties is more satisfactory. In the absence of decisive textual evidence, this provides a prima facie reason for attributing the "joint activity" conception of human consciousness to Aristotle.

This much is certain. Aristotle's conception of noetic activity poses an obstacle to our simply equating the activity of the common sense with consciousness in the modern sense. The first-order awareness of intelligible objects is always a function of the noetic faculty, and the second-order awareness of them is either a function of the noetic faculty acting with the common sense or is a function of the common sense but *kata sumbebēkos*.

Nevertheless, Aristotle's concept of the common sense is such that he can appeal to it to explain the unity of experience. Aristotle has some difficulty accounting for the consciousness of thinking, but as we have found, there are two options open to him; thus even in this case he is not without resources.

2. Reflexive Consciousness

Reflexive awareness is another paradigmatic characteristic of the modern conception of consciousness.[17] Just as in the case of unity, we can distinguish within our notion of reflexive self-consciousness two sorts of reflexive awareness. There is the reflexive awareness of particular psychological states as they occur, for example, a percipient's awareness that he is now seeing red or a thinker's awareness that she is now pondering a philosophical problem. There is also the reflexive awareness of the self. The latter notion is more central to our conception of consciousness than the former. As we might expect of a proponent of the Actuality Principle, Aristotle concentrates on the former.

Aristotle discusses the reflexive awareness of perception in a number of places. In *De Anima* III, 2, he decides that each sense is aware of its own activity and argues for this conclusion on the grounds that the reflexive awareness of sensing is the awareness of a sense object. Were we not reflexively aware of seeing through sight, there would be two senses that apprehend color. However, in the *De Somno* Aristotle appears to reject the conclusion reached in the *De Anima*. There he claims that reflexive awareness is a power held in common (*koinē dunamis*) by all the senses (455a16–21). These conclusions are not as incompatible as they initially seem to be. In the *De Anima*, Aristotle considers each sense separately and in effect concludes that were sight exercised alone or hearing or any of the other senses, each sense would be reflexively aware of its own activity. In the *De Somno*, Aristotle is concerned with the total object of perceptual experience because sleep is the temporary cessation of ordinary perceptual experience, not the inhibition of one or another aspect of it. On the basis of observation and introspection, Aristotle posits the existence of an integrated object of perceptual experience that includes sensible qualities of all sorts. Thus, typically the reflexive awareness of sensing is the awareness of a very complex perceptual object, and this awareness cannot be a function of one or several of the special senses; the awareness of seeing is the awareness of seeing as an inseparable part of the cognitive activity, which includes other forms of sensing.[18] Were the object of experience a collection of sensory fragments instead of an integrated whole made up of different sensible qualities, reflexive awareness would be a function of the individual senses. As it is, the reflexive awareness of sensing through all five senses simultaneously is a function of the common sense.[19] The *De Anima*'s discussion of what was in effect a hypothetical case established that the reflexive awareness of sensing belongs to a perceptual faculty; taking up an actual case of perception and its complex object, the *De Somno* assigns reflexive awareness to the perceptual faculty as a whole.[20]

But, one might ask, what about the reflexive awareness of thinking? In a passage in the *Nicomachean Ethics*, Aristotle explicitly mentions this type of reflexive awareness and apparently makes it a function of the perceptual faculty.

> And the person who sees perceives [*aisthanetai*] that he sees and the one who hears, that he hears and the one who walks, that he walks, and concerning the other activities there is a similar perception that we are active, so that if we perceive, we perceive that we perceive, and if we think, that we think, and perceiving that we perceive or think, we perceive that we exist. (1170a28–33).[21]

The reflexive awareness of thinking, if it is a form of perception, must be a function of the common sense, for it could not be a function of any of the special senses. Were Aristotle to assign the reflexive awareness of thinking to the common sense, he would make the common sense *the* faculty for reflexive awareness, and we could credit him with a unified account of reflexive awareness. However, in *De Anima* III, 4, Aristotle makes certain claims about *nous* that seem inconsistent with attributing the reflexive awareness of *nous* to any faculty other than *nous* itself.[22] According to Aristotle, *nous* is potentially the intelligible object, and *nous* itself is intelligible (429b22–430a3). This statement might mean no more than that the second actuality state of the noetic faculty is the actualization of an intelligible object. If so, the reflexive awareness of thinking is not at issue in *De Anima* III, 4; what is at issue is the first-order apprehension of the intelligible object, which is a function of the noetic faculty (Modrak 1981a, 165–66; cf. sec. 1). On the basis of this interpretation, no conclusions can be drawn about the reflexive awareness of thinking. A different but equally tenable interpretation holds that insofar as the mental activity of *nous* can be isolated from perceptual activities, the reflexive awareness of it belongs to the noetic faculty.[23] If we adopt the first position and we believe that the momentary object of experience is always apprehended through the common sense, we will have every reason to conclude that the reflexive awareness of thoughts is through the common sense (cf. Kahn 1966, 78–80). If we adopt the second position and/or decide that the apprehension of the unified object of experience is through the joint activity of the noetic and perceptual faculties, then we should assign the reflexive awareness of thinking to the joint activity of the two faculties. We cannot decide the question on the basis of textual evidence alone any more than we could resolve the analogous problem conerning the unity of experience.

The modern notion of consciousness includes the reflexive awareness of the self as well as the reflexive awareness of momentary states of consciousness. Aristotle mentions the reflexive awareness of the existence of the self in several passages, including the passage just quoted from the *Nicomachean Ethics* and in the following *De Sensu* passage: "For when someone perceives himself or something else in continuous time, it is not then possible for it to escape his attention that he exists" (448a27–28). Aristotle makes the awareness of one's own existence depend upon the awareness of one's perceptions and thoughts. Similarly, in the *Physics* the perception of time is made to depend upon our other perceptions and the recognition of changing states within ourselves (218b21–33). The reflexive awareness of the self is a product of the reflexive awareness of transitory psychological states. Although this form of reflexive awareness might be a joint function of the noetic and perceptual faculties, it is more likely that it belongs to the common sense alone. The *De Sensu* passage does not even mention thinking, and according to *Nicomachean Ethics* IX, 9, we perceive that we exist. Moreover, at least a weak form of reflexive awareness of the self is involved in memory, and memory is a function of the common sense.[24]

Nagel (1974) argued that "the fact that an organism has conscious experience at all means, basically, that there is something it is like to be that organism" (p. 436). What it is like to be an organism of one type might be radically different from what it is like to be an organism of another type. Aristotle's notion of reflexive awareness can accommodate Nagel's criterion of consciousness. The original cognitive object determines the character of the reflexive awareness of the cognition. Since an animal (Nagel's example is a bat) that had unique experiences would, from our point of view, apprehend unique objects, the reflexive awareness the animal had of its psychological activities would be unique. However, Aristotle hypothesizes that the types of sensible objects are the same for all animals; unless maimed, we all apprehend colors, sounds, odors, flavors, and tactile qualities. Aristotle does allow different species to possess different degrees of sensitivity. Many animals recognize more odors than we do, for instance, and in this respect their conscious experience would differ from ours (cf. *De An.* 421a13–22; *De Sens.* 441a1–2). The physical realization of a perceptual capacity need not be the same for all species; for example, a fish's capacity for smelling is not realized in the same physical structure as a land animal's capacity for smelling (see chap. 2, secs. 3, 4; chap. 3, sec. 1). But this difference in Aristotle's theory does not entail a difference in the object; even though the mechanism is different, fish apprehend odor and so do land animals. Although Aristotle does not envisage radical differences among animals with respect to their perceptual experiences, to the extent that such differences exist they would be reflected in the organism's reflexive awareness of its psychological states. In short, there would be "something that it is like to be a bat."

Of the four features of mental life that we took to be definitive of the modern notion of consciousness, two, namely, the unity of experience and reflexive awareness, have been discussed, and two, namely, intentionality and the interrelatedness of cognitive states, remain to be discussed. The latter pair are often mentioned by modern philosophers in connection with consciousness.[25] Little argument is needed to show that both characterize the activities of the perceptual faculty as a whole.[26]

The intentionality of a mental act consists in its being directed upon or being about an object that, except in the case of self-referential mental acts, is located outside the act. In chapter 2 we compared this conception of intentionality to the Actuality Principle. The Actuality Principle makes the object necessary to the exercise of a cognitive faculty and the most significant factor in determining the character of the cognitive act. Nonetheless, why the mental act is about its object does not seem to be fully explained by the Actuality Principle. However, the relation Aristotle envisages between the first and second actualities of a cognitive object and the cognition fills in this gap. The wine has a certain structure such that it will taste bitter to a healthy percipient. The bitter flavor (the gustatory object) realized in the act of tasting is referred to the wine because it is the actuality of a structure already present in the wine. In the same way, the essence of water that is the object of an act of thinking is the actualization of a noetic form potentially present in a *phantasma* of water; hence the essence is referred to the water. Since the Actuality Principle interpreted in terms of first and second actualities of cognitive objects and capacities applies to all forms of cognition, intentionality is always a feature of conscious experience. Yet there are differences as well as similarities between Aristotle's position and the modern notion of intentionality. In recent treatments, the problem of intentionality is often construed as the problem of how mental properties can be relational properties obtaining between people and propositions. A common solution is to suggest that this relation is mediated through mental representation (cf. Field 1978 and Fodor 1978). Although Aristotle's conception of sensory and noetic representation is such that he too could adopt this solution, he does not define the problem in these terms. In addition, modern philosophers have emphasized the peculiar ontological status of the intentional object. The intentional object is projected into the extramental world by the mind, but it need not exist in the extramental world. (My fear of my own death is, on the one hand, the fear of my actual death, not of my fantasized death; on the other hand, my fear is directed on an object that does not actually exist.)[27] Aristotle recognizes that it is possible for people to have beliefs about future states of affairs and to have false beliefs about past, present and future states of affairs, and to this extent he acknowledges the peculiar character of intentional objects. But this aspect of intentionality receives little comment from him. Aristotle's failure to address the topic of intentional inexistence, however, does not pose a serious obstacle to our attributing a conception of consciousness to him since it is the reference to the intentional object and not the ontological status of the latter that is central to the modern conception of consciousness.

The apperceptual recognition of how various components of one's experience fit together, for example, the recognition that a particular perception confirms or disconfirms a certain belief or the recognition that one and the same physical object tastes sweet and feels sticky, is also a fundamental characteristic of consciousness as we understand it. Aristotle recognizes this feature of experience, and he appeals to the common sense to explain it. The reflexive awareness of the perception of a white, sweet dessert is ipso facto the reflexive awareness of experiencing a single object through sight and taste (cf. *De An.* 425b1–2). The appearance of a monster if accompanied by the reflexive awareness of illness will not produce the belief that there is a monster present because the authoritative or common sense blocks the inference to the creature's existence (*De Ins.* 460b11–16; cf. *De An.* 427b21–24; *De Ins.* 461b1–8). Thus, Aristotle conceives the common sense in a way that includes the fourth paradigmatic feature of consciousness.

The objective was to decide whether and to what extent Aristotle's conception of consciousness resembles the modern conception of consciousness. As a first step, we picked out four paradigmatic features of consciousness in our sense, namely, the unity of experience, self-reflexiveness, intentionality and the interrelatedness of cognitive states. We have found that Aristotle takes all of these features of psychological experience into account in one way or another.

3. Is Aristotle's Conception of Consciousness Different from Ours?

Since Aristotle can explain the paradigmatic features of consciousness, as we conceive it, there is some temptation simply to identify his view with ours. But this would be hasty for there are significant differences between the two positions. Aristotle's conception of the object of experience seems comparable to ours; it can be (typically is for human beings) a very complex object that consists of perceived sensible characters and other sensory representations and thoughts. Aristotle's conception of the coordinated activities of the senses, *phantasia*, and memory seems comparable to our conception of the internal cohesiveness of mental acts occurring at the same time. If there is a disagreement between us, it does not lie in picturing the object of experience differently or in conceiving the psychological constituents of the experience differently. The quarrel concerns the direction of causality. We are inclined to believe that the unity of experience is a consequence of the unity of apperception, that is, the consequence of structures imposed by the mind on its objects. The Actuality Principle leads Aristotle to the opposite conclusion; the unified object of experience produces the unified mental activity.[28] We recognize one form of reflexive awareness that accompanies individual mental acts and a more global form of reflexive awareness that yields a concept of the self as the subject of psychological experiences. Aristotle also recognizes both forms. But for Aristotle, the very possibility of reflexive awareness depends upon the apprehension of a cognitive object of one sort or another. "It seems that knowledge is always of something else and of itself only as a by-product and perception and opinion and thought are also of something else" (*Met.* 1074b35–36). The reflexive awareness of the self is derived from the simple reflexive awareness of specific psychic activities, so it too ultimately rests upon the actualization of the cognitive object (*De Sens.* 448a27–28; *E.N.* 1170a28–33; cf. Oehler 1962, 250–61).

These differences between our position and Aristotle's concerning the causal primacy of the object of consciousness are closely related to a different conception of the psychological activity itself. According to Aristotle, the activity is simply the actualization of its object. A psychological event can be described from the perspective of the object and from the perspective of the psychological subject. The same event can be described as a being actually red on the part of the object or as a seeing red on the part of the subject. Neither description tempts one to analyze seeing as a relation between a *psuchē* and a colored object. Aristotle accepts a constituent analysis of consciousness; that is, consciousness, as he conceives it, consists in the psychic activity and its object.[29] This distinguishes his position from Plato's, from Descartes' and, to the extent that we are the heirs of Plato and Descartes from our conception of consciousness as well.

The importance of this difference has not been lost on modern philosophers. Rorty, for example, writes: "But in Aristotle's conception intellect is not a mirror inspected by an inner eye. It is both mirror and eye in one. The retinal image is *itself* the model for the 'intellect which becomes all things,' whereas in the Cartesian model, the intellect inspects entities modeled on retinal images." (1979, 45) The Aristotelian conception leaves no room for a homunculus who receives the reports of the various faculties and is the ultimate source of consciousness.

If like Rorty we believe that the "I" of modern epistemology and philosophy of mind is a philosopher's myth, we will be pleased that Aristotle propounded a psychological theory that makes self-contained psychological activities the basis of consciousness. If we are discomforted by the notion that the "I" of consciousness is a by-product (*to parergon*) of seeing colors, smelling odors, remembering past impressions, thinking about philosophy, we will agree with Plato that an internal subject is needed (cf. Burnyeat 1976): "It would indeed be strange if the many senses were placed in us just as in wooden horses and did not come together in some one form, either the soul or whatever else one ought to call it, with which through these as through instruments we perceive all the objects of perception" (*Theaet.* 184d).

Philosophers, both ancient and modern, who emphasize the importance of the subject of experience are likely to make the seat of consciousness an immaterial soul or mind. This would be incompatible with the Psychophysical Principles; for Aristotle, the subject of consciousness is the living organism.

A final issue to consider when comparing Aristotle's conception of consciousness to the modern notion is the attribution of consciousness to animals. There is no question that Aristotle's notion of consciousness covers all the higher animals, that is, all the animals possessing the full contingent of the five senses, *phantasia,* and memory (*De An.* 434b11–27; see chap. 4, n. 51). There is also no question that many modern philosophers from Descartes to the present have denied that animals possess consciousness.[30] About this sharply drawn difference little more needs to be said, but there is another question that deserves our attention (cf. Hardie 1976, 401). It is whether Aristotle has a uniform conception of consciousness that applies to both animals and human beings or whether he distinguishes between human and animal consciousness. This has been a point of disagreement between Hardie and Kahn. The latter held that "our personal consciousness as men belongs essentially to our sentient animal nature" (1966, 80). The former suggested that Kahn should have said, "our sentient animal nature is an essential part of our 'personal consciousness as men' (1976, 408–9). Hardie emphasizes the differences between human and animal consciousness; Kahn minimizes them. Each approach has certain strengths.

Aristotle gives a uniform account of the functions of the perceptual faculty for all animal species, including human beings. Some of the simpler animals have fewer senses than the higher animals have; some of the simpler animals are without fully developed imaginations or memories. Nevertheless, the basic model of perceptual function is the same for all animals.[31] Consciousness is, by and large, a function of the perceptual faculty and hence is possessed by many animals besides human beings. On the other hand, the fact that only human animals are capable of noetic activity is the source of certain anomalies. If the consciousness of thought is through the common sense, as Kahn believes, the resulting state of awareness is different from any other animal's, for it embraces the awareness of thinking. If human consciousness involves the joint activity of the perceptual and noetic faculties, the internal structure of human consciousness will not be the same as the internal structure of animal consciousness.

Had Aristotle posited a faculty for consciousness he would have had to confront whether to include animal consciousness in human consciousness or to identify the two. Since the total object of human consciousness is different from the total object of animal consciousness, the Actuality Principle would incline Aristotle toward the former view. However, the Analytic Principle favors the expansion of the functions of a lower-level faculty over the postulation of a new and possibly unnecessary faculty; hence it might have tilted the scale in the opposite direction. If so, Aristotle might have sidestepped the Actuality Principle by making the consciousness of intelligible objects *kata sumbebēkos*. But Aristotle did not posit a faculty for consciousness; he posited a perceptual faculty and assigned the lion's share of the activities belonging to consciousness to the perceptual faculty; he also posited a noetic faculty for thinking and may have included the reflexive awareness of thinking among its functions. We cannot decide on the basis of the textual evidence how Aristotle would have dealt with the differences between human and animal consciousness had he been pressed to do so.

4. Consciousness and the Foundational Principles

In earlier chapters, we found that Aristotle structures the discussion of individual cognitive activities within a single explanatory scheme consisting of certain fundamental assumptions about the nature of the perceptual faculty. Let us now consider the relation between that explanatory scheme and Aristotle's conception of consciousness. Consciousness involves the coordinated activity of the senses, *phantasia*, memory and reflexive awareness, and, in the case of human beings, thought. The Psychophysical Principle makes psychological activity psychophysical activity; the interdependence of bodily systems (recognized by Aristotle) makes psychophysical activity the activity of the biological individual as a whole.[32] The subject of consciousness is the living creature: "it would perhaps be better to say not that the soul pities or learns or thinks, but that the man does these things with the soul" (*De An.* 408b13–15).

The Actuality Principle has profound consequences for Aristotle's ability to account for consciousness. According to this principle, the object of a cognition determines the character of the cognition. If the object is red, round, bitter and hard, then the cognitive act is the simultaneous apprehension of these characteristics. Several perceptual capacities would be involved in this case—sight, taste, touch and the common sense—but since the object is a unity, so too is the cognitive act. The unified exercise of several different senses requires no further explanation because it is a direct result of the Actuality Principle. The reflexive awareness of the perceptual act is included in the original cognition in the same way. The cognitive act is transparent; it is the simple apprehension of the cognitive object, which is identical to the mere presence of the cognitive object as part of the subject's experience (cf. chap. 3, sec. 2). The reflexive awareness of the cognitive act is the reflexive awareness of the object as an object present to oneself. The simple apprehension of the object is central to the reflexive awareness of the cognitive apprehension, and neither would be possible without the object of the experience. The following schema captures Aristotle's conception of the relation between the cognitive object and the cognitive act: Cognition A' is the apprehension of object A; the character of A' is determined by A. Cognition A'' is the reflexive awareness of A'; the character of A'' is determined by A', and hence the character of A'' is ultimately determined by A. A'' includes A' just as A' includes A. There is a single cognition, which includes the cognitive object, its apprehension and the reflexive awareness of its apprehension.

Aristotle's conception of the noetic object reinforces the notion of the unity of experience that follows from the Actuality Principle. The noetic object is an abstract representation of a *phantasma*. In terms of the schema used above, the object of thought, A, contains a (the *phantasma*) employed in the act of thought, A'. The presentation of a is through the perceptual faculty, so a further consequence of the Actuality Principle is the notion of a unified cognition that is primarily noetic but also includes a perceptual component.[33] Having postulated a cognitive object with these characteristics, Aristotle follows the dictates of the Actuality Principle and posits an integrated response on the part of the psychic faculties.

The Sensory Representation Principle is another reason why Aristotle can give an adequate explanation for the unity of perceptual consciousness. Memory, perceiving and imagining are all exercises of the perceptual faculty; thus the apprehension of a complex cognition involving elements from all of these mental states is unified not only by the subject matter of the whole but also by the similar character of the constituent states. Each state is a different aspect of the exercise of the same faculty.

In accordance with the Analytic Principle, the cognitive capacities of sentient beings as Aristotle envisages them are built up out of simpler capacities. Hence, in the case of consciousness, he does not introduce a separate faculty to explain the unity of experience or reflexive self-awareness. He simply extends the notion of the common sense to encompass these psychological features. Since the common sense is constituted by the convergence of the special senses, the five-sense model of the perceptual faculty is expanded to include still more aspects of sentience. Activities such as the discrimination of sensible difference, the recognition of the unity of perceptible objects and reflexive self-awareness are assimilated to the activities of the senses. Having exploited the notion of the common sense as far as possible, Aristotle has recourse to the integrated model of noetic and perceptual activity. This model, which is also motivated by the Analytic Principle, furnishes him with a device for explaining unified states of awareness on the part of a creature that thinks as well as perceives.

The consequences of the foundational principles of Aristotle's theory of perception are such that this theory can be invoked to explain consciousness in our sense, including the unity of experience and reflexive awareness.[34] In this sense, Aristotle has a perfectly adequate account of consciousness. Indeed he should be described as having a concept of consciousness, although this is not to say that he posits a separate faculty for consciousness or even has a term for consciousness. Aristotle's notion of consciousness is embedded primarily in his conception of the perceptual faculty, and to a lesser extent, insofar as distinctly human consciousness is at issue, it is embedded in his conception of the integrated activity of the perceptual and noetic faculties.

III

PERCEPTION, THOUGHT AND KNOWLEDGE

7

The Epistemological Consequences

Aristotle's epistemology is empiricist in that he repeatedly emphasizes the importance of perception to knowledge and psychologistic in that the ultimate validity of our basic concepts depends upon the psychological mechanisms involved in their apprehension (*Pst. Anal.* II, 19; *Met.* I, 1).[1] It is an Aristotelian commonplace that if we perceived nothing, we would know nothing (*De An.* 432a3–10; *Pst.Anal.* 81a37–b6). What Aristotle means by this and related claims is somewhat obscure. He sometimes speaks as if psychological dependence were at issue. To exercise knowledge or even to acquire it, we must think; thinking requires *phantasmata*, and perception is the source of *phantasmata*.[2] Sometimes Aristotle speaks as if conceptual dependence were at issue; the content of our concepts is derived from our perceptions (*De An.* 432a3–6; cf. 431b2; *Pst. Anal.* 100a15–b5). Sometimes he speaks as if perception had a special role to play in the acquisition of the indemonstrable principles that provide the foundation for systematic knowledge (*Pst. Anal.* 88a6–8, 99b34–100b5; *E.N.* 1098b3).

Let us distinguish between several different epistemological stances that might be taken by a philosopher who claims that knowledge depends upon perception: (1) Perception is the source of some or all of our simple concepts, that is, the content of the concepts is derived from perceptions. (2) Not only is perception the ultimate source of our concepts, but certain fundamental propositions are also derived from our perceptions. One might hold, in addition, that we reach these propositions through a process of inductive generalization. (3) The process by which we derive basic concepts and propositions from perceptions is itself a manifestation of the same critical capacity that is exhibited in ordinary perception. These positions are conceptually distinct but a philosopher could endorse all three without inconsistency. I shall argue that this is precisely what Aristotle does. The account of thinking found in the psychological writings supports the first position, which is asserted in the *De Anima* as well as in the *Posterior Analytics* (*Pst. Anal.* 100a15–b5; also see chap. 5). The second position also finds expression in the *Posterior Analytics*, where a distinction is drawn between the indemonstrable first principles of a science and the derived principles. The former are apprehended through induction (*epagōgē*) from particular cases presented in perceptions (81a40–b9, 99b34–100b5). The perplexing yet critically important final chapter of the *Posterior Analytics* (II, 19) describes a cognitive process that develops out of the perceptual capacities and yields the basic concepts and universal principles necessary for knowledge.

Having discussed the general issues concerning the relation between perception and knowledge in the first section, in the second section we turn to II, 19, a chapter of perennial interest to commentators.[3] The difficult argument of this chapter will prove easier to reconstruct from the vantage point of Aristotle's theory of perception and the integrated model of perceptual and noetic activity. In the third section I argue that Aristotle's confident assertion that we have knowledge of the indemonstrable first principles of art and science derives from his confidence in the psychological processes through which the first principles are apprehended. The fourth section discusses how the foundational principles of Aristotle's theory of perception affect his epistemology.

1. Perception as the Source of Knowledge

"And for this reason if one perceived nothing, one would not learn or understand anything, and whenever one contemplates one must contemplate a *phantasma* at the same time. For *phantasmata* are just like sensuous contents [*aisthēmata*] except without matter" (432a7–10; cf. 432a13–14). This passage from *De Anima* III, 8 makes knowledge dependent upon perception, and it gives a psychological explanation for the dependence. The exercise and the acquisition of knowledge is dependent upon thinking. Thinking is not possible without *phantasia* because all thoughts employ *phantasmata*. An *aisthēma* is a sensory representation that the percipient refers to the external object, causing its apprehension (*De An.* 431a15, 432a9; *Met.* 1063b4; *De Som.* 456a26).[4] The *phantasma* is like an *aisthēma* without its matter because the *phantasma* is a sensory representation of an object that need not be concurrently present to the senses. *Phantasmata* are sensory representations that the mind cannot create ex nihilo, for *phantasmata* duplicate sensible features that were once perceived.[5] The psychological dependence of knowledge on perception is one of the many consequences of the integrated model of perceptual and noetic activity.

In addition, all knowledge is dependent upon perception for its objects: "the intelligibles [*noēta*] are in the perceptible forms, both those that are spoken of in abstraction and those that are dispositions and affections of perceptible objects" (*De An.* 432a4–6). All our concepts, without exception, are derived from perceptions. When Aristotle speaks of abstract objects, he usually has in mind mathematical objects—at least as the example par excellence (cf. 431b15–17). In *Metaphysics* XIII, Aristotle discusses the ontological status of the mathematical object. Mathematical objects are not separate substances as the Platonists believe, nor are they separable substances existing in concrete objects. A mathematical object is an abstract representation of a property of a sensible particular. Geometry treats concrete particulars qua lengths and planes, and it investigates the attributes that belong to objects qua planes and qua lengths (cf. *Met.* 1078a2–31; *Pst. Anal.* 81b1–4). A line is an abstract representation of the straight edge of some arbitrarily selected material object (which object is not important so long as the object is represented as having a perfectly straight edge). As we saw in chapter 5, Aristotle gives a similar account in *De Anima* III, 4 of the apprehension of the essence of a natural kind. In both cases, sensible particulars as presented in *phantasmata* are used as arbitrary examples of the property under investigation. The apprehension of a mathematical object or an essence is the apprehension of a concept that is derived from the sensible particulars that exhibit it. The mind is a blank tablet before it confronts the world through perception (cf. 430a1); the content of our basic concepts is derived from our perceptions.

Aristotle makes thinking about concepts dependent upon the thinker's capacity for sensory representation; he makes the content of our concepts dependent upon the content of our perceptions; and he makes perception the ultimate source of the indemonstrable principles of science. According to the *Posterior Analytics*, knowledge in a particular field will be amenable to axiomatization (Scholz 1930; Hintikka 1980; also see Ferejohn 1982; Gomez-Lobo 1976–77). That is, a complete science can be expressed in a series of syllogisms. The premises of some of the syllogisms will be conclusions of other syllogisms. But not all the propositions of a science can be derived (72b18–23; cf. Lear 1980, chap. 5). Some are primitive. Our knowledge of the derived premises depends upon our having a logically valid derivation of them. Aristotle sets a number of other constraints on the premises of a science, such as expressing necessary and universal relations, but here we need not concern ourselves with these conditions.[6] The feature that is relevant to our question is the requirement that a science ultimately rests upon primitive, indemonstrable principles and concepts.

It will come as no surprise that Aristotle, the exponent of the Actuality Principle, holds that the way we know first principles is unique to them. The cognitive activities that Aristotle mentions in connection with the apprehension of the first principles are *nous* or *noēsis*, perception and *epagōgē*.[7]

> Demonstration is from universals, and induction [*epagōgē*] is from particulars, and it is impossible to contemplate universals except through induction . . . and induction is impossible for one not having perception. For perception is of individuals; for it is not possible to have knowledge [*epistēmē*] of these, nor from universals without induction, nor through induction without perception. (*Pst. Anal.* I, 18, 81a40–b9)

> For from many individuals the universal is clear. And the universal is honored, because it reveals the cause. As a result concerning such things, insofar as the cause is something else, the knowledge of the universal is more honored than perceptions and insight [*noēsis*], but concerning the primitives there is a different account. (*Pst. Anal.* I, 31, 88a4–8)

The first passage (I, 18) makes perceptions the basis for the inductions that produce the universal propositions and concepts that are the proper objects of science.[8] The second passage (I, 31) contrasts the knowledge of universals with the apprehension of particulars presented in perception and classified through *noēsis* (cf. *Met.* 1036a2–8). A few lines later, Aristotle describes a case where we see light streaming through a perforated glass and recognize (*noēsai*) that the observed phenomenon instantiates a universal regularity.

Knowledge (*epistēmē*) consists of the apprehension and manipulation of universals; nevertheless, basic (indemonstrable) universals are not arrived at through *epistēmē*. Universals are derived from particulars; particulars are apprehended through perception; thus *epistēmē* is ultimately dependent upon perception. Perception, like *epistēmē*, is limited in scope; its objects are always individuals (*ta kath' hekasta*). A bridge between the *epistēmē* of universals and the perception of individuals is needed. In I, 18, the bridge is provided by induction (*epagōgē*) (*Pst. Anal.* 81a38–b9; cf. *Pst. Anal.* 72b29; *Top.* 105a12–16). Here it is implied, although not stated, that *epagōgē* transforms the particulars presented in perception into the universals required by knowledge. Only at the very end of the *Posterior Analytics* in II, 19, does Aristotle attempt to explain how *epagōgē* brings about this transformation.

Our two passages taken together raise a question about the relation between *noēsis* and *epagōgē*. *Epagōgē* is mentioned in I, 18 but not *noēsis*; however in I, 31, we find *noēsis* associated with perception in a way that suggests both faculties are somehow involved in the apprehension of the first principles. Aristotle often uses *noein*, *noēsis*, and *nous* as generic terms for noetic activity, but here they seem to have a narrower sense, the recognition of the universal through generalization from particular cases.⁹ In the *Posterior Analytics* and elsewhere, Aristotle uses *epagōgē* in the same sense that he uses *noēsis* in I, 31.¹⁰ Aristotle's final explanation of the relationship between *epagōgē* and *noēsis/nous* is also found in II, 19.¹¹

Perception, *noēsis* and *epagōgē* share the characteristic of being inferior to *epistēmē* and *apodeixis* (demonstration), except in the case of first principles. Since a generalization from particular cases to a universal principle provides less support for the universal principle than a deductive argument for the same principle, demonstration, when possible, is superior to *noēsis*. The primitive (indemonstrable) concepts and principles cannot be grasped through demonstration or *epistēmē*. They must be derived through induction and *noēsis*, and these processes take perceptions as their starting point.

In short, noetic activity of all sorts, including the exercise of knowledge, depends on perception; this psychological dependence has an epistemological counterpart. According to the *Posterior Analytics*, knowledge is dependent upon perception in that perception is the ultimate source of universal concepts and indemonstrable first principles.

2. The Genetic Account of the *Posterior Analytics* II, 19

The constraints Aristotle places on knowledge (*epistēmē*) in the *Posterior Analytics*, namely, that the objects of *epistēmē* must be universals and that *epistēmē* must rest on indemonstrable first principles, lead naturally to the question asked at the beginning of II, 19: "Concerning the first principles [*archai*], how do they become known and what disposition [*hexis*] knows them?" (99b17–19). Aristotle has already given us some clues to answering the first question—the knowledge of universals is derived from the perception of particulars, and the universals required by *epistēmē* are initially apprehended through *epagōgē* (see sec. 1). The first question is answered in detail by the "genetic account" (99b34–100b5) that explains the origin of the first principles in terms of a series of cognitive activities, each of which brings the knower closer to the universal generalizations of science, and in terms of a series of abstractions, which produce increasingly general universal concepts.

Aristotle struggles throughout the genetic account to give as perspicuous an account as possible of the cognitive process that leads from the sensible particulars grasped in perception to the abstractions of science. Attempting to clarify his position, he gives several reformulations of it (cf. 100a15). In the course of the discussion, the topic seems to shift from the first principles of science to basic concepts such as man and animal. From the vantage point of modern philosophy and logic, which distinguishes between terms and propositions, Aristotle seems to initiate a discussion of the acquisition of basic propositions but then to describe only the acquisition of primitive terms (cf. Ross 1949, 675). Are the *archai* of II, 19 propositions and first principles or are they primitive terms and basic concepts that are components of indemonstrable first premises? According to Solmsen (1929, 95–101) and more recently to Barnes, (1975, 248ff.) Aristotle vacillates. Yet other commentators have found the genetic account to be primarily about the acquisition of concepts (Ross 1949, 675).

I shall argue, on the contrary, that Aristotle does not distinguish between primitive concepts and indemonstrable propositions. The genetic account is throughout a description of the same cognitive process, namely, how we come to know basic concepts and first principles; it is, however, a twofold description. The first depicts the process from the "outside," from the perspective of the cognitive faculties involved; the second part describes it from the "inside," from the perspective of the cognitive object. As a preliminary step before undertaking the detailed analysis of the genetic account, we should quickly review some of the reasons why any interpretation that finds a distinction between term and proposition, between basic concept and first principle, in the *Posterior Analytics* II, 19, cannot be sustained.[12]

To facilitate the analysis of this passage, let us take a look at it:

> 99b34–100a3: And this appears to belong to all animals; for there is a connate critical capacity, which is called perception. In some animals having perception, a retention of the sensuous content comes about but in others it does not. In the animals in which a retention does not come about either generally or with respect to those cases where it does not come about, there is no knowledge outside of perception. Animals in which the perception persists can continue to retain the percept in the soul. And when many such things come about, some difference arises at once; as a result, some come to have an account out of the retention of such things, but others do not.

> 100a3–9: Then out of perception memory, as we say, comes to be and out of memory occurring frequently with respect to the same thing experience comes to be. For memories which are many by number make up one experience. And out of experience or out of the universal resting as a whole in the soul, the one beside the many, which is one and the same in all of these, comes to be the first principle of art and science—of art, if it concerns coming to be, of knowledge if it concerns being.

> 100a10–14: Neither are these present in us as definite dispositions nor do they come about from other dispositions which are more capable of knowing but from perception. Just as in a battle, when a rout occurs, if

one takes a stand, and another takes a stand, then another, until the original formation is achieved. And the soul is such as to be capable of being affected in this way.

100a14–b3: And what has been said just now [*palai*] but not said clearly, let us say again. For when one of the undifferentiated things takes a stand, the first universal is in the mind (for although one perceives the individual, the perception is of the universal, it is, for instance, of man but not of Callias, the man). Again in these a stand is taken, until the undivided, that is, the universal, stands, for instance, such and such animal stands until animal stands, and in this in the same way.

100b3–5: Indeed it is clear that we must recognize the primitives by induction; for even perception introduces the universal in this way.

The interpretation to be rejected holds that the first part of the genetic account (99b34–100a9) is about the acquisition of first principles and that the second part (100a10–b3) is about the acquisition of concepts.[13] A similar distinction may be read into the closing lines (100b3–5), where *epagōgē* (induction) is mentioned in connection with the apprehension of first principles and perception is mentioned in connection with universals.[14] The arguments against dividing the text in this way are several. First, Aristotle uses a plethora of terms to describe the object that is grasped at the final stage of the process: *katholou*, universal (100a6, 100a16, 100b2, 100b5); *archē*, first principle (100a8), one over many (100a7), one of the undifferentiated objects (100a16), undivided (100b2); *prōta*, primitives (100b4). To this list can be added the terms used in the introductory section, namely, *archai*, principles (99b17), and *prōtai archai*, first principles (99b21). Aristotle's choice of words suggests a single inclusive notion covering both concepts and propositions rather than a notion of primitive concept that excludes proposition or conversely. Moreover, the repeated use of *katholou* throughout the passage and the progression from *archai* to *prōtai archai* to *prōta* argue against the proposed division.

Second, a single metaphor dominates the whole discussion. The metaphor is that of the one that takes a stand, "the universal that has come to rest in the soul" (100a6–7). (This metaphor reappears in *Phys.* 247b11–12; cf. 247b17–18.) The metaphor found first at 100a6–8 occurs again at 100a12–13, at 100a15–16 and at 100b2. There is no tenable scheme of division of 99b34–100b5 that will encompass all of these texts.

Third, a proponent of the view that Aristotle speaks initially about first principles and then about basic concepts might argue that Aristotle's use of *palai* at 100a14 indicates a change in topic. *Palai* has a number of meanings, including "just now," "long ago," and "sometime before."[15] Waitz (1844–46) understands *palai* in the last sense and takes it to refer to the discussion in II, 13 of determining the highest universal. Adopting this reading, one might argue that we should divide the text at 100a14, thus making 100a14–b3 Aristotle's account of the abstraction of the universal. But this division seems to occur at the wrong place. The passage at 100a10–14 makes precisely the same point in much the same language as 100a14–b3. Rather than look for a distant and otherwise unspecified referent for *palai*, it would be better to read *palai* as "just now" and construe 100a14–b3 as a clarification and an expansion of 100a10–14.[16]

It is not surprising that Aristotle fails to distinguish between concepts and first premises in II, 19, for this distinction is alien to his epistemology where the paradigmatic first principle is a definition.[17] A definition is the articulation of a concept.[18] Were we to examine the concept "man" we would find that it was the concept of a rational, two-footed animal or something like that (cf. *Met.* 1037b11). Were we to define *man* we would say that man is a rational, two-footed animal. Although we might differentiate between the verbal expression of the concept in the statement of the definition and the comprehension of the concept, there would seem to be no grounds for distinguishing between the comprehension of the concept and the comprehension of the definition. These are two ways of describing the same cognitive act. Moreover, the definitions that serve as the first premises of a science are indemonstrable expressions of essences that *ex hypothesi* have existential import (pace Ferejohn 1982; see Bolton 1976 and Gomez-Lobo 1976–77). Although Aristotle distinguishes between nominal definitions and existence claims, he also believes that the existence of X is presupposed by the recognition of the essential nature of X (*Pst. Anal.* 93a27–28; cf. 76a32–34). Even were it to turn out that not all first principles were definitions, Aristotle might very well take the line that, in order to be recognized as true without a deductive derivation, a first principle must possess the internal cohesiveness that characterizes primitive concepts. Hence, he ignores the differences between concepts and principles in the genetic account.[19]

Although Aristotle is not concerned to differentiate between primitive concepts and first principles in II, 19, his approach to the topic does change at 100a10. In 99b34–100a9, Aristotle describes the apprehension of basic concepts and principles from the point of view of the psychological activities involved, namely, perception, experience, memory and knowledge. This process is described twice. In the first description (99b34–100a3) only three stages are mentioned; the second description (100a3–9), an expanded version of the first, includes all four stages. In 100a10–b3, Aristotle describes the same process from the point of view of the cognitive object. The cognitive object is initially a sensible particular apprehended through perception, preserved through memory, and classified through experience. This object is somehow transformed into a universal object of knowledge. The second part of the genetic account describes the transformation of the cognitive object and explains how it is possible for the apprehension of particulars to engender the knowledge of universals. This double-barreled attack on the problem of the acquisition of first principles is exactly what we would expect from the author of the Actuality Principle. For Aristotle, the most important feature of the process is the articulation of the universal through the transformation of the sensible particular. Like the first part, the second part of the genetic account (100a10–b3) also describes the same process twice in the hope of making the account clearer.

The genetic account is Aristotle's definitive treatment of the acquisition of first principles and basic concepts. Despite the promissory notes given in the earlier chapters of the *Posterior Analytics*, Aristotle's final explanation seems rather too quick. The topic is broached only once again in the entire extant corpus—in the opening chapters of *Metaphysics* I, and this account, which seems to be a slightly expanded version of the genetic account of the *Posterior Analytics* II, 19, adds little of importance.[20] In the end Aristotle seems satisfied with his position.

Aristotle may have been satisfied; his commentators seldom have been. Part of the difficulty is that the genetic account is not self-contained. Aristotle makes certain assumptions about human cognition that are neither explicitly stated nor explained in II, 19.[21] I propose to draw upon our findings in previous chapters to fill in the gaps in the genetic account.

The genetic account is framed by references to perception and to *epagōgē*. It is introduced in answer to a puzzle about the possibility of acquiring the knowledge of first principles, since the acquisition of knowledge seems to require preexisting knowledge (99b26–30; cf. 71a1–7).[22] Aristotle's solution invokes a distinction between actually having knowledge and having some cognitive capacity that enables us to acquire knowledge:[23] "therefore it is necessary that we have some capacity [for acquiring the knowledge of first principles] . . . and this seems to belong to all animals, for all have an innate critical capacity called perception" (99b32–35).

The final line of the genetic account refers to both perception and *epagōgē*: "Indeed it is clear that we must recognize [*gnōrizein*] the primitives [*ta prōta*] by induction [*epagōgē*]; for even perception introduces the universal in this way" (100b3–5).[24] Not only is Aristotle's theory of perception relevant to interpreting this text, but the integrated model of perceptual and noetic activity supports Aristotle's conception of *epagōgē*. *Epagōgē* has the peculiar property of being a kind of reasoning that initially apprehends sensible particulars and hence seems to be a perceptual power and that ultimately apprehends universals and hence seems to be a noetic power.

The very possibility of *epagōgē* depends upon the retention of the sensory content of a perception (*monē tou aisthēmatos*) that is mentioned at 99b36 and again at 100a3. In the psychological treatises, Aristotle uses *aisthēma* to refer to the sensory content of a perception as distinguished from the external object. The *phantasma* is said to take on the role of the *aisthēma* in thinking (431a14–15, 432a9). In the *De Insomniis*, Aristotle says that *aisthēmata* give rise to *phantasmata* (461a18–19). In the psychological treatises, when the sensory content is again an object of awareness, it is called a *phantasma*. Even though the term *phantasma* does not occur in the *Posterior Analytics* account, it is found in the analogous discussion in *Metaphysics* I, 1.

The retention of an *aisthēma* or a *phantasma* enables us to remember the content of a previous perception. In the *Posterior Analytics* II, 19, Aristotle seems to treat each such retention as a memory. More precisely, according to the *De Memoria* account, the retention of a sensory content makes memory possible; memory proper occurs only if the thinker recognizes the sensory representation as a token of a past experience. In the present context this requirement seems unduly restrictive. However, were Aristotle using *mnēmē* in the narrower sense here, it would strengthen the connection between the cognitive object and the extramental world. In any event, *mnēmē* is the vehicle for the sensory representations required for the subsequent stages of the process.

The next step finds many memories constituting one experience (100a5). Aristotle does not explain how this happens. Some commentators have interpreted his silence as evidence that it comes about mechanically. Le Blond (1939), for instance, holds that the superposition of a number of related sensible images produces a confused, general image. This is unsatisfactory for a number of reasons, among others, the loss of intuitive plausibility.[25] We seldom if ever are aware of sensory aggregates of this sort. Moreover, Aristotle does not talk about confused general images in this context or in any other.[26]

In *Metaphysics* I, 1, Aristotle speaks of experience at much greater length than in the *Posterior Analytics* II, 19, and he gives examples:

"To have an opinion that when Callias was ill with this disease this helped him and similarly Socrates and many other individuals, is to have experience" (981a7–9). Experience is expressed in judgments that are generalizations based on a number of observations.[27] Such judgments recognize similarities among particular cases and thus initiate the articulation of the relevant universal concept or proposition. These generalizations do not involve the kind of insight into causes that would warrant an unqualified judgment of the form "such and such is/will be the case" (981a1–12). The warrant for a judgment made through experience is simply the past and present observations on which it is based, and such judgments can always in principle be reduced to lengthy conjunctions, where each conjunct describes a particular case. Most likely, Aristotle believes that corresponding to each conjunct is at least one *phantasma* that is a sensory representation of that particular state of affairs. Just as experience is articulated in a judgment conjoining several descriptions, it is thought about in a series of *phantasmata*. The sensory apprehension of particulars is then a feature of experience as well as memory and perception, and the continuity of the progression from perception to experience is assured.[28]

The crucial step is the next one, namely, the derivation of a universal from the experience of one or more sensible particulars. The articulation of the universal marks the boundary between knowledge (art and science) and experience.[29] As Aristotle puts it, "to recognize that this has helped such-and-such persons, marked off in one class, when they were ill with a particular disease, is to have art" (981a10–11). The genetic account hypothesizes that the mind is able to move from a particular to a universal. The psychological explanation Aristotle gives for this feature of human rationality is terse: "the soul is such that it can be affected in this way" (*Pst. Anal.* 100a13–14).[30] The transformation of the cognitive object interests him more, and hence he describes the change from sensible particular to abstract universal in greater detail.

Here is Aristotle's final description of the articulation of the universal:

> For when one of the undifferentiated things takes a stand, the first universal is in the mind (for although one perceives the individual, the perception is of the universal, it is, for instance, of man but not of Callias, the man). Again in these a stand is taken, until the undivided, that is, the universal, stands, for instance, such-and-such animal stands until animal stands, and in this in the same way. (*Pst. Anal.* 100a15–b3)

Earlier at 100a6–7, Aristotle mentions the first "universal that comes to rest in the mind, the one beside the many." Here he uses similar language to make the crucial point that there is a sense in which universals are grasped through perception.[31] The universals in question are those that determine the features of the sensible particular; these include features perceived *kata sumbebēkos* as well as those perceived *kath' hauta*. Indeed, in the case of substances, the single most important universal, namely, the substance sortal that the particular falls under, is perceived *kata sumbebēkos*. What is incidental at one cognitive level becomes essential at another (cf. 89a33–37). The essential features of a concrete particular are general characteristics. Hence the perceptible individual is not only the object of perception but is also the vehicle for the apprehension of the universal.

The sensible particular is a token of a type, and we apprehend the type in virtue of apprehending the particular. In Aristotle's metaphysics, the substance type is ontologically prior to the token; the essential characteristics of an individual human being are determined by the substance type, the species *anthropos* (Modrak 1979). We perceive a particular man (i.e., a token of a certain type or species), but the perception is of man (i.e., the type is the ultimate determinant of the content of the perception). Many of the distinctive perceptible features of a particular object are type-dependent. For instance, the difference between a cat and a dog is more easily recognized through perception than the difference between one cat and another (cf. *Phys.* 184a24–b14).[32]

Perceptible individuals exemplify more than one type. Callias is not only a human being, he is also a two-footed, tame animal; he is also an animal and a living thing. As Aristotle describes it, the relation between the perception of Callias and the apprehension of the species, man, is the same as the relation between the apprehension of the species and the apprehension of the genus, animal. We would be inclined to emphasize the difference between the relation of class membership and the relation of class inclusion and hence to distinguish between the relation of Callias to the classes he falls under and the relation between a universal with a narrower extension, for example, man, and a universal with a wider extension, for example, animal.[33] Aristotle, however, emphasizes the connection between perceiving a sensible particular and employing that particular to represent the types it exemplifies. The integrated model envisages the dual use of a sensible particular—as a concrete representation of a unique individual (Callias) and as a component of an abstract representation of a type (man). From the latter perspective, the perception is the apprehension of the species as instantiated by the particular. "When a stand is taken," a more narrowly defined class (man-as-perceived) has been subsumed under a more abstract class (man).

Because Callias is a member of all the classes involved, an exemplification of all the universals under consideration, the perception of Callias and the retained *phantasma* of Callias can serve as the basis for the apprehension of these universals. The *phantasma* is a representation of a sensible particular, which is a token of a number of types, and the more abstract representations represent the types exemplified in the *phantasma*. The relation between species, genus and higher order universals consists in the degree of abstractness with which the features of the particular are conceptualized (cf. *Met.* 1075a1–3).[34] Many more of Callias' characteristics are disregarded when we use a *phantasma* of Callias to represent the universal, living thing, than when we use it to represent the species, man.

Thinking is, according to the integrated model of cognitive activity, a way of comprehending or representing the object presented sensorially through *phantasia* (cf. Sorabji 1982, 303–4). To apprehend the essence of water is to conceptualize a blue, fluid patch in a particular way; it is to represent water in terms of its essential properties. Similarly, if Callias is perceived as tall, thin and balding, the *phantasma* of Callias employed in thinking about the essence of human beings would include (some of) these idiosyncratic characteristics, but the thought would ignore them. To grasp an intelligible form is to reinterpret the content of an appropriate *phantasma*. Nevertheless, the *phantasma* is a necessary component of the thought. Just as in the extramental world essences inhere in matter, essences-as-thought inhere in the *phantasmata* that serve as their material substrata.

We are now in a position to understand Aristotle's puzzling remark that the cognitive process involved in the acquisition of knowledge is like a rout in a battle stopped by first one person making a stand and then another until the beginning formation is reached (100a12–13). Both the cognitive process and the rout involve a movement from discrete individuals considered as such to an orderly arrangement of individuals in which individual differences are irrelevant. During the rout, each soldier is an isolated individual, as are sensible particulars when they are initially apprehended in perception. When the reversal of the rout begins and some soldiers have resumed their battle positions, an ordered whole begins to emerge of which the soldiers are constituents. Similarly, the generalization that is grasped through experience orders a number of individual *phantasmata*—at least to the extent of specifying similarities. When the battle formation is completely restored, the formation can be fully specified in terms of the number, position, and location of the soldiers; individual soldiers of the same type are interchangeable. The *phantasma* employed in thinking about an abstract object is treated as an arbitrary instance of that type of object. The battle formation under a general description constitutes an ordering of individuals and thus is analogous to a universal principle. The cognition of a universal principle orders the particular states of affairs that are subsumed under the universal, and the peculiar features of the *phantasmata* that embody these states of affairs are irrelevant to their role in the cognition (cf. *Met.* 1078a22–31; *De Mem.* 450a1–4). There is no battle formation without soldiers, nor is there a noetic apprehension of a universal without the sensory representation of (some of) its instances; nonetheless, the first member of each pair cannot be reduced to the second member.

At this stage of the investigation, we are also better able to explicate Aristotle's concept of *epagōgē* (induction). Aristotle describes a cognitive process that is the articulation of a universal in successive stages in the *Posterior Analytics* II, 19, and then almost as an afterthought he identifies the process with *epagōgē*: "indeed it is clear that we must recognize the first principles by *epagōgē*" (100b4). The identification, however, makes perfect sense in the context of his epistemology as a whole (see sec. 1). *Epagōgē* is a method of reasoning that enables a thinker to move from particular cases to general claims.[35] The contrast between demonstration and *epagōgē* is drawn in terms of the dependence of the former on preexisting knowledge of the universal, whereas *epagōgē* is the source of universals.[36] The recognition of particular truths as well as the recognition of the conclusions of inductive arguments is assigned to *epagōgē* (*Pr. Anal.* 67a23; *Pst. Anal.* 78a34; *Met.* 1048a36). For instance, Aristotle says that we recognize that nearby celestial bodies do not twinkle by perception or by *epagōgē* (*Pst. Anal.* 78a34). This remark is of special interest because it indicates that *epagōgē* begins with the apprehension of single states of affairs, just as perception does.

The object of *epagōgē* is the apprehension of a universal or a series of universals initially exhibited in a sensory representation and subsequently represented more abstractly. The universal is sometimes a simple concept such as a natural kind; sometimes it is an abstract principle such as a first principle of geometry.[37] In all cases, the cognitive process through which the universal is articulated is the same—the stripping away in successive stages of the particularities of the object as represented sensorially. Aristotle's epistemology rests on the assumption that the mind is capable of undergoing a process that results in the apprehension of universals based on sensible representations.

The theory of perception, especially Aristotle's conception of sensory representation, and the integrated model of perceptual and noetic activity establish the possibility of a cognitive activity such as *epagōgē*. Because we human beings are able to employ sensory representations to represent objects not present to the senses, we are able to reason inductively from particular cases. Because we human beings are capable of representing the content of a sensory representation abstractly, we are able to apprehend the universal displayed in the sensory representation. For example, we use the rippling, blue, irregular shape to exemplify and thus to represent the essence of water. The sensory representation serves as the matter for the noetic representation of the essence (see chap. 5, sec. 4). The genetic account grapples with the same problem as *De Anima* III, 4–8, namely, the origin of the noetic object, though from a different perspective (cf. Kahn 1981). In both contexts, Aristotle's answer turns on the notion of a multilevel representation of the same object; at the basic level it is represented sensorially and concretely; at another level, the object is represented abstractly and universally (cf. *De An.* 429b13–14; *Pst. Anal.* 100a6–b3).

3. Psychologism and Realism

In the final section of the *Posterior Analytics* II, 19 (100b5–17), Aristotle answers the second part of the opening question, namely, What is the disposition that knows the first principles? The answer is *nous*. Commentators have disagreed vehemently about the connection between this answer and Aristotle's answer to the first question, namely, that we recognize the first principles through *epagōgē*. Le Blond (1939, 132–40) read the genetic account as a description of a perceptual process that excluded intellection, and hence he could not find any satisfactory way of connecting it with the final section (cf. Irwin 1977, 214–15). Barnes (1975, 256–59) agreed that there was little connection between the two parts of II, 19; according to him, the first part describes the process of coming to know the first principles while the second part names this kind of knowledge *nous*, thus making a merely terminological point. Kosman (1973) and Lesher (1973) both argued to the contrary that the connection between the two sections is obvious and unproblematic: the first section describes the acquisition of first principles through *epagōgē*; the second section talks about *nous*, which is the *hexis* (disposition) realized through *epagōgē*.[38] More recently, Kahn

(1981) has argued for a broad construal of *nous* that allows us to understand its discussion as a natural development of themes broached in the genetic account.

In the preceding section, we established that the genetic account describes the articulation of the universal in successive stages through *epagōgē*. This finding is compatible with any interpretation of II, 19 that allows for the acquisition of the knowledge of first principles through *epagōgē*. It is incompatible with any interpretation that makes some further act of intuition necessary for the knowledge of first principles. Therefore, our previous findings are consistent with Barnes's interpretation, on the one hand, and on the other, with the different line of interpretation adopted by Kosman, Lesher and Kahn.

Our interpretation, however, is at odds with the traditional interpretation championed by Le Blond (1939) among others. According to that interpretation of II, 19, the genetic account describes a process of empirical generalization that yields general principles of some sort, but these principles fall short of the comprehensiveness and certainty required of first principles. First principles are apprehended through an immediate act of insight (*nous*), and this process is described in the final section. Fortunately, we need not beg the question by resorting to the interpretation of the genetic account given above to find reasons for rejecting the traditional interpretation of the chapter as a whole.[39]

There is no direct textual evidence for the identification of *nous* with a form of self-warranting intuition (cf. Lesher 1973, 50–51). The *De Anima*'s account of *nous* makes it the capacity for thought. Thinking is the actualization of the noetic object.[40] The noetic object is a generalized representation of the sensible particular that is presented in the concommitant *phantasma*. There is no claim made on the part of *nous* to absolute insight into self-evident truths, but rather to a distinct type of cognitive activity that is not limited to sensory representation. A narrower notion of *nous* can be found in the *Posterior Analytics*, which identifies *nous* with knowledge. This notion, however, does not decide the case in favor of the traditional interpretation, for it is consistent with several alternative interpretations, namely, (1) *nous* exists as a dispositional state of knowledge of the first principles reached through *epagōgē*; and (2) *nous* is also the faculty for *epagōgē* and hence is exercised in the process of reasoning from particular cases to general principles.

Proponents of the traditional interpretation sometimes argue from the alleged inferiority of *epagōgē* as a means of obtaining knowledge to the claim that *nous* qua immediate intuition is the ultimate source of first principles. But this argument when scrutinized also gives way.

In a number of different contexts, Aristotle mentions the inferiority of perception, and in some instances the inferiority of *noēsis*, vis-à-vis *epistēmē* and *apodeixis* (*Pst. Anal.* 88a6–8; *E.N.* 1143a35–b5). The genetic account is introduced with the claim that the ability in question develops out of perception, and it concludes with a description of the articulation of the universal through *epagōgē* that associates this process with perception. Nonetheless, *epagōgē* and perception are distinct powers. The object of the genetic account, especially of the third and fourth formulations, is to show how the sensible particular apprehended in perception and presented in a *phantasma* can be used by the thinker to represent a universal. The process by which the universal is abstracted is *epagōgē*, so the fact that we cannot apprehend articulated universals through perception—the fact that accounts for the epistemic inferiority of perception—has no bearing on the reliability of *epagōgē* or on its claim to be the cognitive process through which primitive universals are initially apprehended.

Moreover, the structure of II, 19 counts against the traditional interpretation. The chapter begins with two related questions—How do the first principles become known and what disposition knows them? The first part concludes with the statement that the primitive principles are apprehended through *epagōgē*, and the second part asserts that *nous* is the knowledge of first principles.[41] There is no suggestion in the text that the genetic account has failed to give an adequate answer to the first question. Yet if the answer is satisfactory, the positing of an additional cognitive activity different from *epagōgē* to explain the apprehension of first principles is superfluous. While a seventeenth-century philosopher might believe that *nous* is needed to confirm the apodictic certainty of principles reached through *epagōgē*, Aristotle is not motivated by skeptical considerations; hence for him the interesting issues concern the apprehension of first principles, not the validation of our claim to know them. *Nous* is Aristotle's answer to the second question; it is the *hexis* of knowing the first principles. The two answers fit together nicely on the assumption that *nous* is the cognitive capacity realized in the apprehension of first principles by *epagōgē* as well as the dispositional knowledge of these principles. In sum, both internal and external considerations weigh against the traditional interpretation of II, 19, and we would be well advised to reject it.

In addition, if we appeal to the integrated model of cognitive activity to explicate the relations between *epagōgē* and *nous*, we see why Aristotle would not be troubled by the implication that *nous* is realized through *epagōgē*. Grasping a first principle, like any other form of thinking, will include the apprehension of a *phantasma* that illustrates the principle. *Epagōgē* is merely the cognitive process of coming to recognize a first principle in its sensible manifestations. As cognitive activities, the actualization of a first principle in which *nous* is realized and the actualization of the same first principle in which *epagōgē* terminates would be indistinguishable.

This does not mean that all the problems concerning the final section of II, 19 are solved. Aristotle claims that *nous* is more exact (*akribesteron*) and truer (*alēthesteron*) than *epistēmē* (100b8, 100b11). This position is likely to strike the modern philosopher who believes that *nous* is the knowledge of first principles acquired through *epagōgē* as both inexplicable and unwarranted. The certainty of *epistēmē* is a consequence of the logical and conceptual constraints Aristotle places on demonstration. Demonstrations are valid syllogisms that meet a variety of other conditions; for instance, each premise must express a necessary and universal truth.[42] The criteria Aristotle sets out for demonstrations are so demanding that commentators have questioned whether there is a single, genuine demonstration to be found in the whole Aristotelian corpus.[43] Should we, however, possess a demonstration of some proposition *p*, we would have good reason to claim to know that *p*. There does not seem to be the same sort of argument for the certainty of propositions grasped through *epagōgē*.

All the same, Aristotle's claim that *nous* is more exact than *epistēmē* can be explained. Aristotle envisages a hierarchical ordering of the sciences (*Pst. Anal.* 87a31–35; *Met.* 982a5–28, 1078a9; cf. McKirahan 1978). The more basic the science, the more accurate (*akribesteron*) it is. Arithmetic is more *akribesteron* than harmonics or even geometry (*Pst. Anal.* 87a31–37). In the same sense, the first premises of a demonstrative science are more accurate than the derived propositions because they are more basic. The knowledge of the first principles possesses the feature of being more accurate than the knowledge of the derived principles merely by virtue of being the knowledge of first principles (cf. *Met.* 982a25–27). This feature has nothing to do with the way in which the principles are known.

The worry occasioned by Aristotle's claim that *nous* is truer (*alēthesteron*) than *epistēmē* is more difficult to dismiss. The modern problem of induction seems to come up with a vengeance in Aristotle's case. We might observe 999,999 crows and conclude on the basis of these observations that all crows are black, but the millionth crow may still turn out to be white. How could a philosopher claim that beliefs arrived at in this way are truer than any other beliefs?

In the first place, Aristotle's conception of *epagōgē* differs in crucial respects from our conception of induction. For us, inductive arguments are empirical generalizations; the larger the sample the generalization is based upon, the more reliable the conclusion of the inductive argument. For Aristotle, *epagōgē* is simply the process of coming to recognize a general principle or concept in one or more of its instances (cf. Lesher 1973; Hamlyn 1976; Engberg-Pederson 1979). The arguments Aristotle treats as inductive are not lengthy listings of examples in support of a general thesis; instead they often cite a single instance of the general principle or at most a few instances.[44] The example Aristotle gives in II, 19 of the perception of Callias and the subsequent apprehension of the concepts, human and animal, suggest that the universal can be elicited from a particular instance or a small number of cases. Even in the *Topics*, where Aristotle mentions the recognition of similarities between particular cases as a feature of *epagōgē* (108b10), there is no suggestion that the adduction of numerous examples to establish a universal is characteristic of *epagōgē*.

Pointing out this feature of Aristotle's concept of *epagōgē*, of course, does not help if we think that the only check on an inductive argument is the size of the original sample. From that perspective, to generalize from the perception of Callias to a concept of human being seems like a very slipshod procedure that is quite unlikely to lead to a true conception of the nature of human beings. Yet this is precisely what Aristotle assumes we can do. Aristotle's answer to the "problem of *epagōgē*" turns on psychologism—human rational capacities are such that the process he describes in II, 19 does, at least in favored cases, lead to truths. This answer rests on certain realist assumptions Aristotle makes about the world and our ability to know it. Because he makes these psychological and ontological assumptions, Aristotle holds that we can claim to know the first principles that are apprehended through *epagōgē* because the process through which they are comprehended is such that they correctly represent the extramental reality. The external world acts on us through perception. The inductive process begins in perception; the first universals that we comprehend are implicit in our perceptions. They correspond to real distinctions among extramental objects. The progression from sensible universal to abstract principle is continuous; the object apprehended at each stage is implicit in the preceding stage(s). The continuity of this process maintains the correspondence between our concepts and the world.[45]

Nevertheless, the move from a concept of man that fits all the individual humans we have perceived in the past to a concept of man that fits all human beings seems to require some further justification. Aristotle cannot avoid this difficulty by restricting the concept to those individuals whose perception gave rise to it, for then its definition will not be a commensurately universal proposition of the sort required for demonstration and knowledge.[46] Aristotle's belief in natural kinds probably accounts for his seeming obliviousness to this problem. If the world just is such that individuals form natural kinds, and our minds just are such that we form concepts that correspond to these kinds, then a concept based on a limited sample need not be restricted in application to those individuals.

In the modern epistemological idiom, *epagōgē*, as Aristotle conceives it, is a reliable belief-producing mechanism, that is to say, it is a way of arriving at true beliefs that stand in need of no further justification.[47] If the world and our minds were such as Aristotle believes them to be, then the basic concepts grasped through *epagōgē* would be the objects of justified, true belief.[48] Having in effect described a reliable belief-producing mechanism at 99b35–100b5, Aristotle can then cogently claim that *nous*, which is realized through this mechanism, is knowledge.

The difficulty comes at the next level of justification when we ask: How can Aristotle know that "the mind is such as to be capable of undergoing this" (100a14)? Aristotle has no answer. He makes no attempt to justify the realist assumptions that he makes in the *Posterior Analytics* and elsewhere, namely, that there is an extramental world, that the world is intelligible and that we have knowledge of it.

4. The Epistemological Consequences of the Foundational Principles

As an epistemological foundationalist, Aristotle assumes that knowledge of the first principles is attainable. As a psychologist, Aristotle gives an account of human cognition that complements his account of the apprehension of first principles. Having made certain realist assumptions about the objects of knowledge and the nature of minds, Aristotle propounds a psychological theory that brings the psychological subject into direct contact with the extramental world. The foundational principles of the theory of perception all support the thesis that we humans can apprehend the basic concepts and first principles required for art and science because our minds are just as they are.

According to the genetic account, the knowledge of first principles develops out of our perceptual capacities. The Psychophysical Principle engenders an analysis of perception that makes the extramental world the cause and the source of the content of sensory experience. The content is the actualization of characteristics possessed by the external object of perception, and a causally connected series of events links the external object to changes in the sense organs. Short-term changes in the organs are the substrata of perceptions; long-term changes are the substrata for *phantasmata*. Hence the Psychophysical Principle insures that the cognitive progression described in II, 19 is rooted in the world. From the initial changes in the sense organ and the initial apprehension of the perceptual characteristics of the external object there is an unbroken causal chain connecting the original state with the sensory representations employed by memory, experience and knowledge. Since thinking always employs *phantasmata*, no matter how abstract the ultimate principle, there is always a causal chain connecting the apprehension of that principle to objects in the world.

The Actuality Principle also supports the picture of the relation between perception and the world that is presupposed by the genetic account. The perceptible form actualized in the act of perception is the second actuality of a property that the external object possesses, whether it is perceived or not. Despite the fact that when conditions are not optimal, perceptual errors are possible, the gap between perceiver and perceived is not such that systematic distortions will occur under normal conditions.[49] In addition, the Actuality Principle explains why Aristotle describes the emergence of the universal in such detail in II, 19. As a cognitive object, the universal determines the character of the cognition.

The Sensory Representation Principle provides the basis for the bridge between perception and knowledge that is required by Aristotle's notion of *epagōgē*. The noetic object is an abstract representation of a sensible particular, and the sensory representation is retained as a component of the thought. (This fact causes Aristotle to puzzle at *De An.* 432a10–14 about how to distinguish between primary *noēmata* and *phantasmata*.) The continuity of the reasoning from sensible particulars to abstract universal is guaranteed because the *phantasmata* employed at every stage of the reasoning represent the same type of sensible particular. The (extramental) world is not only the ultimate source of concepts, but sensory representations of features of that world are immediately involved in thinking about any concept whatsoever.

The embedding of simpler perceptual activities in more complex ones and the relationship between perceptual and noetic activities in Aristotle's theory of perception are a consequence of the Analytic Principle. Since at each higher level of complexity, the lower-level faculties are included, either potentially or totally, cognitive responses that involve a number of different faculties acting in a coordinated fashion are anticipated and easily accounted for. The coordinated cognitive activity envisaged by the genetic account, where the apprehension of a sensible particular is simultaneously a perception of Callias and the basis for the representation of the natural kind *anthropos*, is easily explained by reference to the Analytic Principle. When an explanation involves more than one cognitive capacity, the Analytic Principle causes Aristotle to build the explanation up from the ground by assigning as large a role as possible to the lower-level faculty. On the model of cognition found in the psychological treatises, it makes sense to identify the cognitive stages of the genetic account with steps in the articulation of the universal, and this is what Aristotle does in II, 19.

5. Psychological Solutions to Epistemological Problems

At this point, we are in a good position to appreciate the nearly perfect fit between Aristotle's epistemology, his theory of perception, and the integrated model of perceptual and noetic activity.

Commentators have long taken the position that to understand Aristotle's epistemology we must understand the *Posterior Analytics* II, 19. Yet the argument of II, 19 proved to be elusive and recalcitrant. At the heart of these exegetical problems were puzzles about *epagōgē* and puzzles about whether the mind arrives at the knowledge of first principles through the employment of *epagōgē* or in some other way. To solve these problems an interpreter must fix on a tenable interpretation of the genetic account and decide the question of the relation between the genetic account and the closing section of II, 19. By appealing to Aristotle's theory of sense perception and the integrated model of perceptual and noetic activity to interpret the genetic account of II, 19, I explain why Aristotle believes that the knowledge of first principles is acquired through *epagōgē* and why he is not troubled by reservations about knowledge claims based on "induction."

We should also briefly consider another chronic problem for interpreters of Aristotle's epistemology. This problem extends beyond the genetic account and beyond the *Posterior Analytics*. Aristotle repeatedly asserts three theses that do not seem to be compatible: (1) the objects of knowledge are universals; (2) only sensible particulars are apprehended through perception; and (3) perception is the source of knowledge.[50] The tension between these theses can be resolved by appeal to the integrated model of perceptual and noetic activity. The objects presented in perception are indeed particulars, but the mind is able to use sensory representations of particulars as the basis for representations of universals. The conception of a unified cognition that includes a sensory representation and the apprehension of a universal based on that sensory representation is central to Aristotle's conception of the relationship between perception and knowledge. To perceive Callias and simultaneously to recognize that men are two-footed, tame animals is to have a cognition of this sort. The recognition of the essence is based on the perception because the essence is an alternative representation of the individual represented in the perception.

Even if one rejects Aristotle's psychologism or his realism and hence finds his epistemology ultimately unsatisfactory, the conceptual beauty of his comprehensive vision of epistemology and psychology is awesome.

Conclusion

The hypothesis we set out to investigate about Aristotle's descriptions of sense perception, apperceptual comparison, reflexive awareness, *phantasia*, dreams and memory has been confirmed. Simply put, the hypothesis was that Aristotle had a theoretical model of the functions of the perceptual faculty that enabled him to explain many different, psychological activities by subsuming them under the perceptual faculty, and hence that Aristotle's descriptions of these activities were genuinely explanatory. Examining Aristotle's psychological writings, we found the same conception of psychological activity exhibited again and again in Aristotle's characterizations of different psychological states and events. We found Aristotle invoking the same general principles and the same generic concept of the perceptual faculty to account for superficially disparate psychological phenomena. Chief among the general principles are the five foundational principles I abstracted from Aristotle's writings and presented in chapter 2—the Psychophysical Principle, the Actuality Principle, the Sensory Representation Principle, the Analytic Principle and the Normative Psychophysical Principle. All five of these principles make an appearance in the *De Anima* by the end of the second chapter of the third book, that is, by the end of Aristotle's discussion of sense perception. The Psychophysical Principle, the Actuality Principle and the Analytic Principle were, we discovered, implicit in Aristotle's criticisms of his predecessors in *De Anima* I, and they were asserted by Aristotle at the beginning of *De Anima* II as part of his programmatic statement of intent.

The five foundational principles express an ideal of psychological explanation, and Aristotle structures his explanations of the functions of the perceptual faculty in accordance with them. They also provide the theoretical justification for specific explanatory claims and unify Aristotle's treatment of the different functions of the perceptual faculty. Having conceived the perceptual faculty as an umbrella faculty covering a large and diverse group of psychological states and capacities, Aristotle is confronted with the prospect that the perceptual faculty will be an unwieldy conglomerate. The foundational principles engender a unified conception of the perceptual faculty as a complex psychophysical system made up of the five senses, the common sense, the capacity for sensory representation, the individual sense organs and the central sense organ.

Chapters 2 and 3 established that Aristotle had an explanatory framework consisting in the foundational principles and that he presented his account of sense perception in the *De Anima* and the *De Sensu* within this framework. In later chapters we turned to the other uses to which Aristotle put the foundational principles. The principles are evident in Aristotle's account of *phantasia*. *Phantasia* is internalized sensory representation; thus, in accordance with the Sensory Representation Principle Aristotle includes, under the functions of the perceptual faculty, mental activities, such as memory and dreaming, that employ *phantasmata*. Moreover, the foundational principles ensure the comprehensiveness and unity of the theory of the perceptual faculty, and as a result Aristotle is in a position to give an adequate treatment of the phenomena of consciousness without recourse to a technical notion of consciousness as such.

We also considered the consequences of the foundational principles of the theory of perception for Aristotle's analyses of thinking and knowing. As an epistemologist, Aristotle assumes that human beings are capable of exercising the rational and perceptual faculties in a fully integrated manner. As a psychologist, Aristotle successfully explains this aspect of human cognition by appeal to a model of cognition that borrows heavily from his theory of perception.

The explanatory theory expressed in the foundational principles becomes in Aristotle's hands a powerful analytic tool. He employs these principles to explain all the functions of the perceptual faculty, including awareness, *phantasia*, dreams and memory. Aristotle exploits the resources of this theory in his analysis of the noetic faculty and in his account of knowledge.

Abbreviations

Charm.	Charmides
De An.	De Anima
De An. Comm.	De Anima libros Commentaria
De An. Mant.	De Anima cum Mantissa
De Div.	De Divinatione per Somnum
De Gen. An.	De Generatione Animalium
De Gen. et Corr.	De Generatione et Corruptione
De Ins.	De Insomniis
De Int.	De Interpretatione
De Juv.	De Juventute
De Mem.	De Memoria
De Motu An.	De Motu Animalium
De Part. An.	De Partibus Animalium
De Sens.	De Sensu
De Som.	De Somno
DK	H. Diels. *Fragmente der Vorsokratiker*, 6th ed. Ed. W. Kranz. Berlin, 1951.
E.N.	Ethica Nicomachea
Hist. An.	Historia Animalium
Met.	Metaphysica
Phdo.	Phaedo
Phil.	Philebus
Phys.	Physics
Pr. Anal.	Prior Analytics
Pst. Anal.	Posterior Analytics
Rep.	Republic
Rhet.	Rhetoric
Soph.	Sophist
Theaet.	Theaetetus
Tim.	Timaeus
Top.	Topics.

Notes

Chapter 1

1. According to Aristotle, ancient dualism took several forms: one form was materialistic in that the separate psychical substance was identified with a material element; the other was dualist in the modern sense, i.e., the psychical substance was incorporeal. Aristotle is sharply critical of all two-substance views as well as materialist monism.

2. Not only does Aristotle object to physicalist theories on the grounds that they cannot accommodate explanations of actions in terms of intentional states, but he also objects to them on the grounds that they fail to give satisfactory physical explanations (see especially *De An.* I, 3).

3. Mansion 1961, 42–48, is surely right that the point of Aristotle's criticisms of his predecessors is not simply to clear the slate but to make certain substantive points about the philosophy of mind.

4. Cf. *De Part. An.* 641a18–32. An Aristotelian form is the principle of organization manifested in a composite of form and matter. Aristotle identifies the substantial form of a concrete particular with its essence and hence with its substance (cf. *Met.* VII, 4–6; cf. *De An.* 412b10–11). Aristotle distinguishes between substance-as-essence and substance-as-substratum. A composite of matter and form, for instance, a biological individual, is a substance in the second sense. Cf. Modrak 1979.

5. Typically, materialists attribute materialism to Aristotle and dualists attribute dualism to him. Commentators who are unsympathetic to Aristotle sometimes prove to be exceptions to this general pattern. Slakey (1961), for example, believes that a reductionist account of sense perception is philosophically unsatisfactory, and yet he ignores elements of Aristotle's theory of perception that are inconsistent with the physicalist view he ascribes to Aristotle.

6. Cf. Rodier 1900, II: 261, 330; Hicks 1907, xlviii; Ross 1923, 136.

7. The speakers were respectively R. Bolton, "Aristotle on Scientific Method," and M. Burnyeat, "Is Aristotle's Philosophy of Mind Still Credible?" The conference was held at the University of Pittsburgh, March 30-April 1, 1984.

8. The argument for this thesis is made in chap. 2.

9. See sec. 3 for a more detailed account of the apparent similarities between Aristotle's approach and the functionalist approach.

10. For example, sensory discriminations involving the simultaneous ap-

prehension of the objects of several senses are discussed in *De An.* III, 2 and 7, *De Sens.* 7, and *De Som.* 2; perceptual self-awareness is discussed in *De An.* III, 1 and *De Som.* 2; the characteristics of the five senses and their objects are discussed in *De An.* II, 7–11 and *De Sens.* 1–5; and voluntary animal movement is discussed in *De An.* III, 9–11 and the *De Motu An.*

11. The proceedings of the Symposium Aristotelium were published under the title *Aristotle on Mind and the Senses* (Lloyd and Owen 1978). Some of the more interesting papers on Aristotle's psychology published between 1960 and 1975 were reprinted in *Articles on Aristotle,* vol. 4: *Psychology and Aesthetics* (Barnes, Schofield, and Sorabji 1978).

12. *De An.* 412b10–22; *De Part. An.* 640b4–28, 641a18–32; *Met.* 1029a20–32; cf. 1041b8. See Modrak 1984.

13. Both the *De Anima* II's and the *De Sensu's* accounts of sense perception expend considerably more words in setting out the material conditions for perception than in discussing the *logoi* of sensible opposites that constitute the sensible form. (This point too is discussed later in more detail; see especially chaps. 2 and 3.) Furthermore, the physiological causes of bodily movements are discussed at greater length in the *De Motu Animalium* than the cognitive/formal component of action.

14. Ackrill 1972–73, Hardie 1976, and Sorabji 1974 raise different and troubling objections to Aristotle's employment of hylomorphic analyses in psychology. These objections will be discussed in detail in chap. 2, sec. 5.

15. Cf. Ross 1906, 5–7.

16. *De An.* 412b20–22; *De Part. An.* 640b34–641a5; *Met.* 1035b24–26, 1036b30–32.

17. Cf. *De An.* 412b18–22. In chap. 2, sec. 5, I discuss Aristotle's use of *ophthalmos* for the eye and for the matter of the eye. We find a similar willingness on Aristotle's part to use the material definition of a psychological activity instead of the complete hylomorphic definition on occasion (see, e.g., *De Gen. An.* 780a3–4, where sight is defined as the setting into movement of the eye).

18. Aristotle might be a functionalist in a broad sense, i.e., he might define psychological states in terms of their causal roles without accepting the constraint endorsed by the modern psychological functionalist, namely, that the causal role must be specified without reference to anatomy.

19. Sorabji 1974 looks for behavioral-functionalist definitions of this sort. Robinson 1978 argues that Sorabji's project is ill conceived.

20. I have mentioned some of the reasons why the attempt to assimilate Aristotle's philosophy of mind to modern approaches has failed. I argue this point in more detail in subsequent chapters, especially in chap. 2.

21. The first group includes Matthews 1977 and Rorty 1979; the second, Kahn 1966; the third, Hardie 1976 and Robinson 1978.

22. The initial part of *Posterior Analytics* II, 19 is aporetic (99b14–34); the second part (99b34–100b5) describes *epagōgē,* the process by which universals are apprehended; the final section (100b5–17) describes *nous,* the comprehension of first principles.

23. This task will be undertaken in chap. 7. Far too few recent commentators have recognized the relevance of the psychology to the interpretation of *Pst.* II, 19. Berti 1978 and Kahn 1981 are exceptions, but they concentrate on the account of *nous* in *De Anima* III and its implications for the description of *nous* in II, 19. However, Aristotle's theory of perception is equally important in this context and has been totally neglected up until now.

24. Jaeger's classic work, originally published in 1923, was translated by R. Robinson and published in English in 1948. Here I argue against the Nuyens-Ross elaboration of Jaeger's developmental hypothesis, which leads to a division of the psychological writings. However, it is worth noting that Jaeger's argument has been criticized on other grounds as well, most notably by Owen (1965, 129), who rejected the "divorce that Jaeger thought he had made out between the logical and metaphysical partners in Aristotle's early philosophising."

25. Jaeger (1948, 334) refused to venture an opinion on the dating of the *Parva Naturalia*. Unlike Nuyens and Ross, Jaeger assigns the biological writings to the last period of Aristotle's career (see chaps. 12 and 13).

26. Nuyens found the *De Longitudine Vitae* to be later than the *De Juventute* and the *De Respiratione*; he assigned it to the end of the middle period ([1948]1973, 163–70).

27. Although in agreement about the similarities between the *De Somno* and the *De Insomniis* and the biological texts, Lulofs (1943; 1947, preface) and Ross (1955, introduction) drew different conclusions from this finding. It led Lulofs, but not Ross, to distinguish an earlier, physiological part of each work from a later psychological part. More recently, Wiesner 1978 has argued against Lulofs's two-part interpretation.

28. Cf. Slakey 1961, 481–82, which argues that the *De Sensu* is earlier than the *De Anima*.

29. Scholarly opinion seems to favor assigning an earlier date to the *De Juventute* and the *De Respiratione*, but these treatises are not important for my purposes. The *De Juventute's* description (469b16) of the soul as fiery (*psuchē empepureumenē*) is difficult but perhaps not impossible to reconcile with hylomorphism.

30. More recently, scholars have been uniformly opposed to the division of these works. Cf. Wiesner 1978, 242.

31. Recollection is mentioned at *De An.* 408b17 and discussed at length in *De Mem.* 2. A summary account of voluntary motion is found in *De An.* III, 9–11 and a detailed account in the *De Motu Animalium*. Cf. note 10.

32. Since the nutritive faculty includes all the vital capacities shared by living creatures from digestion to reproduction, it is only a slight exaggeration to say that all the biological treatises (e.g., the *De Part. An.* II–IV, the *De Gen. An.*, the *Hist. An.*) are concerned with the functions of this faculty. There are also cross-references; for example, the *De Generatione Animalium* refers to the *De Anima* at 736a37, 779b23, 786b25, and 788b2.

33. *De An.* 426b12–427a15, 431a20–b1; *De Sens.* 447b10–449a22; *De Som.* 455a16–25.

34. At *Met.* 1035b26–28, Aristotle makes a point of saying that whether the heart or the brain is the crucial organ with respect to the *psuchē* makes no difference to his position; he obviously believes that only one organ can stand in this relation to the *psuchē*.

35. Lefèvre 1972, 156–214, and 1978 argued persuasively that hylomorphism and instrumentalist descriptions are compatible.

36. After *eidos* and *entelecheia* in the definition of the soul in *De An.* II, 1, Aristotle does not use either term again in this sense for the remainder of the *De Anima*.

37. Unless otherwise noted, translations are mine.

38. While neither Nuyens nor Ross would be troubled by evidence that the *De Memoria* is contemporaneous with the *De Anima*, they should be troubled by the presence of instrumentalist descriptions in the *De Anima*.

39. Another "dualist" passage from *De An.* II is 420b27–29: So voice is the striking of inhaled air by the soul in these parts on the part called the windpipe. *De An.* III provides numerous examples of "dualist" language; see, e.g., 429a29 and 434b4.

40. Cf. Lefèvre 1972, 1978. See n. 35.

41. The mental predicates of ordinary language have also proved recalcitrant in the face of physicalist attempts at reduction in the twentieth century. See sec. 3.

42. This also explains why Aristotle uses language that suggests he endorses the Platonic distinction between rational and irrational parts in the *Nicomachean Ethics*. Cf. Jaeger 1948, 332–33.

43. Aristotle ultimately decides that *nous* is acquired before birth albeit at a relatively late stage of fetal development. See also Moraux 1955, which discusses this passage at length. Nuyens acknowledges the presence of hylomorphism in the *De Generatione Animalium* and consequently assigns a late date to it, but instrumentalism is also in evidence in the treatise; Aristotle associates heat and *pneuma* with the *psuchē*, and he appeals to soul-heat *(thermotēs psuchikē)* to explain spontaneous generation (762a19–22; cf. 736b30–737a8).

44. Cf. *De Gen. An.* 730b4–25, where the form transmitted in the semen is compared to the form imposed by a carpenter on his materials in the course of constructing a building.

45. For a clear summary of the argument for the unity of science, see Oppenheim and Putnam 1958; cf. Feigl 1958.

46. Many of the important early papers on the Psychophysical Identity Theory are reprinted in Rosenthal 1971; many of the more recent and important papers in the philosophy of mind are reprinted in Block 1980.

47. For a succinct statement of the conceptual difficulties facing the Psychophysical Identity Theory, see Cornman 1962. Smart 1959 anticipated some of these objections and attempted to answer them.

48. Putnam 1967 objects to the Psychophysical Identity Theory on the grounds that psychological laws should not be species-specific. Lewis 1980 makes a similar argument for including Martian pains under our concept of pain.

49. Kim 1966 makes a persuasive case for this claim.

50. The proponents (and critics) of functionalism agree that the functional analyses of mental states does not involve a materialist reduction of these states. They disagree about whether functionalism ultimately supports physicalism or defeats it. For the former view, see Armstrong 1968, 1977 and Lewis 1966, 1972, 1980. For the latter view, see Fodor 1965; Putnam 1966; Block and Fodor 1972.

51. A short, clear statement of the functionalist position can be found in Block 1980, "Part Three Introduction."

52. The association of the *psuchē* with life functions is an ancient doctrine that Aristotle puts to use. See Claus 1981, which through a careful study of Archaic and Classical Greek writers establishes the prevalence of the identification of the *psuchē* with life-force before Plato. Cf. Onians 1951; Snell 1953; Bremmer 1983.

53. This is not to say that Aristotle is a psychological functionalist. Functionalism encompasses a number of related yet distinguishable positions—a feature that is often overlooked by both the advocates and the opponents of functionalist readings of Aristotle's psychology. Robinson's 1978 critique of Sorabji and Kosman would have been more persuasive had he acknowledged that different functionalist stances are possible. Cf. n. 18.

54. Robinson 1978 argues vehemently against attributing functionalism to Aristotle.

55. See Dennett 1978 for a concise sketch of the recent history of the philosophy of mind.

56. Rorty 1965 proposed to use the schema "What people call X's are nothing but Y's" to eliminate mental descriptions in favor of physicalist ones.

57. Cf. n. 50.

58. With the exception of thinking, all of these psychological activities are functions of the perceptual faculty and thinking is dependent upon the perceptual faculty.

Chapter 2

1. According to the *Posterior Analytics*, knowledge in a particular field is organized around a single genus, which is described by the initial definitions and hypotheses. In this instance, the genus is the perceptual faculty. The foundational principles are the comprehensive principles Aristotle uses to explain the cognitive activities assigned to the perceptual faculty. See n. 50 and 51.

2. These principles will be discussed in greater detail in sec. 1. As presented here, the principles are couched in modern terminology; for instance, where Aristotle speaks of the form and matter of states of the soul, the Psychophysical Principle speaks of psychophysical states. Despite the dangers of anachronism, I believe it is better to formulate Aristotle's position in language that has a clear meaning for us rather than in language that, while appearing simply to render the Greek terms in English, in fact has a (post-fourth century B.C.) history of its own, which often serves to obscure rather than illuminate Aris-

totle's meaning. With the exception of the Sensory Representation Principle, all the principles I isolate are explicitly stated by Aristotle. The Sensory Representation Principle is implied by the broad notion of the functions of the perceptual faculty found in the Aristotelian corpus and by the arguments that Aristotle employs to justify this conception. For instance at *De An.* 425b14–15 he argues that since apperceptual judgments involve the apprehension of sensible characters, such judgments are made through a sensory faculty.

3. Direct textual evidence for the Psychophysical Principle is found at *De An.* 403a16–31, 403b7–9, 412a20–22, 412a27–28, 412b18–21; *De Sens.* 436a7–10; *De Som.* 454a7–11. Indirect evidence is provided by *De An.* 406b14–25, 407b17–23, 414a20–25.

4. A psychical state has a physiological realization when the state enforms a particular physiological structure to yield a psychophysical state. The psychical description of the psychophysical state refers to the form of the state, the physiological description to the matter of the state.

5. *De An.* 418a3–4, 422b15–16, 424a1–3, 425b26–31, 429a15–17, 429b30, 430a7, 430a19–20. Cf. *De An.* 402b12–15, 415a18–22; *De Sens.* 449a13–19; *De Part. An.* 641b1–4.

6. *De An.* 425b12–17, 426b14–15; *De Mem.* 451a17–19 (cf. *De An.* 428b10–429a4); *De Ins.* 459a11–22.

7. The focal object is the representation of the intentional object of the cognitive state (except in cases where there is only an intentional object). For instance, red is the focal object of the state of seeing red. Since for Aristotle *phantasmata* (sensory representations) are involved in nonsensory cognitive activities, there are some cases where the focal object of the cognitive state is an intelligible object, even though the thinker employs a sensory representation to think about that object. A thinker might, for example, employ a *phantasma* of a red object to think about the essence of color.

8. *De An.* 414b20–33, 415a12–23. Cf. *Phys.* 184a11–16; *De Part. An.* 641b6–8.

9. *De An.* 403a16–31, 407b17–23, 414a20–25.

10. The one exception is thinking, which Aristotle is reluctant to assign to a bodily organ. Nevertheless, he makes human thought dependent upon the body by making it dependent upon *phantasmata*, which are provided by a perceptual faculty, the faculty of imagination (*De An.* 431a17, 432a13–14; cf. 403a8–10). Plato by contrast appeals to psychophysical states only when absolutely necessary and treats the emotions and desire as mental phenomena (*Phil.* 47a and 35c respectively.)

11. For the sake of clarity I use the following terminology: *psychical* is used for the formal cause of a psychophysical state; *physiological* for the material cause of a psychophysical state; and *psychological* for the composite psychophysical state.

12. The distinction between matter and form is fundamental to Aristotle's account of change and allows him to meet certain difficulties he finds in his predecessors' accounts. See especially *Phys.* I, 7–9.

13. The identification of form with the principle of organization is charac-

teristic of the doctrine of the central books of the *Metaphysics*. See especially VII, 3 and 17, and VIII, 2.

14. *De An.* 412a20. Cf. *De An.* 412a21–22, 412a27–8; *Met.* 1035b14–23.

15. This passage uses *ophthalmos* both for the eye and the matter of the eye. I have followed tradition and substituted "pupil" (*korē*) for the latter in accordance with *De An.* 413a3. Although few commentators would follow Torstrik's suggested emendation of the text, namely, the insertion of *to sunolon, he de korē* at 412b20, most would agree that this is the sense of the passage (cf. Hicks 1907, 317). In sec. 5, Aristotle's disconcerting practice of using the name of a bodily organ for the functional organ and for its matter will be discussed at greater length.

16. A functional description as I am using the term makes reference to the function of the organ in the sense defined by Wright 1973, 161: "The function of X is Z means (a) X is there because it does Z and (b) Z is a consequence (or result) of X's being there."

17. As mentioned (n. 10), there is some tension between Aristotle's desire to give a unified explanation of psychological states on a psychophysical model and his desire to recognize the uniqueness of human rationality. How well he succeeds in reconciling these desires is considered in chap. 5.

18. In chap. 3 I defend the claim that the formal description of the exercise of a special sense is stated in terms of a *logos* of opposite sensible qualities.

19. Cf. *De An.* 424a5–10. For a detailed discussion of color, see *De Sens.* 3. In recent discussions, *melas* and *leukos* are often translated "dark" and "light" respectively following Owen 1965, 98. I prefer to preserve their usual sense as color terms. Black/dark and white/light are used here in keeping with *De Sens.* 439b17–19: "Thus the same conditions which in air produce light (*phōs*) and darkness (*skotos*) in bodies produce white (*leukon*) and black (*melan*)."

20. These issues are discussed in greater detail in chap. 5.

21. In light of the proliferation of articles and books on the topic of functionalism, I list only a few of the more important contributions here: Armstrong 1968; Fodor 1965, 1968; Lewis 1966, 1972, 1980; and Putnam 1960, 1967. See chap. 1, sec. 3.

22. Important defenders of this position are Armstrong 1968, 1977 and Lewis 1966, 1972, 1980.

23. A phenomenal feature is a feature of an object as experienced; it is a raw feel.

24. In this instance I agree with Robinson 1978, which is highly critical of Sorabji's attempt on Aristotle's behalf to find behavioral-functional descriptions of psychological states.

25. Throughout this work, I talk about being aware of sensible qualities; Aristotle's preferred term is *aisthanesthai* (to sense/to perceive), but he uses this verb in contexts where the sense is clearly that of being aware. For instance at *De Mem.* 450b17–18, he speaks of "perceiving" (*aisthanetai*) the memory image. In the *De Somno*, he makes "perceiving" the criterion of being awake (454a2–4). According to Aristotle, we know (*gnōrizomen*) the present through perception (*De Mem.* 449b13–14; cf. *De An.* 427a18–21), and perception is a

kind of *gnōsis* (recognition, knowledge) (*De Gen. An.* 731a30–34; *Met.* 981b11–31; *Pst. Anal.* 99b38–39; cf. *De Mem.* 450a9–12). Lyons 1963 analyzed Plato's use of words for knowing and discovered that Plato uses *gignōskein* for knowing in the sense of being aware of. Aristotle also uses *gignōskein* and its cognates in this sense, and he uses these terms to describe *aisthēsis*. Cf. Kahn 1966, which points out that *aisthēsis* can "cover the whole range of thought, feeling and perception" (pp. 72–73).

26. Cf. *De An.* 412a29–b6. The biological writings also suggest that Aristotle accepts biological functionalism. Aristotle takes into account the contribution of specific systems, such as the perceptual system to the well-being of the animal as a whole, and hence his explanations are functional/teleological in the traditional sense (cf. *De Part. An.* 642a7–13). Robinson 1978, on the other hand, takes modern philosophical functionalism as definitive of functionalism and then argues that Aristotle is not a functionalist.

27. See Modrak 1981d. Cf. Hicks 1907, lxviii–xlix.

28. The claim that the capacities of the percipient organ and the object are realized simultaneously is the crucial premise in Aristotle's argument to show that perceptual self-consciousness is a sensory capacity. Cf. Plato, *Charm.* 167cd, where the notion that there might be a type of vision that is self-aware but not aware of color or a type of hearing that is self-aware but not aware of sound is ridiculed; the passage concludes: "Now consider all the senses taken together. Does it seem to you that there is any sense which is a sense of itself and other senses but which does not perceive any of the objects of the other senses?"

29. This difficult doctrine is discussed in greater detail in chap. 3, as is the literalist reading of it by Sorabji 1974, 72. For an incisive account of the simultaneous actualization of the faculty and its object, see Kosman 1975.

30. *Entelecheia* occurs once in *De An.* I (402a26) in a discussion that foreshadows its later use. Although the definitions of the soul employ *entelecheia*, *entelecheia* and *energeia* are used interchangeably in II, 2 and II, 5; at 431a1–5 they occur in equivalent adverbial phrases. Similarly in the technical account of motion in *Phys.* III, 1, *entelecheia* is Aristotle's preferred term, but he also uses *energeia* in the same sense (201b9).

31. Cf. *De An.* 413b29–31, where the distinction between the perceptual faculty and the doxastic faculty is based on the difference between perceiving and believing. Even in the case where one faculty is a component of another, as in the case of imagination and the perceptual faculty, the difference in function is made the basis for distinguishing between them. Cf. *De Ins.* 459a15–23.

32. The statement that that which is potentially X insofar as it is potentially X cannot become actually X without the intervention of something else is for Aristotle a conceptual truth (cf. *Met.* 1046a23–29; *De An.* 417a17–18). Aristotle argues in *Metaphysics* IX, 8 that actuality is prior to potentiality in definition, substantiality and time.

Because Aristotle distinguishes between potential and actual sense objects, he is able to distinguish between the object as it exists in the world and the impression it creates (cf. *Met.* IV, 5). However, even in the case of hallucinations, Aristotle makes the sensory experience a consequence of some features of the external world acting on our sense organs (cf. *De Ins.* 460b1–23).

33. Brentano 1973, bk. 2, chap. 1. See also Brentano's study of Aristotle's psychology ([1867] 1967).

34. It is arguable that certain moods and fleeting emotions are objectless; cf. Armstrong 1968, 120.

35. Cf. Chisholm 1967. See also the discussion of intentionality in chap. 6, sec. 2.

36. The referent of the memory image, according to Aristotle, is the original perceptual situation that gave rise to the image. See chap. 4, sec. 2.

37. Hamlyn 1968a, 104, would limit the Actuality Principle to the physical/ physiological basis of perception. This is a hard position to maintain in light of the textual evidence. The Actuality Principle is more typically asserted in connection with the faculty *(aisthētikon)* than with the sense organ *(aisthētērion)*; see, e.g., *De An.* 418a3–4, 422b15–16, 424a13, 431b26.

38. The thesis that the object of an apperceptual judgment is a sense object is a direct consequence of the Actuality Principle. The character of a sensing is determined by its object, so the sensing cannot be the object of any further awareness except in relation to the sense object that gives it its character.

39. Cf. Schofield 1978, 99–102, on the differences between our conception of imagination and Aristotle's conception of *phantasia*. The unique character of Aristotelian *phantasia* will be discussed in chap. 4, sec. 1.

40. Talking about "representation" in connection with Aristotle may seem anachronistic, and indeed the terminology is mine not his. Yet this modern terminology seems to capture what Aristotle has in mind when he says that spoken words resemble thoughts *(De Int.* 16a3–4). In a similar vein, Plato proposes to define thinking as internal dialogue *(Theaet.* 189e; *Soph.* 263e).

41. *De An.* 431b2–11, 433a9–12; *De Motu An.* 700b17–25, 701a29–702a20, 703b18–19; cf. *Met.* 980b25–27.

42. Cf. *De An.* 427b28. The latter might be read as a reference to two components of thought, namely, imagination and judgment (cf. Hicks 1907, 460). Since *De An.* 433a10 cannot be read in the same way, it is better to give a uniform reading of these two, very similar passages. According to this reading, *phantasia* is a degenerate form of thinking (a kind of [*tis*] thinking) that does not require the possession of the rational faculty because it employs sensory representation only.

43. These claims will be defended in chap. 4, sec. 4, and chap. 5, sec. 4.

44. A type of representation that employs sensory characters rather than linguistic-like elements, it might be thought, can at best have a very limited function. Such representation is limited to resemblance, it is argued, and resemblance requires recognition and interpretation. These claims have the ring of philosophical commonplaces. Nonetheless, there is good reason to question their cogency. Schwartz 1981 raises a number of telling objections to the "obvious" distinctions, such as the distinction between pictorial and symbolic representation or the distinction between analog and digital systems, which are cited in support of imposing restrictions on sensory representation.

45. A number of philosophers have sought to analyze perception in terms of the acquisition of information, e.g., Goldman 1977, or the acquisitions of beliefs, e.g., Close 1976, 1980; Pitcher 1971; and Armstrong 1961. See chapter 4, n. 69.

46. The present state of the controversy is aptly summed up by Russow 1978, 57: "Of all the doctrines that come under fire from modern philosophy of mind, the idea that we see mental pictures seems to be one of the hardest to get rid of. Despite numerous attacks presented by philosophers from Ryle to Dennett, there are still many arguments to be found in defense of mental images; the issue has by no means been decided." For sample contributions to each side of the debate, see Block 1981.

Recently philosophers have made various accommodations to the findings of psychologists. For example, Fodor 1981 grants that images under a description may represent but refuses to allow them to serve as vehicles of truth.

47. See, for instance, Bruner 1966, chap. 1, which identifies the second stage of human cognitive development, usually reached by the age of one, with "ikonic representation." Fodor 1981 criticizes Bruner on the grounds that thinking is never purely iconic; rather images under one interpretation or another serve as the vehicles of internal representation.

48. For a survey of these findings, see Kosslyn 1980, chap. 3; see also Kosslyn et al. 1981 and Brown and Herrnstein 1981. This is not to say that there is a consensus among psychologists about the correct interpretation of these findings. Pylyshyn 1981, for instance, is very critical of Kosslyn's work.

49. Aristotle is not a thoroughgoing reductionist. He is willing to introduce new elements when necessary to explain higher-order phenomena; for instance, he allows the perceptual faculty as a whole to have certain properties that cannot be reduced to functions of the individual senses making up the perceptual faculty.

50. See especially *Pst. Anal.* I, 2, 6–10. Aristotle's epistemology will be discussed in greater detail in chap. 7.

51. The character and import of the first principles have been insightfully discussed by Bolton 1976, Ferejohn 1982, and Gomez-Lobo 1976–77.

52. For a perspicuous account of the discrepancies see Barnes 1969. The solution that Barnes proposes—that in the *Posterior Analytics* Aristotle is concerned with pedagogy not justification—is subject to a number of difficulties. Most important, it does not resolve the problems with which we started, namely, the discrepancy between Aristotle's practice and the requirements of *epistēmē* as stated in the *Posterior Analytics*. Not only is there a presumption that Aristotle is setting out the results of scientific inquiry in the other treatises, there is also the presumption that he is setting these findings out for students; so if Barnes is right, we would expect the other treatises to conform to the standards of the *Posterior Analytics*. Barnes attempts to head off this objection by distinguishing between formal instruction and reports of research in progress, but there is no reason to believe that Aristotle distinguished between the two. Cf. Burnyeat 1981, 115–20.

53. Aristotle's characteristic way of introducing a particular subject matter,

namely the self-conscious assertion of the boundaries of a particular inquiry and the discussion of methodology, including the recognition of different epistemic standards in different areas (cf. *E.N.* 1094b12–28), attests to his commitment to specialized disciplines.

54. Similarly when Aristotle gets down to business in the third book of the *Metaphysics*, he defines metaphysics as the study of being; in *Top.* I, 1, the subject matter is defined as dialectical reasoning; and the *Poetics* opens with the following line: "Concerning poetry, I propose to speak not only of the art in general but also of its species and their respective capacities" (1447a8–9). In some treatises (the *De Memoria*, for example), the description of the genus is omitted or only alluded to, presumably because it is assumed to be obvious to all, and Aristotle plunges immediately into the differentiation of the species.

55. In *De An.* III, 1–2, the perception of the common objects, perceptual self-awareness, and apperceptual judgments about unity and difference are added to the functions of the perceptual faculty; in III, 3 *phantasia* is added. On the grounds that *phantasia* is an activity of the perceptual faculty, Aristotle ascribes memory and dreaming to the perceptual faculty in the *Parva Naturalia*.

56. *De An.* II, 4 is devoted to a cursory account of the nutritive soul; the mechanisms involved in the nutritive functions (digestion, reproduction, respiration, etc.) are discussed in detail in the biological treatises.

57. While the identification of perception with alteration *(alloiōsis)* may represent the received view (cf. Hicks 1907), Aristotle makes it his own as evidenced by his use of *kinēsis* and its cognates in descriptions of sensing (see, e.g., *De An.* 418a31, 419a10, 419a13–15; cf. *Phys.* 244b2–245a12).

58. Here *alloiōsis* is qualified by *tis*, as it is in a similar passage in the *De Insomniis* (459b6); cf. Aristotle's use of *pōs* and *ti* at *Phys.* 244b11 and 244b13 respectively. See also Barnes 1971–72, 109.

59. Aristotle sometimes mentions an intermediate state of learning where the learner is neither completely ignorant nor knowledgeable (*De An.* 417b12; cf. *Phys.* 255a33–b5).

60. The integral connection between the Actuality Principle and the distinction between two types of alteration is signaled by Aristotle's use of *kathaper eirētai* at *De An.* 418a4. This in fact is the first statement of the Actuality Principle, but Aristotle takes it to be implied by the preceding discussion of alteration. Cf. Philoponus, *De An. Comm.* 309, 11–15.

61. How to interpret Aristotle's statement that the sensible form is received without its matter is a hard question that will be discussed in further detail in chap. 3, sec. 1.

62. For instance, color is a ratio of black to white (cf. *De An.* 422b24), but it is also described as that which moves the transparent medium (*De An.* 418a31) and as the limit of the transparent in a body (*De Sens.* 439b12–13). Cf. *De Gen. An.* 780a3–4.

63. Earlier in the chapter I followed tradition and translated *korē* as "pupil." This translation is somewhat misleading because the pupil is not the organ of sight, but the *korē* is. Of late it has become fashionable to translate *korē* "eye jelly" (following Sorabji 1974, 72, n. 22). Eye jelly is not an altogether happy

choice because the term corresponds to nothing in our physiological vocabulary; another possibility is vitreous liquid. Nonetheless, of the three, eye jelly seems the better choice and will be used here.

64. *De An.* 425a4; *De Sens.* 438a6; *De Part. An.* 656b1–3; *De Gen. An.* 779b23–6; cf. *De Sens.* 438a13–15, 438b6–8.

65. The relation between the physical characteristic that brings about the perception of a proper object and the proper object itself is to be understood as the relationship between potential and actual sense object and simultaneously as the relation between matter and form. Aristotle repeatedly identifies matter with potentiality (see esp. *Met.* IX, 7). In the case at hand, the physical characteristic is a potential sense object and the material cause of the actual sense object. The physical characteristic may be described materially or it may be described formally as a disposition for bringing about a certain sort of experience.

66. In the *De Anima*, color is defined as that which has the capacity to change *(kinētikon)* the transparent; color changes *(kinei)* the transparent medium, and the medium changes the sense organ (*De An.* 418a31, 419a10, 419a13–15; cf. 431a17, 434b27–29). It is noteworthy that when the physical substratum of perception is under discussion, Aristotle is willing to use *kinēsis* and its cognates without further qualification.

67. One might argue that the *logoi* of opposites that constitute the sensible forms are physical characteristics, that the *logos* in question is a property of a pigment, or a property of a sound wave, or a temperature. But Aristotle distinguishes between physical *logoi* and sensible *logoi*. Plants are affected by the physical *logos* of hot to cold, but not by the sensible *logos*; hence plants wilt in the heat but do not feel the heat (*De An.* 424a32–b3). This point will be discussed in greater detail in chap. 3, sec. 1.

68. See n. 19. Aristotle extends the analysis of colors as ratios of black to white to the account of color qua physical characteristic in the *De Sensu* at 439b22–440b25.

69. Although Aristotle seeks to reduce every proper object to a ratio of a fundamental pair of opposites, he expresses some reservations about this project in *De An.* II, 11. In the case of sound, besides the basic pair of sharp and flat, he mentions loudness, faintness, smoothness and roughness (422b30–31). It is noteworthy that all of these are "felt" characteristics of sound.

70. Here again Aristotle mentions other pairs of opposites—the pungent and the astringent, and the acidic and the oily (*De An.* 421a30).

71. *De An.* 422b25–33. Cf. *De Part. An.* 647a16–19. In the *De Generatione et Corruptione*, Aristotle argues that the other tactile qualities reduce to the basic four—hot and cold, wet and dry (329b34, 330a24–26; cf. *De An.* 423b27–29). Brentano concludes on the basis of Aristotle's failure to reduce the proper object of touch to a single pair of opposites that touch is not a single sense faculty for Aristotle ([1867] 1967, 83). It is arguable that Aristotle ought to have drawn this conclusion, but there is little evidence that he did. The unity of the haptic system continues to perplex psychologists. Cf. Gibson 1966, chaps. 6–7, whose "tentative classification of the subsystems of the haptic system"

consists of cutaneous touch, haptic touch, dynamic touching, touch-temperature and touch-pain.

72. The considerable body of textual evidence for this claim is cited in n. 25.

73. The point of this preliminary discussion is to raise doubts about whether Aristotle subscribes to any form of psychophysical reductionism. In the next section I distinguish between two positions that might be attributed to Aristotle: (1) the state referred to by a psychical description is a physiological state and (2) the state referred to by a psychophysical description is a physiological state. I shall argue that Aristotle accepts neither (1) nor (2).

74. Cf. *Top.* 156a30. The open-endedness of the *De Anima* definition and the description of the formal definition as the rhetorician's definition are evidence that the formal definition in the *De Anima* should be treated as an abbreviated version of the definition in the *Rhetoric* and the *Topics*. For a summary of the ancient tradition that takes this definition to be Aristotle's own, see Sandys 1877, II:8.

75. The Platonic soul is a pilot in the body, so the most troublesome of these passages is explicable as a dialectical question raised on behalf of the Platonists. Pace Robinson 1983, which argues that Aristotle takes the analogy quite seriously.

76. I am using *dualism* in the modern sense; it is the doctrine that the soul is a distinct, immaterial substance. Plato subscribes to a two-substance conception of the human being where each substance has a radically different nature (see the *Phdo. passim*). As will be seen, many pre-Socratic accounts are dualistic in another sense in that they posit a distinct psychic substance, albeit a material one that permeates the body.

77. Cf. *De An.* 427a17–19. Aristotle's objective in *De An.* I is to establish the need for a radical new approach to psychological explanation, namely, the need for a psychophysical analysis. To do this, Aristotle amasses a wealth of information about earlier views. Theophrastus carries this project still further in his *De Sensibus*, which again is highly critical of earlier accounts.

78. *De An.* 403b31–404a9, 405a8–13, 406b26–407a20. In a similar vein, Anaximenes identified the soul with air (DK 13, B2) and Heraclitus, with fire (DK 22, B77, B117, B118). The latter has been disputed by Kahn 1979, which argues that Heraclitus also identifies the soul with air.

79. With respect to Plato, Aristotle aims his objections at the physiological account of perception found in the *Timaeus* (45b–46c; 61d–68d). Had he spoken to Plato's claim that the ultimate subject of perception is the *psuchē* (*Theaet.* 184d), Aristotle would no doubt have criticized Plato for failing to explain how physiological changes are communicated to an immaterial soul.

80. See the discussion of the Analytic Principle in sec. 1. See also Oppenheim and Putnam 1958; Smart 1959; Rorty 1965; and Armstrong 1968. Not all philosophers agree that the reduction of psychology will require psychophysical identity statements (see, e.g., Kim 1966); others argue against the very possibility of a successful reduction (see, e.g., Davidson 1970).

81. Cf. *De An.* 403a31–b1: "[anger is] a boiling of the blood or warm substance surrounding the heart."

82. Science as Aristotle conceives it deals with general principles that hold without exception or for the most part; so if Aristotle were interested in establishing psychophysical identities, he would presumably be especially interested in type identities.

83. *De An.* 421b9–422a6; *Hist. An* 492a23–29, 503a2–6, 504a20–23, 505a33–35, 532a5–17; *De Gen. An.* 781b23–24; *De Part. An.* 656a35–37, 657a17–24, 658b27–659b19, 660a16, 678b6–13.

84. In recent discussions, type-type identity statements are understood to hold across species. See, for example, Lewis 1980 and Putnam 1967. However, it would be conceptually possible to soften this position and make type-type identities species-specific. This would avoid some of the standard objections to type-type identity statements.

85. Cf. Gotthelf 1976, which argues that according to Aristotle, a functional system cannot be reduced to the sum of the actualizations of the element potentials, that is, that the formal/final cause of an organism cannot be reduced to the material cause.

86. In *De Sens.* 6, Aristotle discusses the changes brought about in the medium and comments on the difference between the kind of change involved in the case of the visual medium and the media for hearing and smelling. The change in the visual medium is a case of alteration (qualitative change), whereas the change in the case of the other two media is a case of spatial movement (446a20–447a11; cf. *De An.* 434b27–435a8). It might be thought that when Aristotle appears to describe the same psychophysical event as a *kinēsis* and as an *energeia*, he is being sloppy and that were he pressed he would opt for one or the other. However, in *De Gen. et Corr.* I, 4, he seems to countenance the use of *genesis* and *alloiōsis*—terms he had been at pains to distinguish between—for the same change; which term is appropriate is determined by the description of the initial and final states (319b25–31). Cf. Code 1976; Joachim [1922] 1970, 109.

87. In support of the view that Aristotle is a materialist, several commentators recently have tried to formulate his position by reinterpreting or weakening the conditions for identifying the mental with the physical. Hence Hartman 1977 claims that in the case of perception, the physical event and the psychological event are accidentally identical, i.e., that each is necessary and sufficient for the other (pp. 167–219); Charles 1984 attributes ontological materialism to Aristotle where the occurrence of the physical event is non-causally sufficient for the occurrence of the psychological event (pp. 213–36). Neither of these approaches captures Aristotle's insistence upon the primacy of form over matter.

88. Aristotle's conception of the relation between the physiological and the psychological is better captured by the notion of composition than by identity. Cf. Boyd 1980.

89. Even though this type of objection is frequently brought to bear against

the Psychophysical Identity Theory, the issue of coherence can also be raised in the case of composition.

90. The only argument Aristotle gives for the Psychophysical Principle is empirical (*De An.* 403a19–22).

91. The discussion of the different ways of defining anger is preceded by a definition of anger where the definiendum is *to orgizesthai* (to be angry) (*De An.* 403a26). Presumably this definition, which has a formal and a physiological component, is the definition that Aristotle means to recommend; thus the choice of *to orgizesthai* over the noun *orgē* may be Aristotle's way of indicating that occurent anger is the object of the sample definitions. Nor would this be surprising since first actualities should be defined in terms of second actualities.

92. Besides Hardie 1976, critics of psychological hylomorphism include Ackrill 1972–73, which finds the theory hopelessly flawed, and Sorabji 1974, whose objections are not to the doctrine itself but to Aristotle's failure to give satisfactory formal descriptions of psychophysical states.

93. Cf. *Met.* 1023b25, 1035b25, 1036b31–32.

94. Ackrill 1972–73 does not defend the demand for an independent specification of the matter of a compound, except to say that if such a specification is not available it is not possible to "explain what it is that *is* this" (p. 133). While it is undeniably true that a full accounting of the matter of a composite would require such a specification, it is not obvious that the distinction between form and matter depends upon the possession of an independent specification of the matter.

95. Even its harshest critics do not argue that the doctrine is incoherent. Charlton 1970, 129–45, argued at length that Aristotle does not subscribe to the doctrine of prime matter; cf. King 1956; Wieland 1962, 209; Schofield 1972; Jones 1974, 494–97. Solmsen 1958, Robinson 1974, and Dancy 1978 defended the traditional view of prime matter against these critics.

96. The proponent of prime matter, for instance, might argue in this way: "Fire," "earth," "air" and "water" have recognizable referents and the form of each is specifiable, e.g., the form of fire is the hot-and-dry. To say that the matter of fire is prime matter is to say that prime matter is the stuff enformed by the hot-and-dry to constitute fire.

97. On Aristotle's description of embryogenesis in *De Gen. An.* II, organic matter is transformed into increasingly complex organic structures. The nutritive soul is the first to be acquired through the development of the relevant organs; then the sensitive soul is acquired, etc. (*De Gen. An.* II, 3). Cf. *De Part. An.* 646b5–8: "So that it must necessarily be that the elementary material exists for the sake of the homogeneous parts, seeing that these are genetically posterior to it, just as the heterogeneous parts are posterior genetically to them." See also *Met.* 1042b28–31 on the relative complexity of the form of bodily organs.

98. Aristotle would seem to be on well-trodden ground here. The presumption that terms referring to emotions have a "mentalist" sense given by a commonsense psychology has been widely accepted by philosophers both in the past and in the present. For instance, the most frequently asserted objections

to the Psychophysical Identity Theory are based on this feature of ordinary psychological language; cf. Smart 1959.

99. The physiological basis of desire is discussed at length in *De Motu An.* 7–10, where it is identified with the heating and cooling of bodily parts, particularly of the heart. The contraction and expansion of muscles, which comes about as a result of the change in temperature, are the material causes of overt bodily movements.

100. Nor is this feature peculiar to psychological terms; Aristotle allows the context and the interests of the speaker to determine the referent of the names of other composites. Although its primary referent is the composite in question, the name may also refer to the form or the matter. For instance, *house* may mean a shelter made of bricks and stones (the composite) or simply a shelter (the form) or simply the bricks and stones (*De An.* 403b3–7; cf. *Met.* 1043a14–21).

Chapter 3

1. *De An.* 424a2–5, 424a24–b3, 426a27–b7; *De Sens.* 449a20.
2. A sensible quality, as I use the term, is a phenomenal feature; a sensible quality is either a property that a physical object possesses qua object of perception or it is an internal representation of such a property in the absence of an external object of sense.
3. The analysis of sense objects in the *De Sensu* is framed in terms of *logoi* of opposite qualities (439b27, 440a13, 440b19, 442a12–17, 442b17–19, 448a8–12). Compare with *De An.* 426a27–b3; cf. *Met.* 1043a11–12.
4. Bonitz cites a large number of passages where Aristotle uses *logos* in mathematical contexts; *Index Aristotelicus* (Berlin, 1870), 437, a40–b30.
5. See Theophrastus, *De Sensibus*, 59; cf 79.
6. One quality from each pair determines the nature of the basic kinds of matter. Although purer, the elements are analogous to earth (dry and cold), air (hot and wet), fire (hot and dry) and water (cold and wet) *De Gen. et Corr.* II, 3.
7. In *De An.* III, 1, Aristotle argues from the existence of only four elements to the existence of only five senses (424b22–425a13). While the argument appears garbled and the identification of each sense organ with a different element seems to be a view Aristotle takes over from the pre-Socratics (cf. *De Part. An.* 647a8ff.), the very fact that he addresses this issue is further evidence that in Aristotle's mind the physical structure of the world and our perceptual capacities are inextricably bound up together. As post-Kantians, we may be perplexed by Aristotle's understanding of the causal connection here. Rather than supposing that because we have certain perceptual capacities our physical theories have certain characteristics, Aristotle assumes that the world has the characteristics attributed to it by our physical theories, from which it follows that our perceptual system has certain characteristics.
8. In some instances (e.g., in the case of musical sounds and some colors),

the *logos* may be represented abstractly by a numerical ratio (*De Sens.* 439b27–440a6, 440b14–21; *De An.* 426b4–7; cf. *Pst. Anal.* 90a18, 90a20, 90a22).

9. Cohen 1982 argues that for Aquinas the distinctive feature of the reception of sensible form without matter is the association of feelings of pleasure and pain with perceptions; irrespective of the merits of this interpretation as it applies to Aquinas's doctrine, it cannot be extended to Aristotle's account. For Aristotle, the distinctive feature of the reception of the sensible form is the actualization of a *logos* of sensible qualities.

10. Of all the proper objects, color receives the most detailed treatment as a *logos*, but Aristotle believes that similar analyses could be propounded for the others (*De Sens.* 442a12–17; cf. 442b17–19).

11. Cf. *De An.* 426a8–19. Aristotle uses *chroma* for the potential sense object but deplores ordinary language's failure to provide a term for color-as-actualized. See also *Met.* 1010b30–37; cf. *Phys.* 201b4–5. In terms of modern classifications, Aristotle's theory of perception resembles critical realism more closely than any other view; Aristotle's position differs in important respects from the naïve realist's and the representational realist's. Several modern theories reduce the content of a perception to a purely propositional structure and thus eliminate sensuous contents from consideration. The epistemic theory of perception accomplishes this by reducing perceptions to beliefs (Armstrong 1961, 1968; Close 1976, 1980; Heil 1982; Pitcher 1971; Runzo 1977, 1982). The adverbial theory takes sensuous features adverbially; see, e.g., Tye 1984a, 1984b. Neither of these approaches would appeal to Aristotle. See also Wright 1984 for a survey of recent philosophical discussions of perception.

12. Hamlyn 1968a would limit the description of a sense as a *mesotēs* to the relationship between certain physical features of the sense organ and similar features of the external object (pp. 112–13). Sorabji 1974 would identify the unity of the sense and its object with the literal taking on of the physical characteristic in question (p. 72, n. 22; p. 74, n. 28); and Barker 1981 would limit to special cases the claim that hearing is a *logos*.

13. Cf. Hamlyn 1968a; Barnes 1971–72 raises a similar objection to mine (p. 109). Burnyeat ("Is Aristotle's Philosophy of Mind Still Credible?" cited in n. 7, chap. 1) points out that the literalist interpretation is also problematic in the case of touch.

14. This passage (*De An.* 424a32–b3) forecloses the possibility that the *mesotēs* and/or *logos* in question is simply the arrangement of the constituents of the organs. A plant lacks the functional organization characteristic of a sense organ for heat and thus lacks the perceptive *mesotēs*.

15. Sorabji 1974 argues that the eye jelly literally becomes colored. According to him, the literalist interpretation improves Aristotle's account of perceiving by making colorings and soundings and other realizations of sensible qualities physiological (p. 72). If the hand feels heat by becoming hot itself, Aristotle has an explanation for why temperature rather than some other quality is experienced. Cf. Slakey 1961, 474. I cannot agree with these commentators for it is hard to see why the bare fact that the flesh has changed temperature should be a sensing of heat whereas the bare fact of a change in temperature

in a plant or a rock is not. Aristotle makes a similar argument against identifying the image in an eye with the awareness of the reflected object (*De Sens.* 438a10–13).

16. Aristotle explains the fact that *phonē* and its cognates are used of musical instruments by appealing to the similarities between the sounds of musical instruments and the voices of ensouled creatures (*De An.* 420b6–9). A musical sound is then a *phonē* only in a derivative sense.

17. If so, the argument is inductive in the nontechnical sense, that is, it is an argument from particular cases to a universal claim. It does not have the form of an inductive syllogism.

18. Cf. Hamlyn 1968a, 128–29; 1968b, 196. I have shown elsewhere that all these operations are functions of the common sense (Modrak 1981a).

19. Philoponus believes that *koinē aisthēsis* is not used in the technical sense at *De An.* 425a27, but this is because he misconstrues Aristotle's notion of the common sense (*De An. Comm.* 460, 17–19).

20. For a detailed analysis of this argument see Modrak 1981c.

21. The argument at *De An.* 425a14–24 divides into two parts. The first concludes with *hoste delon . . . kinēseōs* (425a20–21). At 425a21 *houto* introduces a further argument, which also concludes with the statement that there is not a special sense for the *koina*.

22. Some commentators have suggested that *kata sumbebēkos* at *De An.* 425a15 is a corruption since it appears to contradict *ou kata sumbebēkos* at 425a28. Philoponus (454, 5–13) makes *kata sumbebēkos* at 425a15 conditional upon the hypothetical claim that there is a sixth sense for the common sensibles, which Aristotle rejects. Torstrik 1862 emends the first phrase to *ou kata sumbebēkos*; this leads both commentators to misconstrue Aristotle's argument, making it turn upon the claim that the *koina* are perceived *kath' hauta*. Ross 1961 suggests (not very helpfully) that Aristotle uses *kata sumbebēkos* at 425a15 to indicate that the *koina* are not special objects and that he uses *ou kata sumbebēkos* at 425a28 to contrast the *koina* with incidental objects. Hamlyn 1968a recognizes that Aristotle's intention is to distinguish between the perception of the *koina* by a special sense and the perception of the *koina* by the common sense (p. 117). Graeser 1978 argues at length for attributing the position asserted at 425a14–15 to Aristotle (pp. 81–85).

23. Since the common sense is made up of the special senses, we would never perceive the *koina* were a prior perception required.

24. The implications that Aristotle's analyses of apperceptual discriminations and reflexive awareness of sensing have for his conception of consciousness will be discussed in chap. 6, secs. 1 and 2.

25. For a detailed treatment of this passage, see Modrak 1981c.

26. Aristotle's theory of perception is formulated for normal percipients. Although discriminating between white and sweet would not be essential to the perceptual experience of a congenitally blind person, this case would not show that such discriminations are not characteristic of perceptual experience.

27. The perception of the difference between white and sweet is a direct result of the faculty's being affected by the white and sweet object.

28. The Sensory Representation Principle explains why Aristotle does not even entertain the hypothesis that the judgment in question is not a case of perception (cf. *De An.* 426b14–15).

29. For a lucid discussion of this argument, see Kosman 1975.

30. Pace Neuhaeuser 1878, which argues that *tēs protēs* (the first) at *De An.* 425b17 refers to the central organ rather than to the peripheral organ (pp. 63–64), but this reading makes Aristotle's argument (425b14–17) unintelligible.

31. Aristotle may also have in mind different cases in the two works. In the *De Anima* he is considering reflexive awareness from the perspective of an isolated sense modality; however, in higher animals such as ourselves, more than one sense is active at any given moment. When more than one sense is active, the object of reflexive awareness would be a perception resulting from the convergence of several senses and hence would fall under the common sense as in the *De Somno*.

32. When several senses perceive the same thing at the same time, they "perceive as one" (*hei mia*) (*De An.* 425a31). Cf. *De Sens.* 449a14–20. Judging as one is to be distinguished from several senses independently discerning the same difference, as is clear from *De Som.* 455a20.

33. Baeumker 1877 argues that in the case of seeing, hearing and smelling, the act of sensing occurs primarily in the peripheral organs (pp. 78–84). Although Baeumker overstates his case, he calls attention to an important truth, namely, that Aristotle treats the peripheral organs as parts of the perceptual system and not as mere transmitters of sensory impulses to the central organ.

34. See also Hamlyn 1968b, which develops this argument in further detail.

35. These reasons are stated at greater length in Modrak 1981a, 162–63. See also Modrak 1981c, 420–22, which establishes that the common sense of *De An.* III, 1 is the same faculty as that which recognizes sensible differences in III, 2.

36. *De An.* 425a27; *De Mem.* 450a11, 451a17; *De Som.* 455a16; *De Sens.* 449a17; cf. *De Sens.* 449a9.

37. *De An.* II, 6; cf. 425a24–b3, *Pr. Anal.* 43a33; *Met.* 1087a19. The *kath' hauto/kata sumbebēkos* distinction is found in a number of Aristotle's works. It typically marks the distinction between essential and accidental attributes. See *Pst. Anal.* 73b4, 74b12, 75a20; *Top.* 102b3, 103b17; *Met.* 1018a1, 1025a14, 1026b32, 1059a1, 1065a1. When applied to perceptual objects, this distinction indicates the causal role of the object in bringing about the perception. A characteristic that acts directly on a sense is perceived *kath' hauto*.

38. Cf. *Met.* 1010b3–11, 1062b33–1063a4; cf. *E.N.* 1176a13–16.

39. Cashdollar 1973 argues persuasively that incidental objects are genuine sensibles. The opposite view finds expression in several earlier commentaries; see, for example, Brentano [1867] 1967, 84; Beare 1906, 286ff.; Hicks 1907, 362–63; Block 1960, 94; Ross 1961, 271; Kahn 1966, 46.

40. C. Kahn has indicated (in correspondence) that he believes the incidental sensibles are properly *noēta*. While I agree that conceptualization is required for many of the incidental objects perceived by humans, I note that Aristotle

refers to them as *aisthēta* not *noēta*. Thus I believe that they are genuine *aisthēta*, which in the case of human beings are often informed by noetic activity but are not themselves noetic objects.

41. Pace Graeser 1978, which concludes after a lengthy investigation of the distinction between *kath' hauta* and *kata sumbebēkos* sensibles that "*kata sumbebēkos aisthēta* cannot claim to be proper *sensibilia* after all" (p. 90).

42. See n. 37.

43. *De Som.* 456a5–6; *De Juv.* 469a5–12, 469b4–7; cf. *De Som.* 455a21–26. In bloodless animals (insects, testacea, crustacea, and cephalopods), the central organ is also located in the middle of the body (cf. *De Som.* 456a12–22). For ease of discussion, I speak as if the heart and the vascular system were common to all percipients. To extend the discussion to the bloodless animals, we would need only to rephrase it in terms of the physiological analogues of the heart and blood in these animals.

44. Neuhaeuser 1878 argues that (in the *Parva Naturalia*) the common organ is not the heart but a psychic substratum existing in the heart (pp. 71–75). However, Aristotle, according to Neuhaeuser, makes the heart the common organ in the *De Partibus Animalium*. I see no reason to attribute two different views to Aristotle when the *Parva Naturalia* descriptions can easily be read as expressions of the same conception of the common organ as the one found in the *De Partibus Animalium* and other biological treatises. Webb 1982 follows Neuhaeuser in placing the common organ in the heart, and he makes the central organ *pneuma* contained in the heart.

45. Cf. Plato, who makes the brain the locus for the rational part of the soul (*Tim.* 69d, 73cd) and the ultimate recipient of sense impressions (64b). Also see Solmsen 1961, 163.

46. *De Part. An.* 666a6–9, 666a14–18; cf. *De Juv.* 469b4–7. At *De Part. An.* 667b23–31, Aristotle argues that the blood must have the same bodily source as perception.

47. Aristotle mentions blood in connection with sensory transmission at *De Ins.* 461a25–b21; *De Part. An.* 648a2–4, 650b19–23, 656b3–7.

48. Aristotle argues that the organ of touch is within the flesh (*De An.* 422b34–423b26; *De Part. An.* 656b34–37), and he puts its center in the heart so he may be toying with the notion that the organ of touch is simply the vascular system as a whole (cf. *De Sens.* 439a1; *De Part. An.* 656a29).

49. Aristotle describes the vascular system in detail in the *Hist. An.* III, 3–4. The role of blood as the source of nutriment is discussed at *De Part. An.* 650a3–b13 and *De Gen. An.* 740a18–b3. Although by and large the blood flows outward from the heart, some backflow toward the heart seems to occur when the animal sleeps (cf. *De Ins.* 461a25–b21).

50. By itself, this is not a serious difficulty. The motion in the sense organ that sets up the movement toward the central organ might be sufficient to overcome the outward motion to the extent necessary for the sensory impulse to reach the heart. Giving this objection a new slant, Webb 1982 argues that the transmission of sensory impulses must be instantaneous and hence cannot be through the blood (pp. 27–28, 32–34). However, the passages he cites as

evidence that Aristotle believes in instantaneous sensory transmission do not establish this point.

51. Following Ogle, Peck 1942 excises *De Part. An.* 656b19–22. It makes little difference whether we agree with Peck and Ogle here or follow Solmsen 1961 in retaining 656b19–22. The passage simply elaborates upon the thesis asserted at 666a17–18.

52. See, for instance, Peck 1942, Appendix B; Solmsen 1961, 171ff.; Verbeke 1978, 198–99; Webb 1982. The latter commentator also believes that the central organ consists of *pneuma* (pp. 33–34).

53. It is to Solmsen's credit that, even though he is a proponent of the *pneuma* interpretation, he notes the paucity of textual evidence for it (1961, 174). Solmsen correctly calls attention to the speculative character of Peck's account.

54. Another passage of doubtful authenticity, *De Gen. An.* 781a21–b6, develops this account in more detail. Cf. Peck 1942, 563–64.

55. Beare 1906 bases his argument, that *pneuma* conveys sensory impulses, almost entirely on *De Gen. An.* 744a2 and 781a21–b6; i.e., he generalizes from the case of hearing and smell to the rest of the senses (pp. 333ff.).

56. *De Som.* 456a13; *De Part. An.* 659b18; *De Motu An.* 703a10–14. Arguing that the latter passage contains a reference to the spurious *De Spiritu*, Bonitz and Zeller based their arguments against the authenticity of the *De Motu Animalium* on it, but most scholars now agree that the *De Motu* is a genuine Aristotelian treatise.

57. In insects, innate *pneuma* also plays the role in smelling played by inhaled *pneuma* in other animals (*De Part. An.* 659b14–19).

58. The organ of smell seems to consist of air in land animals and water in aquatic animals. The air-filled passages *(poroi)* are mentioned at *De Gen. An.* 744a2. Verbeke 1978 bases the claim that *pneuma* transmits sensory impulses on this passage (p. 198). But this does not suffice to establish the *pneuma* doctrine.

59. Cf. Solmsen 1961, 178ff. Solmsen credits Praxagoras, Aristotle's near-contemporary, with developing the notion of psychic *pneuma* as neural agent, although earlier Temkin 1945 had expressed reservations about whether Praxagoras used the expression "psychic *pneuma*" *(psuchikon pneuma)* (p. 55).

60. The conception of psychic *pneuma* is also found in the Stoics and in Alexander of Aphrodisias.

61. Solmsen 1961 bases his entire argument for the rejection of blood as the sensory messenger on its lack of sensation (pp. 172–73). Cf. Lloyd 1978, 234, n. 35.

62. If we attribute the distinction between an internal medium and a sense organ to Aristotle, the conflict between passages making blood a sensory agent and the one rejecting blood's claim to sentience vanishes.

63. Cf. Lloyd's conclusion: "Thus all his references to communications between the heart and the sense-organs, and between the heart and the brain, suffer from a greater or lesser degree of imprecision" (1978, 229).

64. Cf. *De An.* 418a23–24. See *Pst. Anal.* 73b10–15, where the distinction

between *kath' hauto* and *kata sumbebēkos* predications is explained in terms of causal connections.

65. Not only would the possession of fewer senses limit our knowledge, the possession of more would be superfluous (*De An.* 424b27–425a13).

66. For instance, in *An Essay Concerning Human Understanding*, bk. 2, Locke lists extension, figure, rest, motion, solidity and number under primary qualities.

67. Theophrastus gives a detailed account of Democritus' conception of sense objects (*De Sensibus* 49–82). Cf. *De Sens.* 442a29.

68. At *De An.* 428b27–30 Aristotle mentions mistakes that occur due to the perceiver's distance from the object. Ross 1961 appeals to this reference to distance to explain our susceptibility to error with respect to the common objects (p. 39). This is not very satisfactory because the *kath' hauto* perception of a *koinon* requires the employment of several senses, and this requirement diminishes the likelihood of the perceiver's being at a great distance from the object. Hamlyn 1968a states that Aristotle is influenced by Plato's arguments for the relativity of the common objects (p. 135); see also Hamlyn 1959. Even if Aristotle attributes a high degree of fallibililty to the perception of the *koina* because he is convinced by Plato's arguments, he still owes us an explanation of how this susceptibility to error is accommodated on his theory of perception.

69. See sec. 2 and n. 37.

Chapter 4

1. In the *De Sensu*, the *De Memoria* and the *De Somno*, Aristotle also speaks to questions about reflexive awareness in perception and the discrimination of sensible difference. All of these passages were discussed in chap. 3, sec. 2.

2. *Imagination* excludes the immediate awareness of objects in our environment and includes the manipulation of ideas. *Phantasia* (as Aristotle conceives it) includes the former and excludes the latter. Cf. Schofield 1978, 101 and 131–32, n. 15.

3. These explanations are found in a number of different works, most notably in the *De Anima*, the *De Memoria*, the *De Insomniis* and the *De Motu Animalium*.

4. Besides the problem of individuation, which Aristotle addresses, there are other problems that he ignores but that have baffled his commentators. Chief among these are questions about the coherence and consistency of his notion of *phantasia*. Aristotle includes under *phantasia* cases of imagery, i.e., cases of internal representation and cases of appearance, i.e., cases of direct sensory experience. The question of consistency arises because, as the crucial cognitive faculty in goal-directed behavior, *phantasia* must be a reasonably reliable source of information; but Aristotle repeatedly claims that *phantasia* is unreliable. For a more detailed treatment of these issues, see Modrak 1986; cf. Schofield 1978, 99, and Hamlyn 1968a, 131.

5. Here I appeal to standard conditions of the sort typically cited in psychological and philosophical discussions of perception. In the case of sight, these would include illumination by white light and certain constraints upon the distance between percipient and object.

6. I argue for this analysis of *phantasia* at greater length in Modrak 1986.

7. Cf. the definition of *phantasma* in Liddell and Scott's *A Greek-English Lexicon* (Oxford, [1843] 1968). The verb is *phainetai* (it seems or it appears that).

8. Cf. Plato's use of *phantasma* in the *Sophist*, where it is used for the (deceptive) appearance of a large work of art at a distance (236b) and for shadows and reflections (266bc); cf. *Rep* 510a. Schofield 1978 also argues this point at some length (pp. 116–18).

9. Plato occasionally uses *phantasma* for a conceptual object, e.g., at *Soph.* 234e.

10. Again, Plato's use is instructive; at *Soph.* 236c, he speaks of two types of image (eidolo)-making, one which is realistic (eikastikē) and one which is not; Plato describes the latter as *phantastikē*.

11. See the discussion of apperception in chap. 3, sec. 2.

12. As we have seen, the distinction between sense objects that are perceived *kata sumbebēkos* and those that are perceived *kath' hauta* is a distinction between objects in the world that are represented by complexes of sensible characters and the sensible characters. Because *phantasia* has the same objects as perception (*De An.* 428b12–13), it too has a complex of sensible characters as its immediate object. I will use *sensory content* as a generic term to cover the three types of sense object recognized by Aristotle. H. Ishiguro (1966) approaches the concept of imagination from a philosophical standpoint that is significantly different from Aristotle's, yet she too emphasizes the "intimate connection with perception" (p. 170).

13. Just as I have not translated *phantasia* to avoid misleading connotations, I shall not translate *phantasma(ta)*, which is Aristotle's term for the object of *phantasia* (cf. n. 16).

14. While imagination in our sense is not exercised through the peripheral organs, *phantasia* in some instances is. *Phantasia* includes nonveridical appearance, and even in the case of dreams the causal movements often arise in the peripheral organs and then travel to the common organ.

15. Other commentators, mistakenly, I believe, emphasize the amount of interpretation involved in nonveridical appearances and give *phantasia* the job of interpreting sensory information. Freudenthal 1863 says that *phantasia* completes the information supplied through perception (p. 47; cf. pp. 16, 54), and Nussbaum 1978 concludes that *phantasia* and *aisthēsis* are the "two aspects to be discerned in many perceptual activities" (p. 255).

16. Since *phantasia*'s object is always a sensory content, Aristotle uses a single term, *phantasma*, for its object in the preliminary definition of *phantasia* at 428a1–2. When describing cases of appearance, Aristotle typically does not employ *phantasma*, nor does he give the object of *phantasia* any other name.

Alexander's preferred term for the content of *phantasia* is *phantaston* (*De An. Mant.* 68, 25–30). But to my knowledge, Aristotle uses *phantaston* only once and then as an adjective, so following Aristotle's practice, I shall use *phantasma* as the generic name for the object of *phantasia*.

17. See sec. 2 for the detailed treatment of *mnēmē*; the use of a *phantasma* to represent an arbitrary case will be taken up again in chaps. 5 and 7.

18. The peculiar character of *phantasia* as intermediate between perception and thought has often been remarked upon; see, for example, Freudenthal 1863, 59; Schofield 1978, 123–26. More important is its role in mediating between perception and thought (see chap. 5, secs. 2 and 4, and chap. 7).

19. To say the *phantasma* is like an *aisthēma* is to say that it is a sensory content. Aristotle uses *aisthēma* infrequently, and he typically uses it for the sensuous content of a perception in contrast to the external object represented through the content (*De Ins.* 461b23; *Met.* 1010b33; cf. Rodier 1900, 525). *Aisthēma* occurs more frequently in the discussion of dreams than in any other context (*De Som.* 456a26; *De Ins.* 460b2, 461a19, 461b22).

20. Plato, for instance, uses *phantasma* to describe the appearance in a painting of a body that appears to be properly proportioned although the upper parts are actually disproportionally large (*Soph.* 236a–b; cf. *Rep.* 602c).

21. Type (1) cases are cited at *De An.* 428a14–15, 428b3–4; *De Ins.* 458b29, 460b4–18, 462a1–2; type (2) cases at *De An.* 428a6–8, 428a16; *De Ins.* 460b27–462a8.

22. One of Aristotle's favorite examples is the apparent size of the sun (*De An.* 428b3–4; *De Ins.* 458b29; *De Ins.* 460b18); another is the distorted perceptions of the ill (*De Ins.* 460b11–13; *E.N.* 1176a13–14).

23. Cf. n. 4. Freudenthal 1863, 47, gives a different account of this feature. He identifies *phantasia* with an inner picture that is brought into play to complete a perception occurring under nonstandard conditions. This works better for some cases, such as objects seen at a distance, than for others, such as the flavor of wine to a diseased tongue.

24. Let us summarize the differences between *aisthēsis* and *phantasia* stated at *De An.* 428a5–16: (a) *aisthēsis* is common to all animals; *phantasia* is not. (b) *Phantasia* need not be the immediate result of the stimulation of a sense organ by an external object; *aisthēsis* must be. (c) *Aisthēsis* provides reliable information about the world; *phantasia* need not. (See also Modrak 1986, especially nn. 13 and 14.) That *phantasia* occurs under different conditions than *aisthēsis* is implied by both (b) and (c).

25. Because he is reluctant to call a nonveridical sensory experience a perception *(aisthēsis)*, Aristotle uses *aisthēma* rather than *aisthēsis* or *aisthēton* in the causal account of dreaming; dream-*phantasmata* are effects of *aisthēmata* (*De Ins.* 461a19, b22).

26. Commentators have been puzzled by Aristotle's claim at *De An.* 428a11–12 that *aisthēsis* is always true and frequently have read 428b18–19 as a correction (e.g., Hicks 1907; Ross 1961). The puzzle vanishes, however, when we realize that the contrast between *aisthēsis* and *phantasia* is the contrast between

veridical perception and sensory experience occurring under conditions that are not conducive to veridical perception.

27. The distinction between having a sensory experience and experiencing an external object through a sense is explicitly drawn at *De Ins.* 459a2–6: "that one sees nothing in a dream is true, but that the sense is not affected is false."

28. See n. 24.

29. This is *phantasia*'s most important function in Aristotle's theory of the perceptual system, for *phantasia* becomes his device for extending the perceptual faculty to include memory, imagination (in our sense), and the cognitive component of goal-directed behavior.

30. Grene 1963, chap. 5, points out some of the strengths of Aristotle's theory of memory.

31. Only one commentator (Nussbaum 1978, 355) to my knowledge has questioned whether Aristotle endorses the second condition; she agrees that this is his position in the *De Memoria*, but she argues that the remark about memory at *De Motu An.* 702a5 is intended as a correction of his earlier view. While it is possible to read the *De Motu* text as Nussbaum does, it is equally possible to construe it in a way that is consistent with the *De Memoria*. The latter seems the wiser course since memory is mentioned in passing in the *De Motu* and discussed at length in the *De Memoria*.

32. Aristotelian scholars as well as modern philosophers of mind tend to conflate representation by complexes of sensible characters, i.e., sensory representation, with representation through resemblance. Nonetheless, it is possible to distinguish between the two claims (cf. Schwartz 1981, 116, 121–25). Granting this distinction, we need not be concerned by examples purporting to show that an image might represent something it does not resemble. Sorabji 1972 gives the following example (p. 3): a person remembers Smith by contemplating an image of an anvil. Whether such cases pose a threat to Aristotle's account of representation remains to be seen.

33. This is but another ramification of the Actuality Principle, which makes the actualization of the cognitive object determine the character of the cognitive act and hence the character of any subsequent (or simultaneous) apprehension of the cognitive act.

34. Aristotle's use of *epistametha* here suggests that the memory object under consideration is a universal; *ex hypothesi* a universal is never adequately exhibited by a complex of sensible characters.

35. Chap. 5 discusses the relationship between thought and the *phantasmata* employed in thinking.

36. See sec. 1 and chap. 5, sec. 4.

37. Sorabji 1972 draws upon a number of modern philosophical discussions of memory to criticize Aristotle's treatment of the memory image as an *eikōn* (pp. 2–12).

38. Cf. Martin and Deutscher 1966 on the difference between remembering events and remembering information.

39. Sorabji 1972, 10–11, believes that Aristotle answers this difficulty by appealing to a causal link that is a physical trace left by the original experience;

Sorabji then points out that this solution does not work. Fortunately for Aristotle, this is not his position. As is clear from *De Mem.* 1, Aristotle exploits the *eikōn*-condition to this end without mentioning the physiological basis of memory. This is not to deny that Aristotle appeals to a physical *pathos* to account for dispositional memory in *De Mem.* 2.

40. See Modrak 1981a, 165–66. Aristotle includes nonperceptual cognitions in larger perceptual wholes, as will be seen in chap. 6.

41. Presumably Aristotle would allow us to employ the image of a blue-eyed statue to remember a brown-eyed one, but it is unlikely he would allow us to claim that we remember the color of the eyes.

42. Aristotle is intent upon giving an account of *anamnēsis* that distinguishes between *anamnēsis* and learning and hence constitutes an alternative to Plato's doctrine that learning is merely *anamnēsis* (*Meno* 81c–86c). Nonetheless, Aristotle follows Plato in making associations of one sort or another the vehicle for *anamnēsis* (*De Mem.* 452a8–b8; cf. *Phdo.* 72e–73e).

43. Unfortunately, Aristotle's use of *hexis* and *pathos* in the *De Memoria* is not particularly systematic and engenders confusions. For the most part, he uses *hexis* to describe *mnēmē* (450a30; cf., 451a24) and *pathos* to describe the *phantasma* that is the focal object of *mnēmē* (450a11, 450a30, 450b18, 450b32). Neither of these descriptions is problematic; however, Aristotle also uses *pathos* for the structural physical change that is the basis of the *hexis* (453a15, 453a30). The latter is troublesome, for the *pathos* underlying a dispositional memory should not be confused with the *phantasma* that is the vehicle for an occurrent memory (Aristotle obliquely acknowledges the difference at 453a16).

44. Aristotle uses *phantasma* here (the only use of it in *De Mem.* 2) to indicate that the ultimate objective of the search is a cognitive object not a physiological state. The infrequent use of *phantasma* and the omission of *phantasia* from the discussion of *anamnēsis* is a further indication that *anamnēsis* is a cognitive strategy for producing actual memory; it is the process of actualizing a *phantasma*. When actualized, the *phantasma* is the vehicle for *mnēmē*; *mnēmē* is the outcome of a successful exercise of *anamnēsis*.

45. *Anamnēsis*, if successful, terminates in *mnēmē*, when the movement *(kinēsis)* corresponding to the object and the movement corresponding to the time occur simultaneously (*De Mem.* 452b23–24).

46. In chap. 5, I argue that the uniquely human character of rationality motivates Aristotle to posit a faculty for thought distinct from the perceptual faculty. However, Aristotle does postulate a type of desire *(boulēsis)* that is a uniquely human realization of the faculty of desire shared by other creatures, so the case of *anamnēsis* is not completely anomalous. Although Aristotle argues against the Platonic distinction between rational and irrational parts of the soul and Plato's tripartite division of the soul (*De An.* 432a22–b7), Aristotle never abandons the program set out in *De An.* II, 3 of analyzing the soul in terms of four or five basic faculties—the nutritive, the sensitive, the appetitive, the locomotive and the rational (414a31). (Sometimes he mentions the appetitive faculty as a fifth faculty; sometimes he treats it as part of the sensitive faculty.)

47. We investigate the possibility that rationality itself is an emergent property of the perceptual faculty in chap. 5, sec. 2.

48. Technically, the *De Divinatione per Somnum* addresses the question of divination through dreams, but it too is a source of information about Aristotle's notion of dreaming. Aristotle opts for a natural rather than a supernatural explanation of the ability apparently exhibited in some dreams to foresee the future. Cf. the Hippocratic treatise, *Regimen IV or On Dreams*, which was probably somewhat earlier in origin; its author does not deny that dreams might portend future events, but he urges his readers to look for explanations in terms of the body and to treat any incipient illness indicated by a dream.

49. This function of the common sense is discussed in chap. 6, sec. 1.

50. Lulofs 1947 bases his argument that *De Ins.* 2–3 is an earlier work than *De Ins.* 1 in part on the prevalence of physiological explanations in these chapters. Once we recognize that Aristotle's explanation of dreaming does not draw a sharp distinction between psychological and physiological explanations and that the ideal for him is an integrated psychophysical explanation, we can and should read the *De Insomniis* as one continuous exposition of a psychophysical explanation of dreaming. The other piece of evidence Lulofs cites (pp. xxx–xxxiii) is that the theory of vision found at 459b23–460a32 contradicts the theory of vision found in the *De Sensu*, but surely Biehl 1898 was right to question the authenticity of 459b23–460a32. As Biehl pointed out, this passage breaks the continuity of the argument; as Lulofs points out, it is inconsistent with Aristotle's standard account of vision.

51. Other animals besides human beings have memories and dreams. Aristotle attributes memory to animals at *De Mem.* 450a15–16, *E.N.* 1147b4–5, and *Met.* 980b20–28; he attributes dreaming to them at *De Div.* 463b11–12 and *Hist. An.* 536b28.

52. *De An.* 431b2–11, 433a9–12; *De Motu An.* 700b17–25, 701a29–702a20, 703b18–19; cf. *Met.* 980b25–27.

53. Nussbaum 1978 argues for the latter.

54. See chap. 6, sec. 1, where the general features of Aristotle's conception of the relationship between the perceptual faculty and the appetitive faculty are discussed.

55. *De An.* 431b3–9, 433a9–12, 433b12; *De Motu An.* 700b17–20, 703b18–19.

56. The most interesting part of practical reasoning, namely the weighing of pros and cons with respect to the performance of a particular action, is not captured by the practical syllogism. This has led a number of scholars to conclude that the practical syllogism is not meant to be a schematic representation of actual motivations. See n. 57.

57. Recent commentators agree for the most part that the practical syllogism exhibits the reasons motivating an actual action and is not intended as an analysis of deliberation (cf. Anscombe 1957, secs. 33–38; Cooper 1975, 23–33, 46–51; Modrak 1976). *De Motu An.* 7 affords numerous examples of the practical syllogism (cf. *E.N.* 1147a26–36).

58. Past experience plays a more central role in Aristotle's explanation of

animal behavior than in ours because in our explanatory theories we appeal to the notion of instinct—a concept Aristotle does not have.

59. Cf. Philoponus (*De An. Comm.* 498, 29–30), who takes an animal's ability to learn to be a mark of its capacity for perfect *phantasia*.

60. If as the passage at *De Motu An.* 702a16–19 (cf. *De An.* 433b27–28) suggests, *phantasia* is always required for the association of pleasure or pain with a perceived object, then a puzzle arises. The shaping of a present perception through past experience is also a feature of the perception of the *kata sumbebēkos* perceptibles. In this case Aristotle does not invoke *phantasia*; instead he makes the object of *aisthēsis* an interpreted complex of sensible characters. The difference between perceiving a white shape as a cookie and perceiving it as a source of pleasure is not obvious. Nor does Aristotle explain the difference. Other passages affirm the connection between pleasant and painful associations and sensible characters. According to *Phys.* 247a5–18, the pleasures and pains that motivate actions are bound up with perceptible features (cf. *De An.* 431a10–14).

61. I once believed that the textual evidence did not warrant the conclusion that *phantasia* is always involved in goal-directed behavior, but I am now willing to entertain the hypothesis that Aristotle may have opted for this position at the end of the day. Even if *phantasia* is not always involved in the actualization of desire, it typically is and thus *phantasia* has a uniquely important role to play in action contexts.

62. Nussbaum 1978 says that *phantasia* enables a percipient to see *X* as *Y* and provides the animal with "the awareness of something qua what-it-is-called" (pp. 255ff.). These descriptions are not particularly helpful when applied to many of the creatures possessing *phantasia*, for instance, insects. If the "seeing as" idiom means only that one sensation is somehow associated with another through *phantasia*, it is unproblematic but also uninformative.

63. Nussbaum 1978 sometimes identifies the impress of an external object with the *aisthēma*, sometimes with a physiological alteration (see, e.g., p. 258). She does not discuss the relationship between these two seemingly different conceptions of the impress. A further consequence of her interpretation is that it equates my seeing Socrates with my interpreting a change taking place in my eyes.

64. Besides the association of pleasure or pain with objects presented in perception, the only other cases of incidental perception where Aristotle mentions *phantasia* are cases of nonveridical appearance. However, were cases of incidental perception not cases of perception proper (as some commentators have held), then on the most reasonable hypothesis all cases of incidental perception would involve *phantasia*. Cf. chap. 3, sec. 4.

65. Aristotle describes the perceptual faculty as *kritikon* (*De An.* 424a6, 432a16) and as one of the faculties through which we discriminate *(krinomen)* (428a3–4) because animals make rudimentary judgments about their environments through *aisthēsis*. Cf. *Pst. Anal.* 99b38–39, which treats *aisthēsis* as a form of *gnōsis;* cf. *De Ins.* 458b3. See also chap. 2, n. 25, and chap. 5, n. 12.

66. Nussbaum 1978 tends to vacillate between making *aisthēsis* a passive

faculty for sensation and *phantasia* the faculty for interpretation and making *phantasia* the interpretative component of *aisthēsis* (cf. p. 259). Aristotle, on the other hand, includes interpretation under *aisthēsis* without invoking *phantasia*.

67. Although the Actuality Principle as stated by Aristotle seems to be limited in application to cognitive states, Aristotle places a similar constraint on affective states; these are also actualized in relation to their objects.

68. The use of *state of affairs* to refer to anything other than the proposition expressed by a symbolic representation may strike some readers as wrongheaded. Nonetheless, for lack of a better phrase I shall use this term to describe physical occurrences that are the intentional objects of perceptual states.

69. The appeal of epistemic theories of perception for modern philosophers is due in large measure to the widely held belief that the complexity of perceptual judgments exceeds the representational capacity of sensible features. Cf. Armstrong 1968, chap. 10. Other proponents of the epistemic theory are Close 1976, 1980; Heil 1982; Pitcher 1971; and Runzo 1977, 1982. The epistemic theory has been criticized by (among others) Dretske 1969 and 1981, which argue in favor of nonepistemic realism.

70. Concrete particulars instantiate universals, so in a sense we confront universals in perception, but the abstraction and articulation of universals is the work of the rational faculty. Universals as such are not apprehended through perception (cf. *Pst. Anal.* I, 31; II, 19).

71. A balanced account of the arguments for and against attributing beliefs to animals can be found in Stich 1979. Aristotle recognizes the need to attribute some belieflike cognitions to animals in order to explain their behavior, so he construes perception and *phantasia* as faculties for making rudimentary judgments. At *De Motu An.* 700b1–20, these faculties are said to have the same place as *nous* (cf. *De An.* 429a4–6, 433a10). Cf. n. 65.

72. Having recourse to a nonsensory mode of representation, we (humans) are able to arrive at a *phantasma* as the result of deliberation (cf. *De An.* 434a7–12). Aristotle calls the form of *phantasia* that is exercised in connection with reasoning *bouleutikē* (deliberative) or *logistikē phantasia* and the form that is exercised solely through the perceptual faculty *aisthetikē phantasia* (*De An.* 433b29–434a7).

73. Alexander (*De Fato* 168, 6–10) takes a similar position when he argues that not everything that appears to be the case is an instance of *phantasia*. I would like to express my gratitude to M. Burnyeat for calling this text to my attention.

74. It is instructive that Aristotle contrasts white to man at *De Ins.* 458b15; both could be objects of perception, but white must be. Aristotle's point is that a dream possesses characteristics that are incompatible with its being a case of *doxa* and hence dreams are a function of the perceptual faculty.

75. Aristotle cites the conflict between a percipient's belief about the size of the sun and his/her visual impression of its size as evidence that *phantasia* is not perception combined with belief (*De An.* 428b2–9; cf. *De Ins.* 460b18–19). When the object as presented through one sense modality conflicts with

the object as presented through another sense modality, a coherent representation is arrived at through the common sense (cf. *De Ins.* 460b16–23). In this case, the object is presented partially through each sense so Aristotle has no reason to posit a nonsensory mode of representation to accommodate the conflicting perspectives.

76. Cf. Schwartz 1981, which argues that images can bear semantic-type relations to things (pp. 111–12, 126–28). See also Block 1983a, 1983b.

77. Aristotle divides cognitive objects into particulars and universals. The former can be (and typically are) represented sensorially; the latter cannot be. This point will be discussed in further detail in chap. 5.

78. This is a consequence of the Sensory Representation Principle.

79. This is true both of the proponents of mental imagery (cf. Hannay 1971) and of the critics (cf. Dennett 1969).

80. The technical notion of imagery employed by cognitive psychologists is stated in terms of similarity relations (see, e.g., Kosslyn and Pomerantz 1977; cf. Dennett 1969, 132).

81. Aristotle assumes that similarity *(homoiotēs)* causes the dreamer to refer the dream image to an extramental state of affairs (*De Ins.* 461b10; cf. *De Div.* 464b7–10).

82. The *kata sumbebēkos* perception of the proper object of another sense is apparently mediated by the *kata sumbebēkos* perception of the object having both sensible qualities. According to Aristotle, the *kata sumbebēkos* perception of a yellow shape as bile by sight mediates the *kata sumbebēkos* perception of it as bitter by sight (*De An.* 425b1–4).

83. Just as Aristotle assumes that the mind is such that it can abstract universals from sensible particulars (*Pst. Anal.* 100a13), he seems to assume that for the most part incidental objects of perception correctly represent the external objects to which they are referred.

84. Cf. Locke (*Essay*, bk. 4, chap. 4) who also takes the correspondence between our ideas and the extramental reality to be an essential characteristic of knowledge.

85. In chap. 3, sec. 5, we were troubled by Aristotle's making incidental objects the basis for scientific generalizations even though it is possible for us to be mistaken about incidental objects. This is a partial solution to that difficulty.

86. This practice attests to the influence of the Analytic Principle.

87. At *De An.* 428b10–30, Aristotle talks about the change *(kinēsis)* identified with perception giving rise to the *kinēsis* he identifies with *phantasia*. Aristotle allows both movements to occur simultaneously, although he clearly does not allow the full-blown psychophysical states of perception and *phantasia* to occur simultaneously. This difference provides decisive evidence that Aristotle is using *kinēsis* to refer to the physiological changes that give rise to and constitute dispositional *phantasia*. Cf. Modrak 1986.

88. In some cases, a single organ is involved and a single past experience; in other cases, several different causal chains might converge to produce a physiological state that is the joint product of several different stimulations of the same peripheral sense organ or of several different sense organs.

89. The Actuality Principle derives the formal definition of the state from the description of its object; the Sensory Representation Principle brings together under the perceptual faculty all the cognitions that have sensory contents as objects.

Chapter 5

1. In this chapter, I consider Aristotle's account of thinking as found in *De An.* III, 4–8 and elsewhere primarily in relation to his theory of perception. This means I ignore many of the exegetical and philosophical problems that have been discussed in the literature on these texts since these discussions do not bear directly on the relationship between the two faculties.

2. Other interpretations are possible. For instance, the straight line might correspond to thought alone and the bent line to thought and perception (C. Kahn, "Some Problems in Aristotle's Theory of *Nous*," paper presented at the Conference on Aristotle's Philosophy of Mind and Modern Theories of Cognition, April 1985), or the straight line might correspond to perception and the bent to reason (cf. Ross 1961, 293).

3. In the *Posterior Analytics* and in other epistemological contexts (e.g., E.N. VI, 1139b14–17, 1141a3–8), *nous* and *epistēmē* are used in an epistemically restricted sense, namely, to refer to the apprehension of truths of a certain sort. This use is found in the *De Anima* at 428a17 (cf. 404a30), but the broad construal of *nous* is much more common.

4. Simple *noēta* are either grasped or not, so there is no possibility of error only of ignorance (*De An.* 430a26; cf. *Met.* 1051b23–33).

5. *De An.* 413b12, 414a32, 414b18, 431a14; Aristotle also calls the noetic faculty the *noētikon* (429a28–30, 431b2, cf. *De Ins.* 458b1); his preferred term in the *De Anima* is *nous* (408b18, 415b16, 429a17, 429a23, 429b3, 429b22, 429b31, 430a2, 430a25, 430a17, 432a2, 433a9). Rather than differentiating between the *noētikon* and the *dianoētikon*, Aristotle differentiates between the functions of the noetic faculty (cf. Oehler 1982, 159–69).

6. This position, however, is also compatible with the attenuated connection envisaged in *De An.* III where the connection between human thought processes and the organs of the perceptual system is mediated through *phantasia*.

7. See sec. 2. See also *De An.* 407a7, 429a13–17, 431b7, 432a12.

8. Cf. Philoponus (*De An. Comm.* 488, 11ff.), who describes *phantasia* as the *mesē* between perception and thought.

9. Jaeger 1948 found the doctrine of *nous* to be a remnant of Aristotle's earlier Platonic dualism, which Aristotle somehow never discarded (pp. 332ff.). But as we shall see in secs. 2 and 3, the picture is more complicated because the Actuality Principle provides a further motive for Aristotle's conception of *nous*.

10. In sec. 3 I argue that it is possible to interpret *De An.* III, 5 so as to make it consistent with the integrated model of perceptual and noetic functions found in *De An.* III, 4, 6–8.

11. The thesis that noetic states are properties of human beings is compat-

ible with epiphenomalism and other versions of property dualism. We can rule the former out immediately since, according to Aristotle, there is no bodily state necessary and sufficient to bring about an act of thinking. Further investigation will also establish that the latter should not be attributed to him.

12. The association of the *noēma* with an internal state is evident in Aristotle's comparison of the *noēma* with the *phantasma*. In the *De Anima* Aristotle stops short of identifying the *noēma* with the *phantasma*, but he wonders how they differ (432a12–13). Furthermore, the suffix *-mat* (nominative *-ma*) is used to indicate the result of an action.

13. In sec. 2 Aristotle's tendency to assimilate the distinction between the *noēton* and the *aisthēton* to the distinction between universal and particular is discussed.

14. The brevity of Aristotle's treatment of thinking is in sharp contrast to the lengthy treatment of perception, which is discussed in *De An.* II, 5–III, 2 and again in the *De Sensu*, while other functions of the perceptual faculty are discussed in the *De Memoria*, the *De Insomniis* and the *De Somno*. Even in the *Nicomachean Ethics*, where contemplation is identified with perfect happiness (1177a12ff.), practical *nous* which is required for moral excellence is identified with a type of perception (1143b5).

15. From the *Posterior Analytics* to the *De Anima*, Aristotle uses *krinein* (discriminate) and its cognates to describe the perceptual faculty (e.g., *Pst. Anal.* 99b35; *De An.* 424a5, 426b10, 426b14, 427a20, 429b13; *De Sens.* 442b12, 447b25, 447b27; *De Mem.* 460b17; cf. *De Mem.* 460b22). Liddell and Scott define *krinō* as follows: "to separate, divide, put apart hence to pick out . . . to judge of, estimate" (*A Greek-English Lexicon*, comp. H. Liddell and R. Scott. Oxford, [1843] 1968). The meaning of *krinein* in other of Aristotle's contexts is "to judge" (see, e.g., *E.N.* 1094b27, 1099a23, 1109b8, 1135b26).

16. Hamlyn 1968a is very critical of Aristotle's using the model of cognition he has developed for perception in his account of thought (pp. 135ff.). Yet success in this enterprise would strengthen Aristotle's psychology for it would provide him with a comprehensive model of cognition that applies to any cognitive state.

17. Thus he rejects the division of the soul into an irrational and a rational part on the grounds that the *aisthētikon* is not obviously either one (*De An.* 432a30–31).

18. As I read *De An.* 429b13, *alloi* (different) means "different from the perceptual faculty" and *allōs echonti* (differently disposed) means "the perceptual faculty differently disposed." Cf. Hicks 1907, 487: "A. appears to be discussing the question, Are sense and intellect different or are they the same faculty in two different attitudes?" By contrast, Kahn ("Some Problems in Aristotle's Theory of *Nous*") reads the line as follows: "by a different faculty (namely sense) or by the same faculty (i.e. *nous*) differently disposed," and he explains that *nous* differently disposed would be *nous* in combination with sense perception (pp. 24–25). However, apart from the disputed reading of the present passage, there is no textual support for the claim that *nous* apprehends sensible particulars such as water, but there is considerable support for the

claim that the perceptual faculty does. In addition, the tenor of *De Anima* III, 4 tends toward the assimilation of the model of noetic activity to the model of perceptual activity and so it would not be surprising to find Aristotle asking in effect how far this assimilation could be carried—could it be extended to the point at which the distinction between the faculties all but disappears?

19. The same account of the essence of a straight line is found at *Met*. 1043a34 and 1036b12. Cf. Hicks 1907, 412, which also remarks on the similarity of 429b18–21 to 429b10–14.

20. My remarks here are based on a particular interpretation of *Pst. Anal*. II, 19—the interpretation I defend in chap. 7, sec. 2.

21. The epistemological advantages of this conception of noetic activity will be taken up in chap. 7. Conceiving noetic activity as a further development of the cognitive capacity displayed in perception has the additional advantage that it is consistent with Aristotle's rejection of the Platonic division of psychic capacities into rational and irrational capacities.

22. Even if, instead of identifying states of the central nervous system with mental states, we opt for some sort of correlation, the continuum view of cognitive activity is still the most congenial.

23. Cf. chap. 4, n. 46.

24. Cf. *De Ins*. 462a29, where *alētheis ennoiai* may refer to thoughts that contravene the dream imagery.

25. There are two passages that might be thought to assert that universals are apprehended through perception. The first (*Pst. Anal*. 100a15–b1) concerns the perceptual basis for the apprehension of the universal; the second (*Phys*. 184a24–b14) is more obscure but presumably Aristotle's point is similar, i.e., that the general features of a sensible particular determine the shape of the perception, even though universals as such are not apprehended in perception. These issues are discussed further in chap. 7.

26. In his later writings Plato modifies this position somewhat, and in the *Theaetetus* he argues only that the objects of knowledge are not grasped through the senses but through the mind (187a).

27. For a detailed treatment of Aristotle's conception of the hierarchial ordering of disciplines see McKirahan 1978.

28. A number of recent commentators (e.g. Burnyeat 1981) urge us to translate *epistēmē* as "understanding" rather than "knowledge"; I prefer the latter term, which had been the traditional rendering. In the *Posterior Analytics*, Aristotle is concerned to set out the characteristics of a completed science. When applied to a unified body of propositions constituting an explanatory theory, "knowledge" seems the more perspicuous rendering of *epistēmē*.

29. D. Rosenthal persuaded me that the noetic and perceptual faculties are related to each other as formal to material cause. ("Aristotle on Thought: Comments on Deborah Modrak's Aristotle's Theory of Cognition." Paper presented at Conference on Aristotle's Philosophy of Mind and Modern Theories of Cognition, University of Rochester, April 1985.)

30. Cf. Berti 1978, which argues that it is possible to give a nonintuitionist interpretation of the two texts, namely, *De An*. III, 6 and *Met*. IX, 10, which

seem to support an intuitionist interpretation of Aristotle's conception of intellectual activity.

31. This interpretation will be defended in chap. 7, sec. 2. Mueller 1970 raises the question whether for Aristotle geometrical objects are universals or geometric properties imposed on pure extension (intelligible matter). The textual evidence is such that Mueller finds it hard to answer this question. This finding supports my contention that abstract objects are represented simultaneously as universals and as particulars.

32. To simplify this discussion I use the paradigmatic *noēton*—the universal of art and science—as the example of a noetic object.

33. Aristotle's description of active *nous* has puzzled commentators from Theophrastus to the present. See, for instance, Alexander (*De An. Mant.* 106–13) and Philoponus (*De An. Comm.* 535–41). For our purposes, it will not be necessary to address all the complexities surrounding the interpretation of *De An.* III, 5.

34. Although light is a necessary condition for the perception of color, it is not directly involved as a causal agent, for the reflection of light is not part of Aristotle's explanation of sight.

35. For an overview of the ancient tradition, see Ross 1961, 41–48.

36. Jaeger's claim that *nous* is a Platonic holdover can now be eliminated in favor of the more accurate claim that Aristotle's Platonic conception of noetic objects leads him to postulate a separate noetic faculty and ultimately to posit active *nous*, which is a peculiarly problematic notion. Cf. n. 9.

37. I adopt Bywater's reading of *di' hautou* at b9. Cf. Ross 1961, 292.

38. In chap. 7, sec. 2, I argue that *nous* is realized in the cognitive activity of *epagōgē*.

39. At least insofar as human intellection is concerned, intelligible objects exist in the world as the essences of physical objects and their properties or as abstractions based on physical characteristics (*De An.* 432a3–6). Since active *nous* "makes intelligible objects" in the sense that it makes their intelligibility evident, it need not have objects of its own.

40. Cf. Philoponus, pp. 537ff. Although Aristotle uses the expression *nous thurathen* (external mind) in the *De Gen. An.* (736b27, 744b22), the technical notion of the *thurathen nous* is elaborated later by Alexander (*De An. Mant.* 90, 11–91, 6; 108, 19–109, 3). For a detailed discussion of Aristotle's use of the expression, see Moraux 1955.

41. Ross 1961, 296: "it is possible that parts have disappeared which would have made the chapter more intelligible."

42. From the medievals to moderns, dualist commentators have taken comfort in the doctrine of active *nous* and emphasized its dualist elements. See, for instance, Brentano [1867] 1967, 106ff.; Aquinas, *In Ar. Lib. De An. Comm.*, L. III, l. X.

43. In recent discussions of the philosophy of mind, a distinction is often drawn between discursive representation and imagistic representation. This practice is somewhat problematic, as we discovered in chap. 4, sec. 4. Nonetheless, the distinction Aristotle draws between thinking about the essence of

X and apprehending a sensory representation of a token of X is the Aristotelian analogue of the modern distinction. Aristotle's distinction is less problematic than its modern analogue because the integrated model of cognitive activity allows for the symbolic employment of *phantasmata*.

44. This point was made in greater detail in sec. 2.

45. Cf. Hume (*A Treatise of Human Nature*, bk. I, sec. 1): "The image in the mind is only that of a particular object, tho' the application of it in our reasoning be the same, as if it were universal" ([1739] 1963, p. 20).

46. I have adopted Bywater's emendation, which eliminates *hautē de ekeinēn* from the text; however, even if this phrase is retained, the text supports my thesis that rational capacities are distinguished from perceptual capacities on the grounds that the former but not the latter involve inferential processes of a logically complex sort. Nonetheless, as we have discovered, Aristotle often speaks as if the distinction between *noēton* and *aisthēton* were the distinction between universal and particular because the paradigm case of a *noēton* is a universal.

47. In the *Ethica Nicomachea*, Aristotle also emphasizes the connection between executing a cognitive search and rationality, and he describes deliberation *(bouleusis)* as a kind of search *(zētēsis)* (1112b20–24, 1142b1–21, 1144a31–33).

48. Cf. *De An.* 428a19–24, where *pistis* (persuasion) is made the mark of *doxa* and hence of human rationality.

49. See the discussion of *anamnēsis* in chap. 4, sec. 2.

50. An interesting analogy can be drawn between *anamnēsis* and *boulēsis* (rational desire). Both are quasi-rational mental activities that terminate in states of the perceptual faculty as such or the perceptual faculty qua desirative faculty. Aristotle argues from the existence of *boulēsis* to the conclusion that the Platonic division of the soul into a rational and an irrational part is misguided (*De An.* 432b4–7). See also chap. 4, n. 46.

51. Epistemic considerations such as truth and logical considerations such as the difference between universal and particular objects can be invoked to distinguish some of the functions of the noetic faculty from some of the functions of the perceptual faculty but not to explain all cases. For instance, the belief that the sun, a concrete particular, is a certain size or the decision about which action to perform, made through *phronēsis*, can only be differentiated from similar functions of the perceptual faculty on the grounds that different modes of representation are involved.

52. The apprehension of universals often plays a part in deliberation, which frequently involves subsuming a particular under a universal rule or a general desirability characterization. This provides Aristotle with a further motivation for making deliberation a function of the noetic faculty.

53. There is considerable evidence that *phantasia* under a material description is an event in the central sense organ (see chap. 4, sec. 5).

54. Active *nous*, an internal state of continuous intellectual activity, does not in and of itself require *phantasmata*; thus it would seem to be independent of the body in a strong sense. This explains why Aristotle says that "when

separated [*choristheis*] it [active *nous*] alone is just what it is" (*De An.* 430a23–24).

55. See *De An.* 429a15–17, 429b30, 431a1.

Chapter 6

1. Here I use *consciousness* in what Landesman calls the "broad use to designate any mental state or whatever it is about a mental state which makes it mental" (1967, 193–94). Hardie 1976 labels this notion of consciousness "consciousness$_g$" and distinguishes it from reflexive consciousness. I find it more useful to distinguish between the broad conception of consciousness just mentioned and the narrower conception of consciousness found in modern philosophy.

2. Aristotle does not even have a word for consciousness in our sense. Cf. Kahn 1966, 71. Cf. also Bywater's remark about *E.N.* 1170a20ff.: "It is clear that throughout this section the word *aisthanesthai* has, in addition to its ordinary meaning, a more general sense corresponding to our modern term 'consciousness.' In default of a better word Aristotle is obliged to say, for instance, *aisthanesthai hoti badizei* in l.30" ([1892] 1973, 65).

3. Aristotle's psychophysicalism enables him to draw a distinction between the special senses as subfaculties and the senses as components of the common sense. Far too many commentators (from Neuhaeuser 1878 to Block 1964) have assumed that if seeing takes place when the visual impulses reach the central organ, then strictly speaking seeing is a function of the common sense. Aristotle can distinguish on physiological as well as formal grounds between the visual system and the central sense faculty.

4. I am grateful to C. Kahn for calling the first alternative to my attention.

5. *De An.* 426b12–427a15, 431a20–b1; *De Sens.* 447a13–449a22; *De Som.* 455a16–21.

6. When considering a sense or its object on an individual basis, Aristotle refers to the analysis of the other senses only in support of his methodology. For instance, he points out that colors, sounds and flavors can be reduced to *logoi* of a basic pair of sensible opposites to justify applying the *logos* conception of sensible qualities to tactile qualities (*De An.* 422b23–33; cf. *De Sens.* 442a12–16). See chap. 3, sec. 1.

7. There is no reason to assume that the use of *kurios* and other words having the connotation of ruling refer to a rational rather than a perceptual faculty. Throughout the passage at *De Ins.* 460b16–461b26, Aristotle uses *kurios* to describe sense faculties (e.g., 460b21, 461b5); at 461a30–b7, he uses *archē* in a context where, as Ross 1955 says, "*archē* is the governing faculty of perception" (p. 277).

8. This practice is a consequence of the Actuality Principle.

9. Memory and *phantasia* were discussed in chap. 4.

10. In *Rhet.* II, 2–11, Aristotle defines the emotions that are of greatest interest to the orator. In each case, the definition mentions pleasure or pain, as the case may be, and the circumstance under which the pleasure or pain occurs.

Envy, for example, is the pain occasioned by the good fortune of one's peers (1387b22–24). Cf. Fortenbaugh 1975, which emphasizes the importance of the efficient cause as a component of the definition of an emotion.

11. Cf. Aristotle's explanation of moral weakness *(akrasia)* where the a-kratic agent's perception of an object qua pleasurable is tantamount to his actively desiring the object and pursuing it against his better judgment (*E.N.* 1147a26–b17).

12. The subject of *kataphasa . . . pheugei* (*De An.* 431a9) must be supplied. Most translations read as if the subject were *psuchē*, but *psuchē* is not found in the preceding lines. More likely the understood feminine term is *aisthēsis* (cf. Hicks 1907, 527), and I have translated accordingly. Strictly speaking, neither the perceptual faculty nor the soul as a whole pursues or avoids, but rather the animal.

13. Plato also treats the experience of pleasure or pain as a kind of perception (*Theaet.* 156b; *Tim.* 64aff.).

14. Insofar as perceptual capacities are at issue, the higher animals are as psychologically complex as human beings, for they too have all five senses, *phantasia*, and memory, and they experience pleasure and pain.

15. This restriction on thought is quite significant from the point of view of Aristotle's epistemology, as we shall see in chap. 7.

16. According to Kahn 1966, "there is for Aristotle an important distinction, which the traditional concept of consciousness tends to ignore, between the intellectual activity as such and our personal awareness of it . . . reasoning and the awareness of reasoning belong properly to different faculties" (p. 80).

17. Although philosophers often point out that consciousness need not include reflexive awareness (see, e.g., Armstrong 1968, 94), the narrow conception of consciousness that I investigate here does include it. Cf. n. 1.

18. When Aristotle says at *De Som.* 455a18 that we do not see that we see or hear that we hear, he then immediately turns to the case of discriminating between different types of sensible qualities. This suggests that the case Aristotle initially has in mind is a case where seeing and hearing are embedded in a complex cognitive object.

19. The reflexive awareness of sensing has traditionally been included among the functions of the common sense; see, e.g., Rodier 1900, II: 265; Ross 1955, 35.

20. *De An.* 425b12–24 establishes that *a* faculty for the apprehension of color is the source of the apperceptual awareness of seeing, but since sight is a component of the common sense, this requirement is met by the *De Somno*'s common *dunamis*.

21. I accept Bywater's emendation of 1170a31–32, which takes the verb to be *aisthanesthai* throughout ([1892] 1973, 64–65). Cf. Kahn 1966, 78, n. 82; Hardie 1976, 409, n. 1.

22. The problems raised by Aristotle's description of *nous* in *De An.* III, 4 for the commentator who would attribute the reflexive awareness of *nous* to the common sense are discussed in more detail in Modrak 1981a.

23. Even so, the reflexive awareness of a thought will require the joint

activity of the noetic and perceptual faculties because thinking always employs *phantasmata*.

24. The reflexive awareness of the self involved in memory would differ between species; the human being would have a much more clearly defined notion of the self than any of the other animals. Cf. chap. 4, sec. 2.

25. Brentano 1973 made intentionality the definitive feature of the mental (see 2, chap. 1); cf. Chisholm 1967, 201–4; Armstrong 1968, 41ff. See also chap. 2, sec. 1. Nagel 1975 accepts the assumption that in ordinary consciousness the mind recognizes the simpler relations between simultaneous mental events (p. 239).

26. Modrak 1981a discusses these characteristics at greater length.

27. Recently philosophers have taken the failure of extensionality in intentional contexts to be the distinctive feature of intentionality (see, for example, Davidson 1970, 84–85). For instance, if I believe I am Antigone, I may fear Antigone's death but not fear my own death under a true description of it.

28. In sec. 1 we discovered that, when an incoherent picture would result were all the objects presented through the senses at a given moment accorded equal treatment, the common sense shapes the total perceptual experience but only to the extent necessary to produce a unified perception. By comparison to us, Aristotle has an extraordinarily restricted notion of the percipient's ability to structure experience.

29. I use the terms *constituent analysis* and *relational analysis* in the following sense: on a constituent analysis of consciousness, consciousness is understood in terms of a mental act and its object; on a relational analysis, consciousness is understood as the relation between the conscious subject and the object of consciousness. This is an adaptation of a similar distinction that Landesman 1967 makes.

30. Descartes, *Discourse on Method*, [1637] 1967 trans., I, p. 116.

31. In this connection, Aristotle's handling of whether *phantasia* is possessed by all animals is instructive. Some passages (e.g., *De An.* 428a8–11, 428a21–23; cf. 415a10) suggest that the simpler animals do not possess *phantasia*. At the end of the day, however, Aristotle opts for a uniform model of the perceptual faculty, and he concludes that the "imperfect" animals possess *phantasia* in an ill-defined manner *(aoristos)* (434a1–5; cf. 433a9–12).

32. To insure that organs are viewed as functional parts of the living organism, Aristotle asserts the Homonymy Principle (a hand is not a hand unless it is part of a living creature). The Homonymy Principle was discussed in chap. 2, sec. 5; see also chap. 1, n. 16.

33. Even if the apprehension of the momentary object of experience is through the common sense, the very existence of a cognition consisting in thoughts and perceptions presupposes the coordinated activity of both faculties.

34. Kahn 1966 recognized the importance of the common sense to Aristotle's concept of consciousness. I have now shown that Aristotle's conception of the common sense is a consequence of the foundational principles of the theory of perception and hence that the foundational principles explain all perceptual phenomena, including the unity of consciousness.

Chapter 7

1. Aristotle's psychologism finds expression in *Pst. Anal.* II, 19, where the certainty of the first principles of science ultimately rests on how we come to know them. I argue that the first principles are known through *epagōgē*, but even on the traditional interpretation of II, 19, where the first principles are known through *nous* identified with immediate intuition in the Platonic sense, Aristotle's account of the acquisition of first principles is psychologistic.

2. *De An.* 431b2, 432a8–9; cf. 431a15; *De Mem* 449b31–450a6; see also chap. 5, sec. 4.

3. To mention but a few of the more recent discussions of this chapter: Kosman 1973; Lesher 1973; Hamlyn 1976; Engberg-Pedersen 1979; Couloubaritsis 1980; Hintikka 1980; Van Fraassen 1980; Burnyeat 1981; Kahn 1981.

4. Aristotle sometimes uses *aisthēma* elliptically for the physiological trace that is left in the sense organ by a perception (*De Mem.* 450a31; *De Ins.* 460b2, 461a19), but which strictly speaking is a trace *(hupoleimma)* of an *aisthēma* (*De Ins.* 461b22).

5. The decaying sense account of *phantasia* is right up to a point. A *phantasma* either duplicates a previous perception or is made up of features that are derived from previous perceptions. See chap. 4, sec. 4.

6. The salient features of *epistēmē* (scientific knowledge), according to *Pst. Anal.* I, 3–14, are as follows: *Epistēmē* in a particular field is a body of true propositions that define and analyze a particular genus, and the propositions are related to each other as the premises and conclusions of syllogistic series which ultimately terminate in indemonstrable first premises. Each proposition is commensurately universal, that is, the subject and predicate terms pick out coextensive classes, and the predicate belongs essentially to the subject. All the propositions making up a science which are not indemonstrable first premises are established through demonstration. A demonstrative syllogism proceeds through a middle term, which is the cause of the fact asserted in the conclusion. Only eternal relations are demonstrable. Cf. *E.N.* VI, 3.

7. *Epagōgē* is mentioned in connection with the apprehension of first principles at *Pr. Anal.* 68b30–32; *Pst. Anal.* 81a38–b6, 100b4; cf. *E.N.* 1098b3, 1139b28–30. *Nous* is described as the *archē* of *epistēmē* at 88b36, 100b5–17; cf. *E.N.* 1141a3–8. The derived principles are known through *apodeixis*; its role in *epistēmē* is described at length in *Pst. Anal.* I, 3–9.

8. Typically Aristotle uses *katholou* (universal) for universal propositions; we typically use *universal* for general terms or concepts, and Aristotle sometimes uses *katholou* in this sense. I often translate *katholou* as "universal proposition or concept" so as to duplicate Aristotle's usage of *katholou*.

9. In *Pst. Anal.* I, 31, *nous* is not used but *noēsis* is, presumably, to stand for the exercise of *nous*. The broad use of *nous* and its cognates is typical of the psychological treatises as we saw in chap. 5.

10. See, for example, *Top.* 105a13, 108b10, 156b14–15; *Pr. Anal.* 67a23; *Pst. Anal.* 78a34.

11. *Noēsis* occurs only once, in *Pst. Anal.* 88a8. Barnes is surely right to translate *noēsis* by the same term, "comprehension," that he uses for *nous*. Ross 1949 also equates *noēsis* with *nous* in this passage (p. 599).

12. The same arguments also show mutatis mutandis that the genetic account is not limited to either concepts or first principles.

13. Not all proponents of the interpretation in question would divide the text at 100a9–10, some would divide it at 100a14. Why this approach is mistaken will also be discussed below.

14. Cf. Ross 1949: "It would not be difficult to argue that the formation of general concepts and the grasping of universal propositions are inseparably interwoven. But A. makes no attempt to show that the two processes are so interwoven. . . . Rather he seems to describe the two processes as distinct, and alike only in being inductive" (p. 675). But see Kahn 1981, 389–95.

15. Cf. Liddell and Scott, *Greek-English Lexicon*.

16. Cf. Ross 1949, 677, which cites precedents for Aristotle's use of *palai* to refer to the immediately preceding arguments.

17. To grasp a concept, for Aristotle, is to grasp a definition, and definitions are propositions. Cf. *Pst. Anal.* 90b3–4, 90b24; *Top.* 101b13–23, 153a16; and *De An.* 407a25–26, where Aristotle treats definitions as propositions and first principles. See Modrak 1981b; cf. Hamlyn 1976; Hintikka 1980; Kahn 1981. For a radically different construal of the role of definitions in demonstration, see Ferejohn 1982.

18. This is why Aristotle says that a definition is a unified formula in which one term is not predicated of another (*Pst. Anal.* 90b35–37; cf. *Met.* 1037b10–14, 1041a32–b2).

19. Significantly, when Aristotle makes a point of differentiating between concepts and propositions, he does not draw quite the same conclusions we would draw. In the case of truth, he recognizes two types—our usual notion of truth which holds of propositions and another which applies to the simple apprehension of essence (*Met.* 1051b22–26; cf. *De An.* 430b26–31).

20. There Aristotle pays more attention to the distinction between experience and knowledge. When he speaks of animals living by *phantasiai* and memories, he invokes the sophisticated notion of *phantasia* as sensory representation that we find in the psychological treatises. Thus, it seems likely that the account in *Met.* I, 1 is later than the *Posterior Analytics'* account, and it is noteworthy that Aristotle's position remains the same. Although Aristotle refers to the knowledge of first principles elsewhere, he does not concern himself with how such knowledge is acquired or treat the topic in any detail. (Aristotle summarizes the *Posterior Analytics'* findings in *E.N.* VI, 3,6.)

21. Of recent commentators, only Kahn 1981 brings the psychology to bear on the interpretation of *Pst. Anal.* II, 19. Kahn is mainly concerned with the relationship between the active *nous* of *De An.* III, 5 and the role of *nous* in *Pst. Anal.* II, 19, and he reaches conclusions that are different from mine.

22. The puzzle is a variant of the Learner's Paradox, which Plato used as part of an argument for innate knowledge in the *Meno* (80de). According to the Learner's Paradox, we cannot learn what we already know nor can we learn

what we do not know because we will not recognize it, hence we can learn nothing.

23. Among other objectives, Aristotle wants to avoid the Platonist conclusion that all knowledge originates in preexisting knowledge. Although Aristotle accepts this thesis insofar as *epistēmē* is concerned, he is troubled by its broader implications (cf. *Pst. Anal.* 71a1–31; *Met.* 992b30–993a2).

24. I prefer "introduces" as a translation of *empoiei* to Barnes' "instills" or Mure's "implants" because, unlike the latter translations, "introduces" does not suggest that the universal is the product of perception.

25. Cf. George Berkeley, "Introduction," in *A Treatise Concerning the Principles of Human Knowledge*.

26. *De An.* 434a9–10: "dunatai hen ek pleinōn phantasmatōn poiein" could be read as "one has the ability to make one image out of many." However, since this is part of a discussion of rational action, Aristotle is probably referring to experience without naming it, in which case the one in question would be a judgment rather than a *phantasma*.

27. The psychological treatises are not much help when it comes to *empeiria* (experience); presumably from the psychological perspective, *empeiria* is a composite of *mnēmē* and *doxa*.

28. Although commentators tend to treat as unproblematic Aristotle's claim that the objects of experience are particulars, it is actually quite puzzling, for many of Aristotle's examples of experiential judgments may be stated as universal propositions, for instance, "all chicken is wholesome" (cf. *E.N.* 1141b16–22). If this is an abbreviated version of a judgment having the form "chicken-eating contributed to Socrates' health, chicken-eating contributed to Callias' health and . . . ," it would be less puzzling.

29. The doctrine that particulars are grasped through perception and that universals are required for knowledge is a persistent Aristotelian theme. *De An.* 417b23; *Top.* 114a21–25; *Met.* 999b3, 1003a15, 1059b26, 1060b20; *Pst. Anal.* 87b28–39.

30. Aristotle's use of *paschein* at *Pst. Anal.* 100a14 is indicative of the emphasis he places on the cognitive object. The universal emerges; the mind does not create the universal; it is affected by the universal.

31. Cf. *Phys.* 184a25–26, where Aristotle says that the whole *(to holon)*, a kind of universal, is known through perception.

32. According to Aristotle, young children initially call all women "mother" and all men "father," that is, the young child is able to distinguish between men and women before he or she is able to distinguish one woman from another or one man from another.

33. Not only does Aristotle seem oblivious to the distinction between class membership and class inclusion, but Plato's account of definition through division also seems to ignore this distinction (*Soph.* 219–231). Cf. Moravcsik 1973, 330.

34. According to Aristotle, the productive sciences study essences whereas the theoretical ones study *logoi* and thoughts, i.e., the former consists in the

study of essences qua essences of sensible particulars whereas the latter consists in the study of essences qua essences (cf. *Met.* 1075a1–3).

35. *Pr. Anal.* 42a22–24; *Pst. Anal.* 81a38–b9; *Top.* 105a13, 108b10, 156b14–15, 160a38.

36. *Pr. Anal.* 42a3; *Pst. Anal.* 71a5, 72a35, 72b29, 81b1; *Top.* 105a18, 157a20; *Phys.* 252a24; *Met.* 992b33, 1025b15, 1064a9.

37. When we understand the concept of a natural kind such as human being, we grasp the essential features as given in the definition. Nevertheless, Aristotle says that one thing is not said of another in this case (*Met.* 1041a32–b2; cf. 1037b10–14). The logical structure of the object that is apprehended is the same in the case of basic concepts of the sort Aristotle cites as examples in *Pst. Anal.* II, 19 as the logical structure of abstract universal propositions such as geometrical axioms. Cf. Hintikka 1980 and Kahn 1981.

38. Among other considerations, the association of *nous* and *epagōgē* with the knowledge of universals needed for *epistēmē* counts heavily in favor of the thesis that the knowledge of first principles is acquired through *epagōgē* and is realized as *nous*. See also Burnyeat 1981, 130–33.

39. The case against the traditional interpretation has already been argued cogently by Kosman 1973 and Lesher 1973. The considerations I cite here are intended to supplement their arguments. See also Modrak 1981b.

40. While it is true as Barnes 1975, 257, points out that *nous* has a number of uses in the Aristotelian corpus, its primary use in the *De Anima* is for the faculty exercised in thinking. See chap. 5, sec. 1.

41. Since at *Pst. Anal.* 99b21 Aristotle calls the first principles "*prōtai archai*," there is good reason to read "*ta prōta*" at 100b4 as first principles.

42. See n. 6.

43. Barnes 1969 could not find a single perfect example of a demonstration in the entire corpus (p. 124).

44. *Pst. Anal.* 88a4–5 says that the universal is from many *(pleionōn)* and thus seems to be an exception, but here Aristotle does not mention *epagōgē*, and *pleionōn* is open-ended.

45. This conception also holds for abstract objects that, in Aristotle's view, are grounded in the actual properties of physical objects. See, for instance, the arguments of *Met.* XIII against the Platonic account of mathematical objects. Cf. chap. 5, secs. 2 and 4.

46. According to *Pst. Anal.* I, 4, a commensurately universal proposition is one that meets the following conditions: *B* belongs universally to *A* if and only if (1) *B* applies to every object that satisfies the description *A*, because the object satisfies *A* (73b26–29), and (2) there is no other description more comprehensive than *A* under which the object falls that accounts for the satisfaction of (1) (73b34–35). See n. 8.

47. This is not to say that Aristotle would describe *epagōgē* as a "reliable belief-producing mechanism" or that *epagōgē* produces *doxa* and not knowledge. All the same, Aristotle's conception of *epagōgē* fits the modern notion of a reliable belief-producing mechanism.

48. Although all known propositions in Aristotle's sense are cases of jus-

tified, true belief in our sense, the converse is not true. To count as knowledge, for Aristotle a cognitive object must meet additional requirements. Thus, to show, as I have, that *epagōgē* can yield justified, true beliefs is to show that true beliefs reached in this way meet one of the necessary conditions for knowledge.

49. Even when the perceptual distortion is a constant feature of our experience because the conditions are never optimal, we are able to correct this error. For instance, heavenly bodies due to their distance are perpetually too far away for us to accurately perceive their size, yet we recognize this fact (cf. *De Ins.* 460b17–23).

50. *Pst. Anal.* 86a8, 87b28–35, 88a2–11; *De An.* 417b20–26. Cf. n. 29.

References

Ancient and Medieval Authors with Editions Cited

Alexander. *De Anima Cum Mantissa.*
   Bruns, I. 1887. *Commentaria in Aristotelem Graeca*, vol. 2, pt. 1. Berlin.
   ———. *De Fato.*
   Bruns, I. 1892. *Commentaria in Aristotelem Graeca*, vol. 2, pt. 2. Berlin.
   ———. *In Aristotelis De Sensu.*
   Wendland, P. 1901. *Commentaria in Aristotelem Graeca*, vol. 3, pt. 1. Berlin.
Anaximenes.
   Diels, H., and W. Kranz. 1951. *Fragmente der Vorsokratiker*, 6th ed. Berlin.
Aquinas. *In Aristotelis Librum De Anima Commentarium.*
   Pirotta, P. Fr. A., O.P., ed. 1959, Turin.
   ———. Foster, K., and S. Humphries. 1951. *Aristotle's De Anima in the Version of William of Moerbeke and the Commentary of St. Thomas Aquinas.* Trans. London.
Aristotle. *Analytica Posteriora.*
   Barnes, J. 1975. *Aristotle's Posterior Analytics.* Trans. with notes. Oxford.
   Ross, W. 1949. *Aristotle's Prior and Posterior Analytics.* Text with introd. and notes. Oxford.
   ———. *De Anima.*
   Hamlyn, D. 1968a. *Aristotle's De Anima Books II, III* with introd. and notes. Oxford.
   Hicks, R. 1907. Text with English trans., introd. and notes. Oxford.
   Rodier, G. 1900. Aristotle: *Traité de l'âme*, with French trans. and notes. Paris.
   Ross, W. 1956. Oxford.
   ———. 1961. Text with introd. and notes. Oxford.
   Theiler, W. 1959. Aristoteles: *Über die Seele,* with German trans. and notes. Berlin.
   Torstrik, A. 1862. Aristotelis: *De Anima*, Libri III. Berlin.
   ———. *De Generatione Animalium.*
   Peck, A. 1942. Aristotle, vol. 13. Loeb Classical Library. Cambridge, Mass., and London.
   ———. *De Generatione et Corruptione.*
   Joachim, H. [1922] 1970. Aristotle: *On Coming-To-Be and Passing-Away.* Oxford.

———. *De Insomniis et De Divinatione per Somnum.*
   Lulofs, H. 1947. Leyden.
———. *De Memoria.*
   Sorabji, R. 1972. *On Memory*, trans. and notes. Providence.
———. *De Motu Animalium.*
   Forster, E. [1937] 1968. Aristotle, vol. 12. Loeb Classical Library. Cambridge, Mass., and London.
   Nussbaum, M. 1978. Text with trans. and notes. Princeton.
———. *De Partibus Animalium.*
   Peck, A. [1937] 1968. Aristotle, vol. 12. Loeb Classical Library. Cambridge, Mass., and London.
———. *De Sensu.*
   Ross, G. 1906. Aristotle: *De Sensu and De Memoria*. Cambridge.
———. *De Somno et Vigilia.*
   Lulofs, H. 1943. Templum Salomonis.
———. *Ethica Nicomachea.*
   Bywater, I. 1890. Oxford.
   Rackham, H. [1926] 1968. Aristotle, vol. 19. Loeb Classical Library. Cambridge, Mass., and London.
———. *Historia Animalium.*
   Peck, A. 1965. Aristotle, vols. 9–11. Loeb Classical Library. Cambridge, Mass., and London.
———. *Metaphysica.*
   Jaeger, W. 1957. Oxford.
———. *Organon.*
   Waitz, T. 1844–46. Leipzig.
———. *Parva Naturalia: De Sensu, De Memoria, De Somno, De Insomniis, De Divinatione per Somnum, De Longitudine Vitae and De Juventute.* Biehl, W. 1898. Leipzig.
   Ross, W. 1955. Text with introd. and notes. Oxford.
———. *Physica.*
   Charlton, W. 1970. Aristotle's *Physics I, II*. Trans. with introd. and notes. Oxford.
   Ross, W. 1950. Oxford.
———. *Rhetorica.*
   Sandys, J. 1877. *The Rhetoric of Aristotle with E. M. Cope's Commentary*, vols. 1–3. Cambridge.
Heraclitus.
   Diels, H., and W. Kranz. 1951. *Fragmente der Vorsokratiker*, 6th ed. Berlin.
   Kahn, C. 1979. *The Art and Thought of Heraclitus: An Edition of the Fragments.* Text with trans. and notes. Cambridge.
Philoponus. *In Aristotelis De Anima libros Commentaria.*
   Hayduck, M. 1897. *Commentaria in Aristotelem Graeca*, vol. 15. Berlin.
Plato. *Opera.*
   Burnet, J. 1900–3. Oxford.

Theophrastus. *De Sensibus.*
Stratton, G. 1917. Text with trans. and notes. London.

Modern Authors

Ackrill, J. L. 1965. "Aristotle's Distinction between *Energeia* and *Kinesis.*" In *New Essays on Plato and Aristotle*, ed. R. Bambrough. London.
———. 1972–73. "Aristotle's Definitions of *Psuche.*" *Proceedings of the Aristotelian Society* 73: 119–33. Reprinted in *Articles on Aristotle*, vol. 4: *Psychology and Aesthetics*, ed. J. Barnes, M. Schofield, and R. Sorabji. London, 1978.
Anderson, J. R. 1978. "Arguments Concerning Representations for Mental Imagery." *Psychological Review* 85: 249–77.
Anscombe, G. 1957. *Intention.* Ithaca.
Armstrong, D. M. 1961. *Perception and the Physical World.* London.
———. 1968. *A Materialist Theory of Mind.* London.
———. 1977. "The Causal Theory of the Mind." *Neue Heft für Philosophie*, no. 11, pp. 82–95.
Baeumker, C. 1877. *Des Aristoteles Lehre von den äussern und innern Sinnesvermögen.* Leipzig.
Barker, A. 1981. "Aristotle on Perception and Ratios." *Phronesis* 26: 248–66.
Barnes, J. 1969. "Aristotle's Theory of Demonstration." *Phronesis* 14: 123–52. Reprinted in *Articles on Aristotle*, vol. 1: *Science*, ed. J. Barnes, M. Schofield, and R. Sorabji. London, 1975.
———. 1971–72. "Aristotle's Concept of Mind." *Proceedings of the Aristotelian Society* 72: 101–14. Reprinted in *Articles on Aristotle*, vol. 4: *Psychology and Aesthetics*, ed. J. Barnes, M. Schofield, and R. Sorabji. London, 1978.
Barnes, J., M. Schofield, and R. Sorabji, eds. 1978. *Articles on Aristotle*, vol. 4: *Psychology and Aesthetics.* London.
Beare, J. I. 1906. *Greek Theories of Elementary Cognition.* Oxford.
Berkeley, G. 1957. *A Treatise Concerning the Principles of Human Knowledge.* Ed. C. Turbayne. New York. Originally published 1710.
Berti, E. 1978. "The Intellection of Indivisibles According to Aristotle, *De Anima* III, 6." In *Aristotle on Mind and the Senses*, ed. G. Lloyd and G. Owen. Cambridge.
Block, I. 1960. "Aristotle and the Physical Object." *Philosophy and Phenomenological Research* 21: 93–101.
———. 1961. "The Order of Aristotle's Psychological Writings." *American Journal of Philology* 82: 50–77.
———. 1964. "Three German Commentators on the Individual Senses and the Common Sense in Aristotle." *Phronesis*, 9: 58–63.
Block, N. 1983a. "Mental Pictures and Cognitive Science." *Philosophical Review* 92: 499–542.
———. 1983b. "The Photographic Fallacy in the Debate about Mental Imagery." *Nous* 17: 651–61.

———, ed. 1980. *Readings in Philosophy of Psychology*, vol. 1. Cambridge, Mass.
———, ed. 1981. *Imagery*. Cambridge, Mass.
Block, N., and J. Fodor. 1972. "What Psychological States Are Not." *Philosophical Review* 81: 159–82. Reprinted in *Readings in Philosophy of Psychology*, vol. 1, ed. N. Block. Cambridge, Mass., 1980.
Bolton, R. 1976. "Essentialism and Semantic Theory in Aristotle." *Philosophical Review* 86: 514–44.
———. 1978. "Aristotle's Definitions of the Soul: *De Anima* II, 1–3." *Phronesis* 23: 258–78.
Boyd, R. 1980. "Materialism without Reductionism: What Physicalism Does Not Entail." In *Readings in Philosophy of Psychology*, vol. 1, ed. N. Block. Cambridge, Mass.
Bremmer, J. 1983. *The Early Greek Concept of the Soul*. Princeton.
Brentano, F. [1867] 1967. *Die Psychologie des Aristoteles*. Reprint. Darmstadt.
———. 1973. *Psychology from an Empirical Standpoint*. Trans. A. C. Rancurello, D. B. Terrell, and L. L. McAlister from the 1874 German edition. London.
Brown, R., and R. J. Herrnstein. 1981. "Icons and Images." In *Imagery*, ed. N. Block. Cambridge, Mass.
Bruner, J. S., R. Olver, and P. Greenfield. 1966. *Studies in Cognitive Growth*. New York.
Burnyeat, M. F. 1976. "Plato on the Grammar of Perceiving." *Classical Quarterly* 70: 29–51.
———. 1981. "Aristotle on Understanding Knowledge." In *Aristotle on Science: The Posterior Analytics, Proceedings of the Eighth Symposium Aristotelicum*, ed. E. Berti. Padua and New York.
Bywater, I. [1892] 1973. *Contributions to the Textual Criticism of Aristotle's Nicomachean Ethics*. Reprint. New York.
Cashdollar, S. 1973. "Aristotle's Account of Incidental Perception." *Phronesis* 18: 156–75.
Charles, D. 1984. *Aristotle's Philosophy of Action*. Ithaca.
Chisholm, R. 1967. "Intentionality." In *Encyclopedia of Philosophy*. New York.
Claus, D. 1981. *Toward the Soul*. New Haven.
Cleary, J. 1985. "On the Terminology of 'Abstraction' in Aristotle." *Phronesis* 30: 13–46.
Close, D. 1976. "What Is Non-Epistemic Seeing." *Mind* 85: 161–70.
———. 1980. "More on Non-Epistemic Seeing." *Mind* 89: 99–105.
Code, A. 1976. "The Persistence of Aristotelian Matter." *Philosophical Studies* 29: 357–67.
Cohen, S. 1982. "St. Thomas Aquinas on the Immaterial Reception of Sensible Forms." *Philosophical Review* 91: 193–209.
Cooper, J. Forthcoming. "Hypothetical Necessity." In *Aristotle on Nature and Living Things*, ed. A. Gotthelf. Pittsburgh.
———. 1970. "Plato on Sense-Perception and Knowledge: *Theaetetus* 184–186." *Phronesis* 15: 123–46.

———. 1975. *Reason and Human Good in Aristotle*. Cambridge, Mass.
Cornman, J. 1962. "The Identity of Mind and Body." *Journal of Philosophy* 59: 486–92. Reprinted in *Materialism and the Mind-Body Problem*, ed. D. Rosenthal. Englewood Cliffs, N.J., 1971.
Couloubaritsis, L. 1980. "Y-a-t-il une intuition des principes?" *Revue Internationale de Philosophie* 34: 441–71.
Dancy, R. M. 1978. "Aristotle's Second Thoughts on Substance." *Philosophical Review* 87: 372–413.
Davidson, D. 1970. "Mental Events." In *Experience and Theory*, ed. L. Foster and J. W. Swanson. Amherst.
Dennett, D. 1969. *Content and Consciousness*. New York.
———. 1978. "Current Issues in the Philosophy of Mind." *American Philosophical Quarterly* 15: 249–61.
Descartes, R. 1967 trans. *Discourse on Method*. In *The Philosophical Works of Descartes*, ed. and trans. E. Haldane and G. Ross. Cambridge. Originally published as *Le discours de la méthode*, Leiden, 1637.
Dretske, F. 1969. *Seeing and Knowing*. London.
———. 1981. *Knowledge and the Flow of Information*. Oxford.
Engberg-Pedersen, T. 1979. "More on Aristotelian *Epagoge*." *Phronesis* 24: 301–17.
Feigl, H. 1958. "The 'Mental' and the 'Physical.' " In *Minnesota Studies in the Philosophy of Science*, vol. 2. Minnesota.
Ferejohn, M. 1982. "Definition and the Two Stages of Aristotelian Demonstration." *Review of Metaphysics* 36: 375–95.
Field, H. 1978. "Mental Representation." *Erkenntnis* 13: 9–61. Reprinted in *Readings in Philosophy and Psychology*, vol. 2, ed. N. Block. Cambridge, Mass., 1981.
Fodor, J. 1965. "Explanations in Psychology." In *Philosophy in America*, ed. M. Black. London.
———. 1968. *Psychological Explanation*. New York.
———. 1974. "Special Sciences, or the Disunity of Science as a Working Hypothesis." *Synthese* 28: 97–115. Reprinted in *Readings in Philosophy and Psychology*, vol. 1, ed. N. Block. Cambridge, Mass., 1980.
———. 1978. "Propositional Attitudes." *Monist* 61: 501–23. Reprinted in *Readings in Philosophy and Psychology*, vol. 2, ed. N. Block. Cambridge, Mass., 1981.
———. 1981. "Imagistic Representation." In *Imagery*, ed. N. Block. Cambridge, Mass.
Fortenbaugh, W. 1970. "Aristotle's *Rhetoric* on Emotions." *Archiv für Geschichte der Philosophie* 52: 40–70.
———. 1975. *Aristotle on Emotion*. London.
Freudenthal, J. 1863. *Ueber den Begriff des Wortes phantasia bei Aristoteles*. Göttingen.
Gibson, J. 1966. *The Senses Considered as Perceptual Systems*. Boston.
Goldman, A. 1977. "Perceptual Objects." *Synthese* 35: 257–84.

Gomez-Lobo, A. 1976–77. "Aristotle's Hypotheses and the Euclidean Postulates." *Review of Metaphysics* 30: 430–39.
Gotthelf, A. 1976. "Aristotle's Conception of Final Causality." *Review of Metaphysics* 30: 226–54.
Graeser, A. 1978. "On Aristotle's framework of *sensibilia*." In *Aristotle on Mind and the Senses: Proceedings of the Seventh Symposium Aristotelicum*, ed. G. Lloyd and G. Owen. Cambridge.
Graham, D. W. 1980. "States and Performances: Aristotle's Test." *Philosophical Quarterly* 30: 117–29.
Gregory, R. 1970. *The Intelligent Eye*. New York.
Grene, M. 1963. *A Portrait of Aristotle*. Chicago.
Hamlyn, D. 1959. "Aristotle's Account of Aesthesis in the *De Anima*." *Classical Quarterly* 9: 6–16.
———. 1968b. "Koine Aisthesis." *Monist* 52: 195–209.
———. 1976. "Aristotelian Epagoge." *Phronesis* 21: 167–80.
Hannay, A. 1971. *Mental Images: A Defense*. Atlantic Highlands, N.J.
Hardie, W. 1964. "Aristotle's Treatment of the Relation between the Soul and the Body." *Philosophical Quarterly* 14: 53–72.
———. 1976. "Concepts of Consciousness in Aristotle." *Mind* 85: 388–411.
Hartman, E. 1977. *Substance, Body, and Soul: Aristotelian Investigations*. Princeton.
Heil, J. 1982. "Seeing Is Believing." *American Philosophical Quarterly* 19: 229–39.
Hintikka, J. 1980. "Aristotelian Induction." *Revue Internationale de Philosophie* 34: 422–40.
Hirst, R. 1967. "Primary and Secondary Qualities." In the *Encyclopedia of Philosophy*. New York.
Hume, D. 1739. *A Treatise of Human Nature*. Ed. L. Selby-Bigge. [1888] rep. 1963. Oxford.
Irwin, T. 1977. "Aristotle's Discovery of Metaphysics." *Review of Metaphysics* 31: 210–29.
Ishiguro, H. 1966. "Imagination." In *British Analytical Philosophy*, ed. B. Williams and A. Montefiore. London.
Jackson, F. 1977. *Perception: A Representative Theory*. Cambridge.
Jaeger, W. 1948. *Aristotle: Fundamentals of the History of His Development*. Trans. with the author's corrections and additions by R. Robinson. Oxford. Originally published in 1923 as *Aristoteles: Grundlegung einer Geschichte seiner Entwicklung*.
Jones, B. 1974. "Aristotle's Introduction of Matter." *Philosophical Review* 83: 474–500.
Kahn, C. 1966. "Sensation and Consciousness in Aristotle's Psychology." *Archiv für Geschichte der Philosophie* 48: 43–81.
———. 1981. "The Role of *Nous* in the Cognition of First Principles in *Posterior Analytics* II, 19." In *Aristotle on Science: The Posterior Analytics, Proceedings of the Eighth Symposium Aristotelicum*, ed. E. Berti. Padua and New York.

Kim, J. 1966. "On the Psycho-Physical Identity Theory." *American Philosophical Quarterly* 3: 227–35. Reprinted in *Materialism and the Mind-Body Problem*, ed. D. M. Rosenthal. Englewood Cliffs, N.J., 1971.

King, H. 1956. "Aristotle without Materia Prima." *Journal of History of Ideas* 17: 370–89.

Kosman, L. 1973. "Understanding, Explanation, and Insight in the *Posterior Analytics*." In *Exegesis and Argument*, ed. E. Lee, A. Mourelatos, and R. Rorty. *Phronesis* supp. vol. 1. Assen.

——. 1975. "Perceiving That We Perceive: *On the Soul* III, 2." *Philosophical Review* 84: 499–519.

Kosslyn, S. 1980. *Image and Mind*. Cambridge, Mass.

——. 1983. *Ghosts in the Mind's Machine: Creating and Using Images in the Brain*. New York.

Kosslyn, S., S. Pinker, G. E. Smith, and S. P. Shwartz. 1981. "On the Demystification of Mental Imagery." In *Imagery*, ed. N. Block. Cambridge, Mass.

Kosslyn, S., and J. Pomerantz. 1977. "Imagery, Propositions, and the Form of Internal Representations." *Cognitive Psychology* 9: 52–76.

Landesman, C. 1967. "Consciousness." In the *Encyclopedia of Philosophy*. New York.

Lear, J. 1980. *Aristotle and Logical Theory*. Cambridge, Mass.

Le Blond, J. 1939. *Logique et méthode chez Aristote*. Paris.

Lee, H. D. P. 1935. "Geometrical Method and Aristotle's Account of First Principles." *Classical Quarterly* 29: 113–24.

Lefèvre, C. 1972. *Sur l'évolution d'Aristote en psychologie*. Louvain.

——. 1978. "Sur le statut de l'ame dans le *De anima* et les *Parva naturalia*." In *Aristotle on Mind and the Senses*, ed. G. Lloyd and G. Owen. Cambridge.

Lesher, J. 1973. "The Meaning of *Nous* in the *Posterior Analytics*." *Phronesis* 18: 44–68.

Lewis, D. 1966. "An Argument for the Identity Theory." *Journal of Philosophy* 63: 17–25.

——. 1972. "Psychophysical and Theoretical Identification." *Australasian Journal of Philosophy* 50: 249–58.

——. 1980. "Mad Pain and Martian Pain." In *Readings in Philosophy of Psychology*, vol. 1, ed. N. Block. Cambridge, Mass.

Lloyd, G. 1978. "The Empirical Basis of the Physiology of the *Parva naturalia*." In *Aristotle on Mind and the Senses*, ed. G. Lloyd and G. Owen. Cambridge.

Lloyd, G., and G. Owen, eds. 1978. *Aristotle on Mind and the Senses: Proceedings of the Seventh Symposium Aristotelicum*. Cambridge.

Locke, J. [1894] 1959. *An Essay Concerning Human Understanding*. Ed. A. Fraser. Oxford. Originally published 1690.

Lowe, M. 1983. "Aristotle on Kinds of Thinking." *Phronesis* 28: 17–30.

Lyons, J. 1963. *Structural Semantics: An Analysis of Part of the Vocabulary of Plato*. Publications of the Philological Society, no. 20. Oxford.

McKirahan, R. 1978. "Aristotle's Subordinate Sciences." *British Journal of the History of Science* 11: 197–220.

Mansion, S. 1961. "Le rôle de l'exposé et de la critique des philosophies anterieurs chez Aristote." In *Aristote et les problèmes de méthode*, ed. S. Mansion. Louvain.

Martin, C., and M. Deutscher. 1966. "Remembering." *Philosophical Review* 75: 161–96.

Matson, W. 1966. "Why Isn't the Mind-Body Problem Ancient?" In *Mind, Matter and Method*, ed. P. Feyerabend and G. Maxwell. Minnesota.

Matthews, G. 1977. "Consciousness and Life." *Philosophy* 52: 13–26.

Metzler, J., and R. Shepard. 1971. "Mental Rotation of Three-Dimensional Objects." *Science* 171: 701–03.

Modrak, D. 1976. "*Aisthesis* in the Practical Syllogism." *Philosophical Studies* 30: 379–91.

———. 1979. "Forms, Types, and Tokens in Aristotle's *Metaphysics*." *Journal of the History of Philosophy* 17: 371–81.

———. 1981a. "An Aristotelian Theory of Consciousness?" *Ancient Philosophy* 1: 160–70.

———. 1981b. "Aristotle on Knowing First Principles." *Philosophical Inquiry* 3: 63–83.

———. 1981c. "*Koine Aisthesis* and the Discrimination of Sensible Differences in *De Anima* III. 2." *Canadian Journal of Philosophy* 11: 405–23.

———. 1981d. "Perception and Judgment in the *Theaetetus*." *Phronesis* 26: 35–54.

———. 1984. "Forms and Compounds." In *How Things Are*, ed. J. Bogen and J. McGuire. Dordrecht.

———. 1986. "*Phantasia* Reconsidered." *Archiv für Geschichte der Philosophie* 68:47–69.

Moraux, P. 1955. A propos du *nous thurathen* chez Aristote. In *Autour d'Aristote*, ed. A. Mansion. Louvain.

Moravcsik, J. 1973. "The Anatomy of Plato's Divisions." In *Exegesis and Argument*, ed. E. Lee, A. Mourelatos, and R. Rorty. *Phronesis* supp. vol. 1. Assen.

Mueller, I. 1970. "Aristotle on Geometrical Objects." *Archiv für Geschichte der Philosophie* 52: 156–71.

Nagel, T. 1965. "Physicalism." *Philosophical Review* 74: 339–56.

———. 1974. "What Is It Like to Be a Bat?" *Philosophical Review* 83: 435–50.

———. 1975. "Brain Bisection and the Unity of Consciousness." In *Personal Identity*, ed. J. Perry. Berkeley.

Neuhaeuser, J. 1878. *Aristotles' Lehre von dem sinnlichen Erkenntnissvermögen and seinen Organen*. Leipzig.

Nuyens, F. [1948] 1973. *L'evolution de la psychologie d'Aristote*. Reprint. Louvain.

Oehler, K. 1962. *Die Lehre vom noetischen und dianoetischen Denken bei Platon und Aristoteles*. Munich.

Onians, R. B. 1951. *The Origins of European Thought*. Cambridge.

Oppenheim, P., and H. Putnam. 1958. "Unity of Science as a Working Hypothesis." In *Minnesota Studies in the Philosophy of Science*, vol. 2, ed. H. Feigl, M. Scriven, and G. Maxwell. Minneapolis.

Owen, G. 1965. "Inherence." *Phronesis* 10: 97–105.

Penner, T. 1970. "Verbs and the Identity of Actions: A Philosophical Exercise in the Interpretation of Aristotle." In *Ryle: A Collection of Critical Essays*, ed. O. Wood and G. Pitcher. Garden City, N.J.

Pitcher, G. 1971. *A Theory of Perception*. Princeton.

Putnam, H. 1960. "Minds and Machines." In *Dimensions of Mind*, ed. S. Hook. New York.

———. 1966. "The Mental Life of Some Machines." In *Intentionality, Minds and Perception*, ed. H. Casteneda. Detroit.

———. 1967. "The Nature of Mental States." In *Art, Mind and Religion*, ed. W. H. Capitan and D. D. Merrill. Pittsburgh. Originally published as "Psychological Predicates."

Pylyshyn, Z. 1981. "The Imagery Debate: Analog Media versus Tacit Knowledge." In *Imagery*, ed. N. Block. Cambridge, Mass.

Randall, J. 1960. *Aristotle*. New York.

Rees, D. A. 1971. "Aristotle's Treatment of *Phantasia*" In *Essays in Ancient Greek Philosophy*, ed. J. Anton and G. Kustas. New York.

Robinson, H. M. 1974. "Prime Matter in Aristotle." *Phronesis* 19: 168–88.

———. 1978. "Mind and Body in Aristotle." *Classical Quarterly* 28: 105–24.

———. 1983. "Aristotelian Dualism." *Oxford Studies in Ancient Philosophy* 1: 123–44.

Rohde, E. [1920] 1972. *Psyche*. Trans. W. B. Hillis. Reprint. New York. Originally published in German in Leipzig, 1834.

Rorty, R. 1965. "Mind-Body Identity, Privacy, and Categories." *Review of Metaphysics* 19: 24–54. Reprinted in *Materialism and the Mind-Body Problem*, ed. D. Rosenthal. Englewood Cliffs, N.J., 1971.

———. 1979. *Philosophy and the Mirror of Nature*. Princeton.

Rosenthal, D., ed. 1971. *Materialism and the Mind-Body Problem*. Englewood Cliffs, N.J.

Ross, D. 1923. *Aristotle*. London.

Runzo, J. 1977. "The Propositional Structure of Perception." *American Philosophical Quarterly* 14: 211–20.

———. 1982. "The Radical Conceptualization of Experience." *American Philosophical Quarterly* 19: 206–14.

Russow, L. 1978. "Some Recent Work on Imagination." *American Philosophical Quarterly* 15: 57–66.

Ryle, G. 1949. *The Concept of Mind*. London.

Schofield, M. 1972. "Metaph. Z.3: Some suggestions." *Phronesis* 17: 97–101.

———. 1978. "Aristotle on the Imagination." In *Aristotle on Mind and the Senses*, ed. G. Lloyd and G. Owen. Cambridge.

Scholz, H. 1930. "Die Axiomatik der Alten." *Blatter für deutsche Philosophie* 4: 259–78. Translated and reprinted in *Articles on Aristotle*, vol. 1: *Science*, ed. J. Barnes, M. Schofield, and R. Sorabji. London.

Schwartz, M. 1981. "Imagery—There's More to It Than Meets the Eye." In *Imagery*, ed. N. Block. Cambridge, Mass.

Shoemaker, S. 1975. "Functionalism and Qualia." *Philosophical Studies* 27: 271–315. Reprinted in *Readings in Philosophy of Psychology*, vol. 1, ed. N. Block. Cambridge, Mass., 1980.

Slakey, T. 1961. "Aristotle on Sense Perception." *Philosophical Review* 70: 470–84.

Smart, J. 1959. "Sensations and Brain Processes." *Philosophical Review* 68: 141–56. Reprinted in *Materialism and the Mind-Body Problem*, ed. D. Rosenthal. Englewood Cliffs, N.J., 1971.

Snell, B. 1953. *The Discovery of the Mind: The Greek Origins of European Thought*. Cambridge, Mass.

Solmsen, F. 1929. *Die Entwicklung der aristotelischen Logik und Rhetorik*. Berlin.

———. 1958. "Aristotle and Prime Matter: A Reply to Hugh R. King." *Journal of the History of Ideas* 19: 243–52.

———. 1961. "Greek Philosophy and the Discovery of the Nerves." *Museum Helveticum* 18: 150–97.

Sorabji, R. 1971. "Aristotle on Demarcating the Five Senses." *Philosophical Review* 80: 55–79. Reprinted in *Articles on Aristotle*, vol. 4: *Psychology and Aesthetics*, ed. J. Barnes, M. Schofield, and R. Sorabji. London, 1978.

———. 1974. "Body and Soul in Aristotle." *Philosophy* 49: 63–89. Reprinted in *Articles on Aristotle*, vol. 4: *Psychology and Aesthetics*, ed. J. Barnes, M. Schofield, and R. Sorabji. London, 1978.

———. 1982. "Myths about Non-propositional Thought." In *Language and Logos: Studies in Ancient Greek Philosophy Presented to G. E. L. Owen*, ed. M. Schofield and M. Nussbaum. Cambridge.

Stich, S. 1979. "Do Animals Have Beliefs?" *Australasian Journal of Philosophy* 57: 15–28.

Strawson, P. 1959. *Individuals*. London.

Temkin, O. 1945. *The Falling Sickness*. Baltimore.

Tye, M. 1984a. "The Adverbial Approach to Visual Experience." *Philosophical Review* 93: 195–226.

———. 1984b. "The Debate about Mental Imagery." *Journal of Philosophy* 81: 678–91.

Van Fraassen, B. 1980. "A Re-examination of Aristotle's Philosophy of Science." *Dialogue* 19: 20–45.

Verbeke, G. 1978. "Doctrine du pneuma et entelechisme chez Aristote." In *Aristotle on Mind and the Senses*, ed. G. Lloyd and G. Owen. Cambridge.

Watson, G. 1982. "*Phantasia* in Aristotle, *De Anima* 3.3." *Classical Quarterly* 32: 100–113.

Webb, P. 1982. "Bodily Structure and Psychic Faculties in Aristotle's Theory of Perception." *Hermes* 110: 25–50.

White, M. J. 1980. "Aristotle's Concept of *Theoria* and the *Energeia-Kinesis* Distinction." *Journal of the History of Philosophy* 18: 253–63.

Wieland, W. 1962. *Die aristotelische Physik*. Göttingen.

Wiesner, J. 1978. "The Unity of the Treatise *De Somno* and the Physiological Explanation of Sleep in Aristotle." In *Aristotle on Mind and the Senses*, ed. G. Lloyd and G. Owen. Cambridge.
Wittgenstein, L. 1953. *Philosophical Investigations*. Bilingual edition. English trans. by G. Anscombe. New York.
Wright, E. 1984. "Recent Work in Perception." *American Philosophical Quarterly* 21: 17–30.
Wright, L. 1973. "Functions." *Philosophical Review* 82: 139–68.

Index

Passages

Analytica Posteriora

I, 18: 8, 77, 123, 160, 221 n.9
I, 31: 160, 161, 211 n.70, 221 n.9
II, 19: 8, 9, 77, 80, 123, 124, 125, 157, 161–71, 175, 178, 184 n.22, 185 n.23, 211 n.70, 221 n.1, 222 n.21
71a1–31: 165, 223 n.23, 224 n.36
72a35: 224 n.36
72b18–23: 159
72b25: 224 n.36
72b29: 160
73b4: 201 n.37
73b12–15: 203 n.64
73b26–29: 224 n.46
73b34–35: 224 n.46
74b12: 201 n.37
75a20: 201 n.37
76a32–34: 164
78a34: 170, 221 n.10
81a37–b9: 78, 113, 157, 158, 159, 160, 221 n.7, 224 n.35
81b1: 224 n.36
86a8: 225 n.50
87a31–37: 174
87b28–39: 223 n.29, 225 n.50
88a4–8: 157, 160, 173, 222 n.11, 224 n.44
88b36: 221 n.7
89a33–38: 131, 168
90a18–22: 199 n.8
90b3–4: 222 n.17
90b24: 222 n.17
90b35–37: 222 n.18
93a27–28: 164
99b14–34: 184 n.22
99b17–19: 161
99b21: 222 n.41
99b26–30: 165
99b32–35: 119, 165, 214 n.15
99b34–100b5: 157, 158, 161, 163, 171, 176

99b34–100a3: 162, 164
99b38–39: 190 n.25, 210 n.65
100a3–9: 162, 165, 166, 167
100a9–10: 222 n.13, 223 n.30
100a10–14: 125, 162, 163, 165, 167, 169, 212 n.83, 222 n.13
100a14–b3: 157, 161, 163, 167, 215 n.25
100b3–5: 166, 170
100b5–17: 171, 184 n.22, 221 n.7

Analytica Priora

42a3: 224 n.36
42a22–24: 224 n.35
43a33: 201 n.37
67a23: 170, 221 n.7
68b30–32: 221 n.7

De Anima

I,3: 184 n.2
II, 1: 31, 186 n.36
II, 2: 11
II, 3: 11, 38
II, 4: 193 n.56
II, 5: 31, 36, 38, 39
II, 6: 201 n.37
II, 11: 194 n.69
III, 1: 63, 66, 72, 76, 184 n.10, 193 n.55, 201 n.35
III, 2: 30, 66, 71, 145, 184 n.10, 193 n.55, 201 n.35
III, 3: 3, 33, 193 n.55
III, 4: 42, 113, 116, 118, 124, 159, 215 n.18
III, 5: 116, 125–27, 213 n.10, 222 n.21
III, 6: 215 n.30
III, 7: 184 n.10
III, 8: 84

239

INDEX

III, 10: 95
402a26: 190 n.30
402b10–14: 29
403a5–10: 28, 42, 115
403a16–21: 14, 25, 188 nn.3, 9
403a19–25: 25, 197 n.90
403a26: 197 n.91
403a30–31: 26, 42
403a31–b1: 196 n.81
403b3–7: 198 n.100
403b7–9: 188 n.3
403b25–28: 44
403b29–405a29: 44, 195 n.78
404a30: 213 n.3
405b31–407b26: 44
406b14–25: 1, 188 n.3
406b24–25: 25, 42, 44
406b26–407a20: 195 n.78
407a7: 116, 213 n.7
407a25–26: 222 n.17
407b12–24: 1, 27, 188 nn.3, 9
408b5–16: 115, 153
408b15–18: 13, 14, 92
410a7–10: 44
412a15–22: 1, 50, 188 n.3, 189 n.14
412a29–b6: 190 n.26
412b6–8: 27
412b10–22: 27, 51, 52, 183 n.4, 184 nn.12, 16, 17, 188 n.3, 189 n.15
413a3: 189 n.15
413a8–9: 14, 42
413b12: 213 n.5
413b29–31: 190 n.31
414a12–13: 188 n.8
414a14–20: 27, 31, 52
414a20–25: 27, 188 nn.3, 9
414a31: 208 n.46
414a32: 213 n.5
414b18: 213 n.4
414b20–33: 15, 35, 188 n.8
415a10: 220 n.31
415a18–22: 29
415b8: 13
416a9–10: 13
417a17–18: 190 n.32
417a27–b8: 38
417b13–16: 38
417b20–26: 223 n.29, 225 n.50
418a3–4: 188 n.5, 191 n.37, 193 n.60
418a12: 79
418a15: 79
418a17–20: 62
418a20–24: 63, 69, 203 n.64
418a24–25: 83
418a31: 193 nn.57, 62, 194 n.66
418b4–20: 32

419a10: 193 n.57, 194 n.66
419a13–15: 193 n.57, 194 n.66
419b9: 40
420a3–20: 5
420b5–14: 60, 200 n.16
420b27–29: 186 n.39
421a7–10: 43
421a13: 147
421b9–422a6: 196 n.83
422a7: 32
422a34–422b10: 32
422b15–16: 188 n.5, 191 n.37
422b23–33: 194 nn.69, 71, 218 n.6
422b23–24: 28, 193 n.62
422b34–423b26: 202 n.48
423b27–29: 41
424a1–5: 188 n.5, 198 n.1
424a5–10: 59, 189 n.19, 210 n.65, 214 n.15
424a13: 191 n.37
424a17–25: 40, 57
424a24–b3: 198 n.1
424a25–32: 48, 56, 61
424a32–b3: 59, 194 n.67, 199 n.14
424b3–5: 47
424b22–425a13: 198 n.7, 204 n.65
425a4: 32, 194 n.64
425a6–7: 75
425a14–24: 37, 58, 62, 63, 64, 71, 76, 200 nn.21, 22
425a24–b3: 201 n.37
425a27: 65, 200 n.19, 201 n.36
425a28: 200 n.22
425a30–b4: 62, 71, 101, 136
425a31: 201 n.32
425b1–4: 149, 212 n.82
425b12–24: 66, 188 nn.2, 6, 219 n.20
425b14–17: 66, 107, 201 n.30
425b22–23: 59
425b23–24: 40
425b25–30: 83, 188 n.5
425b26–426a19: 30, 48, 66
426a2–4: 59
426a8–19: 59, 199 n.11
426a20–25: 29
426a27–b7: 60, 61, 63, 198 n.1, 198 n.3
426a31: 61
426b4–7: 199 n.8
426b8–23: 65, 136, 139
426b10: 214 n.15
426b12–427a15: 33, 62, 65, 185 n.33, 218 n.5
426b14–15: 188 n.6, 201 n.28, 214 n.15
427a10–14: 66, 136
427a17–22: 117, 189 n.25, 195 n.77, 214 n.15

INDEX

427a21–28: 120, 191 n.42
427b11: 79
427b13: 114
427b17–20: 100
427b21–24: 149
427b24–26: 100, 114
427b28: 100
428a1–2: 82, 205 n.16
428a3–5: 100, 210 n.65
428a5–16: 206 n.24, 220 n.31
428a11–12: 206 n.26
428a12–15: 33, 83, 85, 206 n.21
428a16: 206 n.21
428a17: 213 n.3
428a18–25: 100, 217 n.48
428a20–23: 34, 100, 220 n.31
428b2–9: 101, 121, 211 n.75
428b3–4: 206 nn.21, 22
428b10–429a4: 188 n.6, 212 n.87
428b12–13: 205 n.12
428b18–30: 98
428b18–19: 79, 206 n.26
428b24–25: 79
428b27–30: 204 n.68
429a4–6: 211 n.71
429a10–13: 114
429a13–17: 213 n.7
429a15–17: 124, 188 n.5, 218 n.55
429a23: 114
429a24–25: 115
429a28–30: 118, 186 n.39, 213 n.5
429b5–9: 126
429b10–21: 28, 113, 116, 117, 118, 171, 214 nn.15, 18, 215 n.19
429b22–430a3: 146
429b22: 213 n.5
429b30: 124, 188 n.5, 218 n.55
429b31: 213 n.5
430a1: 159
430a2: 213 n.5
430a7: 188 n.5
430a17: 213 n.5
430a19–20: 188 n.5
430a23–24: 218 n.54
430a25: 213 n.5
430a26–28: 101, 116, 213 n.4,
430b26–31: 79, 222 n.19
431a1–5: 124, 190 n.30, 218 n.55
431a8–11: 141, 219 n.12
431a10–14: 141, 210 n.60, 213 n.5
431a14–15: 84, 158, 166, 221 n.2
431a16: 89
431a17: 122, 188 n.10, 194 n.66
431a19: 59
431a20–b1: 185 n.33, 218 n.5
431a22: 66

431b2–11: 191 n.41, 209 nn.52, 55
431b2: 89, 122, 157, 213 n.5, 221 n.2
431b6–8: 116, 129, 213 n.7
431b15–17: 159
431b18–19: 116
431b21–24: 117, 121, 122
431b26: 191 n.37
432a2: 213 n.5
432a3–14: 89, 116, 120, 122, 127, 141, 157, 159
432a3–6: 216 n.39
432a7–10: 8, 84, 89, 158, 166, 221 n.2
432a12–13: 213 n.7, 214 n.12
432a13–14: 158, 188 n.10
432a15–16: 117, 210 n.65
432a22–b7: 208 n.46
432a31–b2: 83
432b4–7: 217 n.50
433a9–12: 209 nn.52, 55, 213 n.5, 220 n.31
433a10: 34, 100, 191 n.42, 211 n.71
433b27–29: 95, 96, 194 n.66, 210 n.60
433b29–434a7: 120, 211 n.72
434a1–5: 95, 220 n.31
434a5–12: 100, 129, 211 n.72, 223 n.26
434b4: 186 n.39
434b11–27: 151
434b27–435a8: 196 n.86

De Divinatione per Somnum

463a8–10: 137
463a25–30: 94
463b11–12: 209 n.51
464a32–b5: 94
464b7–10: 212 n.81

De Generatione Animalium

II,3: 197 n.97
730b4–25: 186 n.44
731a30–34: 190 n.25
734b24–31: 50
736a14–21: 74
736a37: 185 n.32
736b5–29: 15, 216 n.40
736b30–737a8: 186 n.43
740a18–b3: 202 n.49
743b36–744a12: 73, 74
744a2: 203 nn.55, 58
744b22: 216 n.40
762a19–22: 186 n.43
779b23–26: 185 n.32, 194 n.64
780a3–4: 193 n.62

781a21–b6: 203 nn.54, 55
781b23–24: 196 n.83
786b25: 185 n.32
788b2: 185 n.32

De Generatione et Corruptione

I, 4: 51
II, 2–5: 57, 79
II, 3: 198 n.6
321b28–32: 50
329b16–330a29: 57, 194 n.71
330a24–26: 194 n.71

De Insomniis

1: 209 n.50
2–3: 209 n.50
458b1: 213 n.5
458b3: 210 n.65
458b15: 211 n.74
458b10–459a23: 33, 83, 101
458b28–29: 121, 206 nn.21, 22
459a1–8: 93, 207 n.27
459a11–23: 81, 82, 93, 188 n.6, 190 n.31
459b6: 193 n.58
459b11–20: 93
459b23–460a32: 209 n.50
460b1–23: 191 n.32
460b2–3: 93, 206 n.19, 221 n.4
460b3–13: 83, 101, 140
460b4–18: 206 n.21
460b11–16: 149, 206 n.22
460b16–26: 94, 101, 137, 138, 206 n.22, 212 n.75, 218 n.7
460b17–23: 225 n.49
460b18–19: 211 n.75
460b27–462a8: 93, 206 n.21
461a7–30: 94
461a18–19: 166, 206 nn.19, 25, 221 n.4
461a24–30: 72, 101
461a25–b31: 202 n.47
461a30–b7: 218 n.7
461b1–8: 138, 149
461b5–31: 138
461b10: 212 n.81
461b22–23: 206 nn.19, 25, 221 n.4
462a3–8: 121, 206 n.21
462a19–26: 85
462a29: 215 n.24
462b4–8: 94

De Interpretatione

16a3–6: 128, 191 n.40
16a11: 101

De Juventute

469a5–12: 202 n.43
469b4–7: 202 nn.43, 46
469b16: 185 n.29

De Memoria

1: 208 n.39
2: 208 n.39
449b13–14: 189 n.25
449b23–24: 90
449b31–450a6: 221 n.2
449b31: 89
450a1–9: 84, 121, 127, 170
450a9–15: 33, 89, 127, 139, 190 n.25, 201 n.36
450a11: 208 n.43
450a15–16: 90, 209 n.51
450a19–23: 90
450a23–25: 84, 89
450a30–31: 208 n.43, 221 n.4
450b1–10: 108
450b12–451a18: 88
450b17–18: 189 n.25, 208 n.43
450b23: 87
450b25–27: 90
450b32: 208 n.43
451a2: 87, 89
451a5–7: 90
451a11–12: 87, 89
451a14: 89
451a15–19: 83, 87, 89, 139, 188 n.6, 201 n.36
451a24: 208 n.43
451a28–29: 89
452a8–b8: 208 n.42
452b23–24: 87, 208 n.45
453a7–14: 34, 92, 100, 129
453a14–19: 94
453a15–31: 92, 108, 208 n.43
460b17: 214 n.15
460b22: 214 n.15

De Motu Animalium

7: 95, 209 n.57
700b1–20: 211 n.71
700b17–25: 191 n.40, 209 nn.52, 55
701a18–22: 96
701a29–702a20: 191 n.41, 209 n.52
701a32: 95
701b2–702a10: 5
702a5: 207 n.31
702a15–19: 95, 97, 210 n.60

INDEX 243

703a10–14: 203 n.56
703a18–19: 191 n.41
703a19–28: 74
703b18–19: 209 nn.52, 55

De Partibus Animalium

640b4–28: 184 n.12
640b34–641a5: 184 n.16
641a18–32: 183 n.4, 184 n.12
641b1–4: 188 n.5
641b6–8: 188 n.8
642a7–13: 190 n.26
646b5–8: 197 n.97
647a3–23: 32, 73, 194 n.71, 198 n.7
648a2–4: 202 n.47
650a3–b13: 202 n.49
650b19–23: 202 n.47
656a28: 40
656a29: 202 n.48
656a35–37: 196 n.83
656b1–3: 194 n.64
656b3–7: 202 n.47
656b17: 75
656b19–22: 73, 203 n.51
656b34–37: 202 n.48
657a17–24: 196 n.83
657b18: 203 n.56
658b27–659a19: 196 n.83
659b14–19: 203 n.57
660a16–30: 196 n.83
666a6–9: 202 n.46
666a14–18: 202 n.46
666a17–18: 73, 203 n.51
666a19–23: 73
666a35–36: 73
667b23–31: 202 n.46
678b6–13: 196 n.83

De Poetica

1447a8–9: 193 n.54

De Sensu

6: 136
7: 136, 143
436a7–11: 14, 25, 188 n.3
438a6: 194 n.64
438a10–13: 200 n.15
438a13–15: 194 n.64
438b6–8: 194 n.64
438b10: 42
438b25: 40

438b26–439a4: 32
439a1: 202 n.48
439a22–30: 32
439a30–31: 40, 58
439b12–13: 193 n.62
439b17–19: 189 n.19
439b22–440b25: 194 n.68, 198 n.3
439b27–440a6: 199 n.8
440b14–21: 199 n.8
441a1–3: 43, 147
441b19: 41
442a12–17: 198 n.3, 199 n.10, 218 n.6
442a18–20: 57
442a29–b3: 44, 204 n.67
442b8–10: 79
442b10–24: 79
442b12: 214 n.15
442b17–19: 199 n.10
446a20–447a11: 196 n.86
447a13–18: 138, 139, 142
447b10–449a22: 185 n.33, 218 n.5
447b25: 214 n.15
447b27: 214 n.15
448a8–12: 57, 198 n.3
448a23–24: 136
449a9: 201 n.36
449a13–20: 66, 136, 198 n.1, 201 n.32
449b17–18: 91, 201 n.36
451b3–6: 92
451b22–31: 92
453a15–16: 92

De Somnum

2: 68, 184 n.10
454a1–7: 41, 189 n.25
454a7–11: 13, 188 n.3
455a13–21: 65, 66, 67, 145
455a16–26: 40, 185 n.33, 201 n.36, 202 n.43, 218 n.5, 219 n.18
455a20: 201 n.32
455b8–13: 137
456a5–6: 202 n.43
456a13: 203 n.56
456a21–22: 137
456a26: 158, 206 n.19
458a29–30: 72

Ethica Nicomachea

VI, 3: 221 n.7, 222 n.20
VI, 6: 222 n.20
IX, 9: 147
1094b27: 214 n.15
1098b3: 157, 221 n.7

1099a23: 214 n.15
1109b8: 214 n.15
1112b20–24: 217 n.47
1135b26: 214 n.15
1139b14–17: 213 n.3
1139b28–30: 221 n.7
1141a3–8: 213 n.3, 221 n.7
1142b1–22: 217 n.47, 223 n.28
1143a35–b5: 173, 214 n.14
1144a31–33: 217 n.47
1147a26–b17: 219 n.11
1147a26–36: 96, 209 n.57
1147b4–5: 209 n.51
1170a28–33: 146, 150, 219 n.21
1174b15–1175a1: 97
1176a13–16: 201 n.38, 206 n.22
1177a12: 214 n.14

Historia Animalium

III, 3–4: 202 n.49
536b28: 209 n.51

Metaphysica

I,1: 8, 77, 123, 125, 157, 166, 222 n.20
IV, 5: 190 n.32
VII, 3: 189 n.13
VII, 17: 189 n.13
VIII, 2: 189 n.13
IX, 7: 194 n.65
IX, 8: 190 n.32
IX, 10: 215 n.30
980a26–981a7: 119
980b20–28: 191 n.41, 209 nn.51, 52
981a1–12: 167
982a5–28: 174
986b27–34: 57
992b30–993a2: 223 n.23, 224 n.36
999b3: 223 n.29
1003a15: 223 n.29
1009b1–1010a5: 29
1010b3–11: 201 n.38
1010b30–37: 199 n.11, 206 n.19
1018a1: 201 n.37
1023b25: 197 n.93
1025a14: 201 n.37
1025b15: 224 n.36
1026b32: 201 n.37
1029a20–32: 184 n.12
1032a28–b14: 26
1035b14–23: 189 n.14
1035b24–26: 184 n.16, 197 n.93
1035b26–28: 13, 186 n.34
1036a2–8: 160

1036b31–32: 197 n.93
1037b10–14: 164, 222 n.18
1041a32–b2: 222 n.18, 224 n.37
1041b8: 184 n.12
1042b10: 52
1042b28–31: 197 n.97
1043a11–12: 198 n.3
1043a14–21: 26, 198 n.100
1046a23–29: 190 n.32
1048a10–24: 95
1048a36: 170
1050a10–11: 31
1051b1: 101
1051b22–33: 213 n.4, 222 n.19
1059a1: 201 n.37
1059b26: 223 n.29
1060b20: 223 n.29
1062b33–1063a4: 201 n.38
1063b4: 158
1064a9: 224 n.36
1065a1: 201 n.37
1074b35–36: 150
1075a1–3: 169
1078a2–31: 159, 170
1078a9: 174
1087a19: 201 n.37

Physica

I, 5: 57
I, 7–9: 188 n.12
III, 1: 190 n.30
184a11–16: 188 n.8
184a24–b14: 168, 215, 223 n.31
201b4–5: 199 n.11
218b21–33: 147
219a23–29: 91
244b2–245a12: 193 n.57
244b11: 193 n.58
244b13: 193 n.58
247a5–18: 210 n.60
252a24: 224 n.36
255a33–b5: 193 n.59

Rhetorica

1378a30–b2: 42, 140
1385b13–19: 140
1387b22–24: 219 n.10

Topica

I, 1: 193 n.54
101b13–23: 222 n.17

102b3: 201 n.37
103b17: 201 n.37
105a12–16: 160, 221 n.10, 224 n.35
105a18: 223 n.36
108b10: 175, 221 n.10
114a21–25: 223 n.29

153a16: 222 n.17
156a30: 195 n.74
156b14–15: 221 n.10, 224 n.35
157a20: 224 n.36
160a38: 224 n.35

Persons and Topics

Ackrill, J., 5–6, 49–52, 184 n.14, 197 nn.92, 94
Action, voluntary, 5, 95–99
Actuality *(entelecheia)*, 30, 186 n.36, 190 n.30; distinction between first and second, 31
Actuality Principle, 24, 29–32, 37–38, 46, 61, 76–77, 82, 87, 91, 94, 120, 124, 126, 130–31, 135, 148, 150, 152–54, 159, 177, 180, 191 nn.37–38, 193 n.60, 207 n.33, 211 n.67, 213 nn.89, 9, 218 n.8; Plato's version of, 29–30
Aisthēsis. See Perception
Aisthētikon. See Perceptual faculty
Alexander of Aphrodisias, 203 n.60, 205 n.16, 211 n.73, 216 nn.33, 40
Analytic Principle, 24, 35–37, 55, 67, 76–77, 87, 94, 109, 131, 154, 177–78, 180, 195 n.80
Anamnēsis. See Recollection
Anaximenes, 195 n.78
Anderson, J., 102
Anger *(orgē)*: definition of, 18, 26, 42, 53, 140, 195 n.74, 196 n.81, 197 n.91; distinction between dispositional and occurrent, 48–49
Anscombe, G., 209 n.57
Apperception. See Common sense
Armstrong, D., 18, 37, 187 n.50, 189 nn.21, 22, 191 n.34, 192 n.45, 195 n.80, 211 n.69, 219 n.17, 220 n.25

Baeumker, C., 201 n.33
Barker, A., 60–61, 199 n.12
Barnes, J., 5, 6, 9, 162, 192 n.52, 193 n.58, 199 n.13, 222 n.11, 224 nn.40, 43; and M. Schofield and R. Sorabji, 184 n.11
Beare, J., 39, 201 n.39
Berti, E., 185 n.23, 215 n.30
Block, I., 10, 201 n.39, 218 n.3
Block, N., 186 n.46, 187 n.51, 192 n.46, 212 n.76; and J. Fodor, 18, 187 n.50
Blood, role of, in sensory transmission, 73–75, 94, 202 nn.47, 50, 203 n.62
Bolton, R., 164, 183 n.7, 192 n.51
Boyd, R., 196 n.88

Brain: events in 16–18; as seat of *psuchē*, 13, 73, 186 n.34
Bremmer, J., 187 n.52
Brentano, F., 32, 191 n.33, 194 n.71, 201 n.39, 216 n.42, 220 n.25
Brown, R., and R. Herrnstein, 192 n.48
Bruner, J., 192 n.47
Burnyeat, M., 151, 183 n.7, 192 n.52, 199 n.13, 211 n.73, 215 n.28, 221 n.3, 224 n.38
Bywater, I., 206 n.37, 217 n.46, 218 n.2, 219 n.21

Cashdollar, S., 201 n.39
Charles, D., 196 n.87
Chisholm, R., 191 n.35, 220 n.25
Claus, D., 187 n.52
Code, A., 196 n.86
Cognition, general faculty of, 117–18. See also Perceptual faculty; Noetic faculty
Cohen, S., 199 n.9
Common sense *(koinē aisthēsis)*, 62–71, 134–38, 140–42, 144, 154, 200 nn.18, 19, 23; discrimination of sensible difference, 12, 33, 65–66, 136; organ of, 71–76, 137; reflexive awareness, 66–67, 71, 145–50, 201 n.31, 204 n.1, 219 n.19; single concept of, 68–69; unity of experience, 134–44. See also Consciousness
Consciousness, 133–54, 200 n.24, 218 n.1, 220 nn.29, 34; Cartesian concept of, 8, 133, 151
Cooper, J., 46, 209 n.57
Cornman, J., 186 n.47
Couloubaritsis, L., 221 n.3

Dancy, R., 197 n.95
Davidson, D., 18, 195 n.80, 220 n.27
De Divinatione per Somnum, 93
De Generatione et Corruptione, tangible opposites in, 57, 79, 194 n.71
De Insomniis, 83, 93
De Memoria, 87–93
De Motu Animalium, 95–99, 141
De Sensu, 147

De Somno, on common *dunamis* of the senses, 67–68, 145–46
Definition, 164, 222 n.17, 224 n.37; and phenomenal features, 29; formal, 26; in psychology, 26–28, 48; material, 26, 184 n.17
Democritus, 25, 44, 78, 204 n.67
Dennett, D., 187 n.55, 191 n.46, 312 nn.79, 80
Desire, 95, 140–41, 198 n.99, 208 n.46
Doxa (opinion), 100–101, 114, 128–29, 217 n.48
Dreams, 72, 83, 93–94, 101, 137–38, 207 n.27, 209 nn.48–51, 211 n.74, 212 n.81
Dretske, F., 211 n.69
Dualism: ancient, 1, 27, 183 n.1, 195 n.76; Platonic, 10, 44; Cartesian, 15; Aristotle's use of language of, 13, 42

Empedocles, 44
Engberg-Pedersen, I., 9, 175, 221 n.3
Entelecheia. See Actuality
Epagōgē (induction), 8–9, 126, 160–61, 163, 165–66, 170–78, 187 n.1, 221 nn.1, 7, 224 nn.38, 44, 47
Epistēmē (knowledge), 114, 122, 159–61, 173, 192 n.50, 213 n.3, 221 nn.6, 7
Epistemology: Aristotle's 8–9, 106, 123, 157–79; and the theory of perception, 78–80; modern, and justification, 174–76. See also *Posterior Analytics*
Eye, 5–9, 27, 47, 189 n.15, 193 n.63

Feigl, H., 186 n.45
Ferejohn, M., 159, 164, 192 n.51, 222 n.17
Field, H., 148
Fodor, J., 103, 248. See also Block, N.
Fortenbaugh, W., 140
Freudenthal, J., 205 n.15, 206 nn.18, 23
Functionalism: biological, 190 n.26; psychological, 2, 5–6, 16–18, 28, 184 n.18, 187 nn.50, 53, 54

Gibson, J., 107, 194 n.71
Goldman, A., 192 n.45
Gomez-Lobo, A., 159, 164, 192 n.51
Gotthelf, A., 196 n.55
Graeser, A., 200 n.22, 202 n.41
Gregory, R., 107
Grene, M., 16, 124, 133, 207 n.30

Hamlyn, D., 7, 68, 175, 191 n.37, 199 nn.12, 13, 200 nn.18, 22, 201 n.34, 204 nn.68, 4, 214 n.16, 221 n.3, 222 n.17

Hardie, W., 8, 49, 133, 151–52, 184 nn.14, 21, 197 n.92, 218 n.1, 219 n.21
Hartman, E., 196 n.87
Heart, as seat of *psuchē*, 12, 13, 72–74, 76, 186 n.34, 202 n.43. See also Blood
Heraclitus, 44, 195 n.78
Hicks, R., 60, 183 n.6, 189 n.15, 190 n.27, 193 n.57, 201 n.39, 206 n.26, 214 n.18, 215 n.19, 219 n.12
Hintikka, J., 159, 221 n.3, 222 n.17, 224 n.37
Hylomorphism: psychological, 4–6, 25–26, 31, 45; and instrumentalism, 10, 12–15, 186 n.35; criticisms of, 49–54, 184 n.14

Imagination. See *Phantasia*
Induction. See *Epagōgē*
Inference, and rationality, 34, 128–30
Instrumentalism. See Hylomorphism; Unitarian approach
Intellect. See Noetic faculty; *Nous*
Intentionality, of the mental, 32, 134, 148–49
Irwin, T., 171
Ishiguro, I., 205 n.12

Jaeger, W., 9–10, 185 nn.24, 25, 186 n.42, 213 n.9, 216 n.36
Joachim, H., 196 n.86
Jones, B., 197 n.95

Kahn, C., 1, 8, 9, 133, 146, 151–52, 171–72, 184 n.21, 185 n.23, 195 n.78, 201 nn.39, 40, 213 n.2, 214 n.18, 218 nn.2, 4, 219 nn.16, 21, 220 n.34, 221 n.3, 222 nn.14, 17, 21, 224 n.37
Kim, J., 186 n.49
King, H., 197 n.95
Koinē aisthēsis. See Common sense
Kosman, A., 7, 9, 171–72, 187 n.53, 190 n.29, 201 n.29, 221 n.3, 224 n.39
Kosslyn, S., 103, 192 n.45, and J. Pomerantz, 212 n.80

Le Blond, J., 9, 171–72
Lee, H., 9
Lefèvre, C., 186 nn.35, 40
Lesher, J., 9, 171–72, 175, 221 n.3, 224 n.39
Lewis, D., 18, 186 n.48, 187 n.50, 189 nn.21, 22, 196 n.84
Lloyd, G., 203 nn.61, 63; and G. Owen, 4, 184 n.11
Logos, 198 n.4, 203 nn.61, 63; in definition of sense, 56–62, 199 n.14; of sen-

sible qualities, 47, 56–57, 189 n.18, 194 n.67, 198 n.3, 199 nn.9, 10, 218 n.6
Lulofs, H., 11, 209 n.50
Lyons, J., 190 n.25

Mansion, S., 183 n.1
Martin, C., and M. Deutscher, 207 n.38
Materialism, 15; modern reductive, 5–6, 15, 28, 42, 45; in comparison to Aristotle's philosophy of mind, 45–47, 183 n.2; pre-Socratic, 1, 43–44. *See also* Psychophysical identity theory
Matson, W., 1, 133
Matter, 194 n.65; of biological individual, 49–51; specification of, and homonymy, 50–52
Matthews, G., 133, 184 n.21
McKirahan, R., 174, 215 n.27
Memory *(mnēmē)*, 83–84, 87–92, 104, 139, 165, 208 nn.43, 44, 209 n.51
Mental representation. *See* Representation
Mesotes (mean). *See Logos*
Metaphysics, hylomorphism in, 13, 26
Mnēmē. *See* Memory
Moraux, P., 186 n.43, 216 n.40
Moravcsik, J., 223 n.33
Movement, voluntary, of animals. *See* Action
Mueller, I., 216 n.31

Nagel, T., 147, 220 n.25
Neuhaeuser, J., 201 n.30, 202 n.44, 218 n.3
Noetic faculty (intellect), 8, 34–35, 113–17, 146, 213 n.5; and psychophysicalism, 28, 42, 115–16; objects of, 113–14, 116–18, 120–25, 130, 153–4; relation of, to perceptual faculty, 117–24, 178. *See also* Inference; Thought
Noētikon. *See* Noetic faculty
Normative Psychophysical Principle. *See* Psychophysical Principle
Nous: active, 116, 125–27, 216 nn.33, 39, 217 n.54, 222 n.21; and first principles, 8, 172–74, 184 n.22, 221 n.1, 224 n.38; generic concept of, 114; *noēsis*, 160–61, 222 n.11
Nussbaum, M., 2, 7, 17, 98, 106, 207 n.31, 209 n.53, 210 nn.62, 63, 66
Nuyens, F., 10–13, 185 nn.24, 25, 26, 186 nn.38, 43

Oehler, K., 150
Onians, R., 187 n.52
Ophthalmos. *See* Eye

Oppenheim, P., and H. Putnam, 37, 186 n.45, 195 n.80
Owen, G., 185 n.24, 189 n.19. *See also* Lloyd, G.

Parmenides, 57
Parva Naturalia, in relation to *De Anima*, 10–15
Peck, A., 203 nn.51, 52, 54
Perception *(aisthēsis)*: causal theory of, 58; definition of, 38–39, 99–100; psychophysical model of, 39–41. *See also* Perceptual faculty; *Phantasia*
Perceptual faculty *(aisthētikon)*: compared to doxastic faculty, 190 n.31; functions of, 2–4, 8, 23–110, 152, 187 n.58, 214 nn.14, 17; theory of, 2–4, 19, 23–54, 132, 180, 183 n.10, 220 nn.31, 34. *See also* Common sense; *Phantasia*; Noetic faculty
Phantasia (imagination), 7, 33–34, 81–110, 191 nn.39, 42; and *aisthēsis*, 85–86, 98, 101, 108, 114, 206 n.24; deliberative, 211 n.72; nominal definition of, 82; propositional content of, 103; role of, in animal movement, 95–99, 141; role of, in thinking, 115, 122–25, 131, 169; Sensory Content Analysis of, 82–87, 94, 98. *See also* Dreams; Memory; Recollection
Phantasma, 7, 83, 86, 90–93, 97, 102–7, 120–30, 139, 143, 157–58, 166–70, 173, 177, 188 nn.7, 10
Philoponus, 60, 193 n.60, 200 nn.19, 22, 213 n.8, 216 nn.33, 40
Physics; hylomorphism in, 26, 188 n.12
Physiology: of common sense, 71–76; of dreaming, 93–94; of *phantasia*, 107–8, 212 n.87, 217 n.53; of sleep, 72; of special senses, 40–41
Pitcher, G., 199 n.11, 211 n.69
Plato, 39, 57, 120–22, 150, 204 n.68, 208 n.46; *Charmides*, 190 n.28; *Meno*, 208 n.42, 222 n.22; *Philebus*, 42, 188 n.10; *Republic*, 30, 121–22; *Sophist*, 191 n.40, 205 nn.8, 9, 10, 215 nn.21, 26, 223 n.33; *Theaetetus*, 30, 67, 79, 100, 151, 191 n.40, 195 n.79, 215 n.26, 219 n.13; *Timaeus*, 44, 195 n.79, 202 n.45, 219 n.13. *See also* Actuality Principle; Dualism
Pleasure, 97, and pain, 210 nn.60, 64, 218 n.10
Pneuma, 186 n.43; role of, in perception, 74–75, 203 nn.52, 55, 57, 58, 59
Posterior Analytics: on requirements of

science, 36; role of perception in knowledge, 77–78, 122–23
Praxagoras, 75, 203 n.59
Pre-Socratics, 39, 57; and the Actuality Principle, 29. *See also* Dualism, ancient; Materialism
Principles, foundational. *See* Actuality Principle; Analytic Principle; Psychophysical Principle; Sensory Representation Principle
Psuchē (soul), 1–2, 11, 13–14, 16–17, 27, 44, 187 n.52; as subject of mental attributes, 14, 42
Psychophysical identity theory, 15–18, 186 nn.46, 48, 196 nn.84, 89, 197 n.98; compared to Aristotle's approach, 45–47, 195 n.78. *See also* Materialism
Psychophysical Principle, 24, 25–29, 37, 62, 68, 76, 85, 94, 107–8, 120, 130, 135, 151, 153, 176–77, 180, 187 n.2, 188 n.3, 197 n.90; Normative, 24, 27, 37, 49, 52
Psychophysicalism, Aristotle's. *See* Hylomorphism, psychological
Putnam, H., 186 n.48, 187 n.50, 189 n.21, 196 n.84. *See also* P. Oppenheim
Pylyshyn, Z., 192 n.48

Randall, J., 9
Realism, 175–76
Recollection *(anamnēsis)* 92–93, 129, 185 n.31, 208 nn.42, 44, 45, 217 nn.49, 50
Rees, D., 7
Reflexive awareness. *See* Common sense
Representation: mental, 35, 127–30; sensory, nature of, 33, 99–107, 127, 144; pictorial mode of, 35, 191 n.44; through resemblance, 104–7; truth values of, 101–3; symbolic, 102
Rhetoric, definition of anger in, 42
Robinson, H., 53, 184 n.19, 21, 187 nn.53, 54, 189 n.24, 195 n.75, 197 n.95
Rodier, G., 183 n.6, 206 n.19, 219 n.19
Rorty, R., 37, 133, 151, 184 n.21, 187 n.56, 195 n.80
Rosenthal, D., 186 n.46, 215 n.29
Ross, D., 10–13, 69, 162, 183 n.6, 185 nn.24, 25, 27, 200 n.22, 201 n.39, 204 n.68, 206 n.26, 213 n.2, 216 nn.37, 41, 219 n.19, 222 nn.14, 16
Ross, G., 184 n.15
Russow, L., 192 n.46
Ryle, G., 17, 192 n 46

Sandys, J., 195 n.74
Schofield, M., 7, 86, 191 n.39, 197 n.95, 204 nn.2, 4, 205 n.8, 206 n.18. *See also* Barnes, J.
Scholz, H., 159
Schwartz, R., 191 n.44, 207 n.32
Sense, special, 55–62; of hearing, 60–61; of sight, 27–28; 46, 47, 58–60; of smell, 43, 46, 47; of touch, 59
Sense object: common *(koinon)* 62–65, 78–80; incidental *(kata sumbebēkos)*, 64, 69–71, 77, 79–80, 98, 100, 105, 107, 212 n.82; proper *(idion)*, 41, 55–58, 65, 77–79, 105, 107. *See also Logos*
Sense organ, 40, 50, 107–8; and Actuality Principle, 32; and psychophysicalism, 40. *See also* Common sense, organ of; Physiology
Sensory Content Analysis. *See Phantasia*
Sensory Representation Principle, 24, 32–35, 37, 55, 77, 82–83, 87, 94, 109, 130–31, 154, 177, 180–81, 188 n.2, 201 n.28, 213 n.89
Shoemaker, S., 18
Slakey, T., 1, 5, 183 n.5, 185 n.28, 199 n.15
Sleep, 72, 137
Smart, J., 37, 186 n.47, 195 n.80, 197 n.98
Snell, B., 187 n.52
Solmsen, F., 1, 162, 195 n.95, 202 n.45, 203 nn.51, 52, 53, 59, 61
Sorabji, R., 2, 5, 6, 7, 11, 17, 52–53, 169, 184 nn.11, 13, 19, 187 n.53, 189 n.24, 190 n.29, 197 n.92, 199 nn.12, 15, 207 nn.32, 37, 39. *See also* Barnes, J.
Soul. *See Psuchē*
Stich, S., 211 n.71

Temkin, O., 203 n.59
Theophrastus, 195 n.77, 198 n.5, 204 n.67, 216 n.33
Thought, 100–101, 113, 142; asomatic character, 115; epistemic aspect of, 113–14. *See also* Noetic faculty; *Nous*
Torstrik, A., 189 n.15, 200 n.22

Unitarian approach: case for, 9–15; instrumentalism and, 10, 13
Universals, 100, 119, 121–22, 126–27, 160, 163, 165–71, 207 n.34, 211 n.70, 212 n. 77, 216 nn. 31, 32, 221 nn. 6, 8, 223 nn. 29, 30, 31, 224 nn. 44, 46

Verbeke, n.G., 203 nn.52, 58

Waitz, T., 164
Watson, G., 7
Webb, P., 202 n.50, 203 n.52

Wieland, W., 197 n.95
Wiesner, J., 185 nn.27, 30
Wittgenstein, L., 17
Wright, E., 199 n.11
Wright, L., 189 n.16